Ego

# Ego

## *The Ghost In Your Machinery*

Louis D. Cox, Ph.D

*Epigraph Books*
*Rhinebeck, New York*

Book layout and cover design by Colin Rolfe.

Paperback ISBN: 978-1-948796-00-2
Hardcover ISBN: 978-1-948796-01-9
eBook ISBN: 978-1-948796-02-6

Library of Congress Control Number: 2018936223

Epigraph Books
22 East Market Street, Suite 304
Rhinebeck, NY 12572
(845) 876-4861
EpigraphPS.com

"The relevance of Freud to our time is largely his insight...that the *ordinary* person is a shriveled, desiccated fragment of what a person can be.

"As adults...we hardly know of the existence of the inner world....We respect the voyager, the explorer, the climber, the space man. It makes far more sense to me as a valid project—indeed, as a desperately and urgently required project for our time—to explore the inner space and time of consciousness. Perhaps this is one of the few things that still makes sense in our historical context. We are so out of touch with this realm that many people can now argue seriously that it does not exist."

R.D. Laing, *The Politics of Experience* (1967)

"If you bring forth that which is within you, that which you bring forth will save you.

"If you do not bring forth that which is within you, that which you do not bring forth will destroy you."

Saint Thomas, "The Gnostic Gospels"

"We begin to hear the self we actually are emerging out of our shadow selves, our counterfeit selves, our pretended selves. We become aware of what is in us, the best and the worst. Our best parts, if left unlived, can be as poisonous as our worst, if left unhealed."

Ann & Barry Ulanov, *Primary Speech* (1982)

# Contents

# Introduction
## Waking Up and Waking Down

For several decades now, discovering what I am *unaware* of about myself has been my ongoing challenge and passion. And, as I have come to see it, this is the ongoing challenge for any conscious person.

It always strikes me as funny, in a humbling kind of way, that being a *conscious* person means accepting that I am also an *unconscious* person! This means accepting as fact that *in any given moment* there will be more going on within me than I'm aware of—"more" than what I already know or "see." For example, in a conversation with a friend, I may be speaking in an angry tone of voice that I am completely unaware of, while he is being impacted and reacting exactly to that tone. Or, in another moment, I may be feeling unnecessarily hopeless because of an unconscious belief I am powerless, when in fact there are several options for action on my part. Those options will remain "out of view" as long as I don't notice that disempowering belief and step away from it. The specific "more" that is hidden from me may be something that I am delighted to find out about, or it may be something that horrifies me, even scares the bejesus out of me!

So, to me, a "conscious person" is not someone who has his or herself all figured out or abides in some "enlightened" state of mind. "Conscious," in my use of the word, does not indicate a permanent mental or emotional state. For me, being a conscious person is a moment to moment evolving and emerging inner experience. Living as a conscious person means two things: First, I have given up the belief that I am ever fully aware of everything that is available inside of me; and, second, that I remain interested in focusing my attention inside of me, in a curious and friendly way, as a continuous practice. I do this in order to discover what the hidden "more" that exists inside of me may be—*both in any given moment of my day-to-day experience, and also when I chose to sit down and give myself some dedicated time to look inward.*

Of course, as with any person, there are certain things about me that I am more or less permanently aware of. For example, I may be consistently aware that I can count on my creativity to help me solve complicated problems, or I may have an abiding awareness of loving my wife and children. Being a conscious person in my definition just means that in a given moment there is always more going on inside of me, and inner capacities available to me, than I ever notice at first glance, even about that "known" love and creativity.

## Waking Up and Waking Down

In what is considered "normal" moment-to-moment experience, awareness stays focused on whatever content is already "within" it. The normal, deeply-held belief in our culture is that there are no inner experiences going on within us—and no inner capacities we might call on—that may lie outside the edges of the current focus of our attention. If you think of awareness as a spotlight, the belief would be that whatever the spotlight shines on includes everything there is to be seen or accessed. There is nothing that exists in the darkness outside of the spotlight.

I am aware that acting as a conscious person (in my definition) steps out of the norms for our culture. In our culture, normal is:

"I know who I am."
"I have nothing to hide."
"What you see is what you get."
"What I'm giving is all I've got."
"I already know everything I think, feel, and believe."
"I have no inner capacities that I am not already accessing in this current moment."

The recognition by a conscious person that none of the above "normal assumptions" are ever actually totally true takes that conscious person out of the tribe of "normals" and puts him or her in what the culture would consider some category of "abnormal," "weird," or unacceptable.

So besides the potential of being empowering and liberating, being a conscious person who expresses curiosity about his inner life can also be socially risky. Much of what is written in the body of this book is meant to generate respect and compassion for what it takes to live as a conscious person within groups (or tribes) that are deeply deluded about the reality of the following duality: *the co-existence of our awareness in the moment, and of our unawareness in that same moment.* There are great benefits to holding this duality consciously, but it often takes courage to be open to the co-existence of both, and to the personal truths that can arise into awareness as a result of this openness. It can take willingness to suffer interpersonal judgments and blows to our self-image when one encounters uncomfortable personal truths.

## New Tribes

As so many of us have discovered, becoming a conscious person places us in a new tribe—a tribe of committed "awareness expanders." Finding other members of this tribe can be a challenge, but, when we do, it can feel like finally finding a true home. This book is in part a call to create more of these conscious collectives. The members of this tribe have let go of being "normal." They know that "normal" means "stay out of your insides." Members of this tribe of awareness expanders have turned "normal" on its head. They know that a dedicated practice of looking within is believed by the general culture to be abnormal, dangerous, weird, or self-indulgent, but they have discovered that this cultural belief is inaccurate, that it is a distortion of our natural, felt connection to all of our inner experiences and to all of our inner capacities. We suffer profound losses as a result of this cultural aversion to turning our attention to the experience of our inner world, including disconnection from inner capacities such as insight, intuition, creativity, and emotional intelligence. The dominant cultural belief brings about the thievery of the essential guidance provided to us by these inner capacities.

"Awareness expanders" have discovered that the avoidance of looking within results in creating and maintaining an experience of endarkenment, rather than promoting the experience of expanding enlightenment. They are committed to continuously expanding the perimeter of that aforementioned "spotlight" into the darkness that lies beyond it in any given moment of personal experience. Those of us who have become lifetime members of *this* tribe know this means we will be consistently using our own *awareness* to look into our own *unawareness*, and we will be discovering what we are not aware of about ourselves *for the rest of our lives!!*

This book is dedicated to the many, many tribes of committed awareness expanders. If you are a member of such a tribe, whether a beginner or an elder, then you know we have all entered into a continuous process of "waking up" from learned illusions and delusions about who we are and who we are not, and (hopefully) a process of "waking down" into direct contact with the trustworthy guidance of our own inner knowing moment to moment. This is our 'path.' We know that 'walking' this path can be both liberating and harrowing. We know too that while walking this path we can find our way and lose it many times over. A double wish embedded in writing this book is to help shorten the time spent "lost" and to help lengthen the moments we live within the liberating times of being "found."

## Questions On My Path

After fifty years or so of using psychotherapy, meditation, and various other methods of expanding and deepening my own self-awareness, what has come to interest me most is captured in the following questions:

- What are the forces within me that "endarken" me rather than "enlighten" me?
- From where do they arise?
- Why do they want to control what I am aware of?
- Why do they want to keep me blind to certain self-truths?
- How do they control my self-awareness?
- Why are they so persistent?
- Do I have any control over their presence within me?
- Can I get rid of them ... in a given moment? ... or permanently?
- Why do they keep coming back after periods of feeling free of them?
- Is there a place inside of me that is free of their control?
- If it exists, how do I find and access that place?
- What can I do to preserve my contact with that place moment to moment?

This is not a book about our simple ignorance about ourselves—that kind of ignorance, or not knowing, can be cured by someone simply pointing out what you don't know. That's easy. This book will surely give you some additional help seeing what you don't know about yourself. But, more crucially, this is a book that will help you see more clearly what it is within you that *actively and continuously* keeps you from seeing a great deal of what is true about yourself and is available to you for personal guidance. Yes, it is a book to assist you in waking up to how much more is available to you within, but, again more importantly, the book's purpose is to help you to wake up to how much your awareness in each moment is in fact being determined by inner forces that operate automatically and outside your ordinary awareness. Let me give you an example of such a moment of my own waking up early in my life to the presence of these forces.

## A Wake Up Moment

A twenty-seven-year-old psychology graduate student is standing, stunned and frozen, in front of the door to his first psychotherapist's office. That student was me, fifty years ago. I was about to have my second session, and even though his office was only five blocks from the hospital where I worked, I almost didn't make it there. Let me tell you what led to my standing in front of his office door in that stunned and frozen state of mind. It was one of my early experiences of what I am calling "waking up" to the forces of endarkenment.

My first session with my therapist had taken place a week earlier. In that session, I had revealed to him that I had a persistent feeling of not being 'good enough,' of some unknown thing being wrong with me. This was an embarrassing secret for me to reveal. He re-cast this revelation into the statement: "It sounds like you're walking around with a measuring stick." He made it sound like I was in some kind of competition. For reasons I didn't understand at the time, I felt a surge of shame rise within me as a reaction to his interpretation. Without thinking about it, I automatically covered over the feeling of shame as quickly and effectively as I could, making light of the moment. I had no idea how powerful that moment was until it was time for my second session, scheduled a week away at noon.

On the appointed day, I didn't remember my second appointment until a quarter past noon...*already* fifteen minutes late. I dashed out of the hospital to walk the five blocks to his office. I knew very well where his office was and how to get there, but I ended up walking a block past the street his building was on before I realized I had missed the turn. I made the correction and then proceeded to walk down his street, right past his office building for fifty yards or so again before realizing I had done so. After I finally made it into his building, I exited the elevator and headed down the hallway to his office. But again, without realizing it, I *had turned the wrong way once more* and was heading in the opposite direction of his office.

It was after correcting that final wrong turn that I ended up standing stunned in front of his office door before ringing to go in. It dawned on me in that moment: "Wow! Some part of me does not want to get to this session!" On top of almost "forgetting" my appointment, there were just too many wrong turns for me to miss the message from my interior. *Some part of me, a part that I was **not conscious** of until that moment, was **actively** trying to prevent me from keeping that second appointment. How come?* Apparently that part of me had a mind and will of its own!

That early experience of being run by inner forces I was not aware of, and that I was not in control of, was one of many such experiences to follow. In the fifty years since, my respect and appreciation has continued to grow for just how frequently my *conscious* feelings, choices, beliefs, attitudes, thoughts, and reactions are actually being influenced, and often determined in limiting and harmful ways, by inner forces I am *not conscious* of. And so as well has my respect and appreciation for the persistence and tenacity of those endarkening forces' efforts to keep me *unconscious of their presence.*

With time, help, and experience, I became more and more aware of how those forces had placed disabling limits on my capacities for loving, for intimacy with others, for standing up for myself, for knowing when a relationship is safe or not, for inner strength and calm, and for the development of my own personal authority, amongst other impacts. Those forces also kept me blind to my own hostility and hurtfulness, to my prejudices, to my coldness, to my arrogance, to my shame and self-doubt, as well as to my need for others and my vulnerability to their rejection and disapproval. Becoming aware of these forces has enabled me to step out of their grip and step into a continuing expansion of my authenticity, openness, compassion, connection to others, and empowerment.

My need to hide my feeling of shame from myself and from my therapist in that first session was an introduction to the power of shame within me, and to the desperate need to avoid feeling it myself, much less admitting its presence to someone else. A primary challenge I continue to meet at the leading edge of the growth of my own self-awareness and the evolution of my own authentic personhood is to find the courage and the compassion to tolerate the unique discomfort and fear of pushing past shame—the shame I have carried, and still carry, about acknowledging and expressing many core and natural aspects of myself.

Something like what happened to me has happened to many of you. Something woke us up, made us realize that indeed we were doing a version of sleepwalking; made us realize we were not aware of whole pieces of our native selves; realize that we had been selectively endarkened to those pieces. We realized there was more to us than meets the "I." As part of this awakening, we have frequently been blessed with pleasant and enlightening discoveries about ourselves—for example, discoveries of unknown capacities for love, joy, creativity, self-assertion, courage, and inner peace. But we have also hated and feared what we've discovered because those hidden aspects of ourselves were dosed with shame and fearfulness (the "bad me"). Some examples of these types of wake-ups might include reconnecting to inner powers we have been terrorized or shamed out of using or trusting. Or they might include previously unfelt and forbidden feelings of anger, fear, hurt, and grief. Many of us have also discovered unresolved interpersonal traumas, often dosed with crippling shame.

## The Power of Active Unconsciousness

I've joked around with colleagues and friends about my being more interested in "endarkenment" than I am in enlightenment. There is truth in the kidding, though, in the sense of my intense curiosity about what un-enlightens me, and others; about what keeps me blind to some things about myself that may be plainly visible to others, both inner strengths and inner flaws. My curiosity arises from a deep knowing that exposing the endarkening forces within me to the light of my own awareness is one of the essential keys to continuing my movement into greater personal freedom, power, and authenticity.

Like I said earlier, what is kept hidden from me by these forces could be something I would be glad to claim for myself, or alternatively could be something I am horrified to discover may be true of me. But I know my conscious self has little to do with the choice to keep something hidden in the first place. It has become my focus to uncover what the "something" is within me that decides *for me* what to let me see and what to keep hidden from me, what it is in me that, after the liberating experience of an emotional or spiritual breakthrough, manages to shut my experience down again. I have come to see this post-awakening experience of being shut down by the endarkening forces as virtually a predictable event.

Growing numbers of us "awareness expanders" have discovered the existence within us of a "something" that enforces our endarkenment, a "something" that tells us who we are and who we are not; who we're supposed to be, and who we're not supposed to be. This discovery is a bit like waking up from a hypnotic trance. This "something" had functioned in fact like a permanent "altered state of consciousness"—one that somehow became our second nature. We ended up identifying with this altered state. And this endarkened version of ourselves came to be simply "me." This altered or adjusted version of ourselves is what we as a culture consider "normal."

This altered, endarkened state was "permanent" until we were somehow "snapped out of it." Of course we had no idea we were in some kind of trance. We had thought: "I'm just me; this is who I am." As long as we were content with, even proud of, that 'me,' we just sailed along. And if we were unhappy and ashamed of that 'me,' well, we suffered and slogged along, endlessly trying to be more acceptable to ourselves and to those who mattered to us.

Initially we may have wandered along this bumpy path of waking up and self-recovery feeling more or less confused about what this new information about ourselves meant, and about what to do with it. If I am not who I thought I was, then who am I really? And is who I really am acceptable? And what do I do about the experiences of finding positive aspects of myself and then losing contact with them again? And what makes me fear certain aspects of myself, even abhor them? And what makes sustaining change in my relationship to myself such an iffy process?

Many of us now know that waking up is a process. We also know we can actively participate in the process of our own waking up, and in the release from the grip of our conditioned, self-destructive, socially-accepted altered states of consciousness, that we can make deliberate, conscious choices about healing the division in us into a "good me" and a "bad me," and we can keep moving towards regaining our wholeness. So we have continued to meditate, practice self-inquiry, use psychotherapy, find teachers and coaches, do workshops and retreats, practice yoga, pray, chant, listen to our bodies, join groups of fellow travelers, and so on.

But still we suffer. We slip and slide. We seem to regress as we seek to progress. We bump into dark matter we didn't know was within us. Old and familiar demons arise to push us backwards or hold us in some stagnant or self-defeating place. Disappointment, despair, resignation, or depression can take hold. The forces of endarkenment too often seem to regain control of our evolution.

## The Ghost in the Machinery

This endarkening "something" became a major focus of my self-exploration. I have for many years been dedicated to making it more conscious. Its presence in every human being with whom I have ever had a deep relationship— be it my wife, friends, clients, colleagues, my siblings, or my own children— has become an undeniable fact for me. I have come to understand that its universal presence must be accepted and made conscious. If it is not, we will forever remain in its grip, individually and collectively. Its methods of keeping us endarkened in the first place, and then un-enlightening us when we do wake up, must be made visible. How it retakes inner ground we have gained, or robs us of what we have repossessed about ourselves, must be exposed. This "something" must be seen for the active, controlling, and independent inner force that it is. It has a mind of its own. It is the ghost in our inner machinery. If we don't see it, we will be caught in the self-destructive trap of blaming ourselves for that within us that is automatically self-destructive, diminishing, and out of our control.

## Being Seasoned On The Path

In spite of the efforts of this inner endarkening force to push us off the path of waking up, growing numbers of us have stuck it out. We have discovered that it ends up being much more painful to quit the path of waking up than to stay on it. I kid my clients when they realize they can't quit. I tell them they are now "doomed to consciousness." Recognition of that truth usually brings a rueful, knowing laugh.

I had a client who had for many years been on his own wake-up path from living in the grip of his bully mentality, which was devoted to power and intimidation. Painful losses of friendships and marriages had deepened this client's realizations of how the early development of his super-auton-omous, bully thinking and behavior had painfully distorted his life experience. His clarity also grew regarding how the old ways of operating still fought his current intention to develop kindness and compassion for himself and others.

Besides moving through the challenges he had met confronting his bully ways, he was also dealing with a life-threatening progressive physical illness. This physical illness was just one of several instances of life "intruding" and pushing him towards waking up to a need for greater self-compassion and honesty about his vulnerability. This awareness did not surface within him without a variety of inner "attacks." For example, there was criticism for not waking up sooner, as well as a critical voice asking him, "Why bother so late in life?" He was seventy-seven years old. His bully belief that "need-iness" was weak created feelings of shame when experiencing his own vulnerability. He called himself a "sissy." This part of him saw his movement toward openheartedness and trust as setting him up for nothing but pain and victimhood.

At the same time, he had never felt happier or more intimately connected to himself and others. His more current experience of being loved and loving was new to him, and treasured. He was finding his own way of walking the line between being open to love and loving while also learning when and how to protect his heart from the insensitivity of others. Love and loving was new to him, but so were new ways to use his "power" to protect himself. For example, he now exercised his power not by dominating and frightening people, but by simply expressing to them the hurt or disappointment they had caused him.

When I would ask him how he was doing, he would often say, "Never better, never worse." This expression fit the two-sided nature of his waking-up process—of opening and closing, of joy and pain, of remembering and forgetting, and of the back and forth between the grip of his conditioned inner shame and the freedom of living in accordance with his inner truth, moment to moment. His humor also reflected the "seasoning" of his awareness. He often started our sessions, half kiddingly, with, "Well listen, you know I don't want to feel any sucky feelings, right? You know what I am here for, right? Permanent bliss! Can you give it to me?" I'd laughingly tell him "no," and he would respond, "Well alright then, let's get down to business."

Many of us have been matured and seasoned while walking this path of expanding our awareness of our inner selves. The path has taken us deeper and deeper into the truth of our own inner experience. We know the benefits of this deepening but we also know the costs. We have discovered our path is not laid out before us. Our unique path cannot be known ahead of time, by us or anybody else. Our path is created and discovered as we walk it. It emerges with each conscious or unconscious foot we put in front of the other. Someone once described it as "building the bridge as you're walking across it." It emerges in our finding our own unique balance between our need to belong and our need for autonomy. This balance shifts from one moment to the next. We've learned that our steps will create a balanced and authentic path of waking up as long as we continuously remember to stop, look, and listen for our own deep inner knowing...and hopefully remember to do so sooner rather than later.

## But How Come?

But how come we so easily and regularly "forget" to stop, look, and listen? How come we go back into what many call a "trance state?" How come we keep getting it and losing it; remembering who we really are and then forgetting? How come we abandon the voice of inner truth? How come waking up can be so difficult and tricky? We all may have experienced spontaneous moments of grace, revelation, and release. Still, in so many ways the path looks and feels like a battlefront—a battlefront with powerful, insidious, unseen forces determined to keep us endarkened, keep us lost, confused, or even put us back to sleep. These forces can fill us with fear, shame, and self-doubt, or do the opposite and fill us with new self-righteous convictions and blind psycho-spiritual arrogance—like the colleague who told me he was "fully psychoanalyzed" and was no longer unconscious of anything about himself!! These are forces that we cannot see clearly; like ghosts lying in ambush for us along the path, ready to pull us into the thickets of undeserved shame and/or false defensive pride.

## The Ego

I am clear that what I will be calling the "ego" is the inner "ghost in the machinery" in charge of these "endarkening forces." I am clear that our egos are acting out interpersonal survival strategies we learned as youths. They are trying to keep us both safe within our tribes and self-respecting at the same time. Our egos use repression, believed beliefs, and certain rewards and punishments to keep us deluded about who we really are.

I am also clear that for most of us there is a great deal that remains unseen and confusing about what I am calling an ego. If we can't see that our egos are both real *and* not who we really are, then we will be at their mercy. If we can't see clearly the shadow forces the ego uses to keep us deluded, we will fight a losing battle, and we will continue to be plagued by the belief that our lack of progress or failures on the path of waking up to our real selves are our own fault—*that we are doing it to ourselves; that somehow we prefer suffering and delusion to living in the truth of who we are; that there really is something wrong with us.* This actually couldn't be further from the truth. We are deluded into assuming we are in control of our change process when we are not. And we are deluded into believing we can't change when we can. This is why we need to make this ghost in our inner machinery and its tactics of deception and endarkenment more visible, to take off its cloak of invisibility.

The ghost, what I am calling the ego, wants to stay invisible. It wants to keep us deluded. A successful delusion is one you don't see. The ego wants to keep us split and twisted within ourselves, but make us believe this state is our true nature. Its job is to keep us in its altered state of consciousness. and to keep us *unconscious* of our *unconsciousness* about ourselves. What a neat trick. And it is also dedicated to keeping us unaware of and disconnected from what I call our inner "Truthplace." The Truthplace is the place within us where we access our true selves from moment to moment. The ego keeps us disconnected for what *it* believes to be our "best interest," regarding both our need for acceptance by those who matter to us, as well as for the sake of maintaining some sense of acting from free choice. *The ego's success in doing its job effectively depends on it operating in stealth mode.*

But if the ego *is* an actual internal reality, could we uncover its essential nature, structure, and purpose? I have called it "the ghost in the machinery" of our interpersonal operating systems. Could this ghost be uncovered in a way such that each of us could actually "see" it operating within us? Could we become clear not only that each of us has an ego, but also learn what our own personal ego is actually like? And if we do all have one, can we get clearer about why? What it is good for? What are its limits and downsides?

Equally important, if we are something more than what our egos tell us we are, what might that "something more" include? If that "something more" is a more accurate, more expanded version of who we really are, how do we draw closer to *that*? If that "something more" is a positive asset, how do we nourish its emergence? And if the "more" is something we have learned to be afraid or ashamed of, how do we work through those conditioned reactions? These are the questions for which this book seeks to provide answers.

## My Intention

My guiding intention for this book is this: I want to make a contribution to our process of self-recovery and self-realization that makes this process both more user-friendly and more potent. I have watched too many people, myself included, get caught by the forces of endarkenment; caught in nasty, self-destructive cycles of confusion, self-doubt, and self-hatred in the process of doing good, honest work on their inner lives. I have witnessed an almost universal blindness to the presence of the ghosts in our machinery—our egos—as they stealthily do their work.

*What the ego is actually trying to accomplish for its host has remained unclear and confused, and shrouded in unhelpful negative judgments. We need to decriminalize having an ego. Everyone has one. The fact that its job is to find a way to preserve our safety and acceptability in our tribes, while simultaneously preserving our sense of self-respect and autonomy, has not heretofore been spelled out. And how the ego accomplishes this dual task—how it actually works within us; how it controls us—has remained mysterious, hidden from our view. Our egos have remained largely in stealth mode.*

So the first part of my contribution will be to more clearly identify what the ego is and how it has been both friend and foe within us regarding our process of self-development, and how to more clearly identify the difference between what is me and what is my ego. It is meant to be an owner's guide to the mechanics of the ego, as well as a guide to its disempowerment.

The "job description" of the ego that is laid out in the first half of this book, through a combination of documents and dialogues, is designed to help you "see" your own ego "in living color," *as it operates within you*, to help you not only know that you do have one, but to know what yours is like and how it works. It is designed to make the ghost visible and palpable, to bring your ego out of stealth mode. Then you can decide how you want to relate to your own ego. Then you can move from being possessed by your ego to *possessing it*—from being mostly ego-possessed to being more and more self-possessed. And with more and more self-possession comes more and more authenticity and empowerment.

The second part of my contribution to our process of self-recovery and self-realization is this: to provide supports that insure the process of separating "me" from my "ego" is securely grounded in greater access to our potent inner resources of felt, trustable, direct knowing and self-discovery—more grounded in skillful access to what I will be calling our Truthplace. When I am connected to my Truthplace I experience being in the flow of a powerful "something" that opens, reveals, clears, clarifies, creates, appreciates, undoes what needs to be undone, and ties together what needs to be reunited within me.

To turn these intentions into the lived experience of individual and collective self-recovery and self-realization, I offer not just the "maps" describing the unique inner "territories" of both the ego and the Truthplace, but also the tools for navigating these territories. These tools or methods can be used both as an individual and within groups of like-minded fellow travelers. Over the past fifty plus years of my work as a psychotherapist, organizational consultant, and awareness trainer, I have found these maps and methods to be helpful to the hundreds of individuals and groups, and to the many organizations, I have been privileged to work with and learn from.

Using these practices accomplishes several outcomes: more conscious, more accurate visibility of the ego at work within us, and more clarity that *my ego is not me and I am not my ego*. This awareness and clarity then fosters a release from its constricting grip. Once the ego's endarkening grip is weakened, our awareness is freed to be used to find deeper, more reliable access to the *already present* internal source of all the inner qualities which we seek: *more compassion, authenticity, authority, personal power, open-mindedness, trustworthy inner self-guidance, and loving connection with ourselves and others*. This ever-present inner source, our inner Truthplace, is where we find the clarity, compassion, capacity, and courage to live from one moment to the next in conscious awareness of both our deep need for each other's embrace and our deep need to be true to ourselves—without denying or minimizing the power of either need.

## Book Format

The book is divided into two sections with several chapters in each. The first section is named "My Ego And My Self." This section is devoted to the description of what the ego does and how it does it, and to the differentiation between "me and my ego." The second section is called "My Truthplace And My Self." This section is devoted to the description of what the Truthplace is, what it contains, what it does, where it is, and how to consciously and deliberately access it.

The exploration and mapping of the ego and the Truthplace taken up in this book alternates between the didactic documents written by me, and dialogues in response to those documents between myself and several participants in a fictional workshop. The workshop, the participants, and the dialogues are fictionalized. The participants are composite characterizations of some of the many real people I have known and worked with as individuals and in groups over my fifty plus years as a professional. The dialogues, while not real, are meant to capture the substance and feel of the thousands of real dialogues that have occurred between myself and my individual clients, and with those clients who have participated in the many workshops I have led. Chapter One introduces the workshop participants through their dialogues with me about their current understanding of what an ego is. The following chapters alternate between descriptive documents written by me, followed by dialogues between myself and the members of the workshop in response to those documents.

I have chosen this format for the book to provide the reader not only with the verbal maps of the ego and the inner Truthplace, but also with the experience of those maps being translated into living experiences by people sharing how those maps either fit or don't fit as descriptions of their own inner territories—and how they illuminate their inner experience or fail to do so. Maps are helpful, even necessary, for the guidance they provide. But they are not the actual territory they depict. The map may help you find your way into and around the territory, but it will never reveal what you will discover when actually traversing the territory. You can learn a lot from a map about a physical landscape you are about to hike through, but you will not *know* the landscape until you actually walk it. I believe you, the reader, will find much to identify with within the experiences of the different workshop participants. You will also find that what is described within the documents is clarified and fleshed out through the participants entering and traversing the different *actual inner terrains of experience* while using my maps of both the ego and the Truthplace. I view my descriptive documents as the equivalent of mapping one's DNA, and the dialogues as an expression of that DNA in embodied experience.

# Section One

## My Ego and My Self

Section One

# chapter one

# What Do You Think An Ego Is?

## The Workshop Begins

**Lou:** You have all chosen to be a part of this workshop out of both a curiosity about the notion of an "ego" and from a desire to find a way out of some way you are feeling stuck in your own personal development. Thank you for being here and for your curiosity. Let's first see about collecting some descriptions of your experiences that might relate to the concept of "ego." There is much confusion around the word "ego" and what it points at. There is also much confusion about whether one has an ego or not, and whether there is any difference between my "me" and my ego. Let's explore some of that confusion. What does the word "ego" conjure up for you?

**Matt:** I'm pretty clear that I have an ego. But I am confused about whether an ego is a good thing or a bad thing. On the one hand, having an ego seems to mean having self-confidence and self-esteem. On the other hand, it seems to mean being arrogant, self-righteous, and a bully. Are there good and bad egos?

**Lou:** This is part of the confusion. If having an ego, meaning having self-confidence and self-esteem, is a good thing, can there be too much of a good thing? And your question about "good and bad" egos raises the notion of types of egos. Maybe all egos are not the same?

**Mary:** Where I come from the ego is nothing but a problem. The ego is a bad thing, and it just gets in the way of my being helpful to others. In my world getting rid of the ego is the goal.

**Lou:** This is another point of view, especially in many religions and spiritual practices. In these systems of thinking the ego is a very real internal force and is seen as "private enemy number one." This perspective is held in many team situations too, isn't it? That expression, "Leave your ego at the door," captures this same belief. The ego is seen as self-centered in a negative and destructive way to good teamwork.

**Willa:** Several years ago I had what I will call a spiritual experience. It was profound and is hard to describe without sounding crazy. I had been a meditator for many years and had many experiences of the benefits of my practice. A few years ago I began studying with a meditation master, an Indian from a Hindu tradition. In one group session this incredibly beautiful blue light appeared inside me and filled me with a deep sense of peace, vast spaciousness, ecstasy, and love. It was amazing and yet felt natural at the same time. I knew this experience was an expression of my true nature, that this was my real being expressing itself, and that this was not just some nice idea but a real, live experience.

I was a different person after that meditation. I was happy, at ease with myself. I found joy and pleasure in the simplest of things, like just sitting in the sun or watching kids play. I carried that experience with me for at least a year—until I fell in love with someone. At first that was all bliss all the time too. But then we started having fights and pretty quickly I crashed and the relationship blew up and I felt worse and worse. I couldn't get back to what I thought was my true nature and those wonderful feelings. I thought I had finally been freed from all my negative thinking and feeling. I don't know if those thoughts and feelings were my ego. Now I wonder whether those good feelings were even real. I wonder what is real. Nothing good seems reliable to me. And I feel like I screwed up a beautiful gift, like somehow I may not be meditating the right way or with enough devotion or something. I feel lost and depressed about it.

**Lou:** A huge disappointment.

**Willa:** For sure.

**Lou:** And lots of confusion about what's going on inside you, whether or not it has anything to do with ego. As well as some sense you're to blame for losing that state of bliss and getting caught in negativity again. If this is the ego at work, why would it come back again? And how could it make you forget what you felt you knew so clearly? Right?

**Willa:** Right.

**Lou:** So if it is the ego, your experience of the ego would certainly be a painful, negative one.

**Willa:** Absolutely!

**Lucas:** I just want to piggyback onto what Willa just shared. My experience feels similar, but different too. I have been to shrinks on and off over the years for panic attacks and dips in my self-confidence, and it has been helpful. Well, at the beginning of last year I had a real crash in confidence after being thrown out of a partnership in a hedge fund. A friend of mine had gone to an intensive therapy workshop, and some time after my being kicked to the curb he was telling me about how it changed him. I decided it might be the right thing for me at the right time. I didn't know what else to do. I was feeling pretty desperate.

The workshop was five days and evenings of group therapy, role playing, psychodrama, and lectures. I was very skeptical at first. We all went back into our family histories and got to re-experience what it was like to be a kid in our families. To my surprise, it got so much clearer both that I've always had trouble really feeling alright inside of myself and about why I have had so much trouble feeling okay. It was like a dam broke inside me. I discovered feelings I didn't know I had. I didn't know how much rage I had pent up inside me, or how much buried shame I was carrying. I won't go into the whole story. Well, by the end of the workshop I was flying. I felt free. I felt all right, really all right as a person, for the first time in my life, without having to perform. It was really different. I couldn't wait to get home and share my new found self with my wife. I wanted to connect with her with my new self and recover some of the love we felt for each other in the beginning of our relationship. She couldn't feel what I was feeling, couldn't connect with me. Truth is she's been pretty pissed at me for quite a while. I felt that disconnection and it pissed me off. With that I closed down.

I felt so crushed to go from that high to so closed down. They warned us at the end of the workshop that we were probably in for a rollercoaster ride of feelings. But wow! I didn't expect to be slammed that way. That's a year ago. I think I'm different from the workshop, but I never got that really free feeling back again. Like Willa, I don't really know what happened and whether or not that was my ego coming back. I know what came back was really familiar, just a hell of lot more painful now that I had been free of it for a moment. At least Willa got a year. I got about twenty-four hours of freedom post-workshop.

**Lou:** Again, horribly disappointing.

**Lucas:** And scary...like I'm doomed or maybe have depression.

**Lou:** Yes. And again, if this is the ego at work, what is it doing? Why shut you down? You didn't sit down with yourself and consciously choose to shut down. It happened to you. It was automatic. If this "something" we are calling the ego shut you down, it would appear it has a mind of its own, wouldn't it?

**Lucas:** Sounds a little schizophrenic.

**Lou:** Or like multiple personalities, I know!

**Gabe:** I think the ego is necessary for functioning in life. I wouldn't have called it my ego. For me, my ego was my sense of self, my sense of belonging here, of my right to take care of myself. If I didn't have a good sense of self I'd be at the mercy of others' agendas and I wouldn't have any self-motivation or self-respect. If that's my ego, then my ego was an ally, a strength. That strength has helped me be successful in my life and protected me from being taken advantage of. The only reason I'm curious now about the notion of ego is because I've lost a sense of meaning in my life. Actually, I don't know if I ever had it. I just did what I was supposed to do as a man, and did it well. That's all good. I've been very successful as an entrepreneur. I'm proud of all that. But in this part of my life—I'm forty-eight now—I seem to be coming up empty on the inside and I don't like the feeling. I have a hunch this somehow relates to this notion of an ego.

**Lou:** This is another way the word is used...to point to something that gives us a strong sense of self and that motivates us to take care of ourselves, to respect ourselves. In this sense of the word, the ego *is* an ally, a part of our survival equipment. It can give us a sense of entitlement and worth. And most importantly, it creates a sense of acceptability and safety within the groups that matter to us, our tribes.

I think your hunch is accurate. I think when we see more clearly how the ego operates inside us, we will see that it twists our experience of meaning and purpose to accommodate its own purpose. It seems that for whatever our egos give us that may have value, it demands that we give up something else of value about ourselves in exchange.

**Gabe:** Being a man, I find I am often getting some kind of feedback about my "male ego." From my guy friends, that feedback is my male ego is a good thing and I should be more that way. From women, it's that my male ego is getting in the way of our relationship. But then the women don't seem to like it if I am not masculine enough. Very confusing.

**Lou:** So here "ego" points to a certain admired way of being for membership in a particular group: the male community. There are certain qualities you are supposed to have and behaviors you are supposed to exhibit if you are a man. And those qualities get you accepted by your male tribe, but may get you rejected by others. I would also assume that when you are amongst your guy friends and you are feeling you're meeting those expectations of maleness that you feel pretty good inside.

**Gabe:** Sure. I feel like I belong. Sometimes I feel superior to some of the other guys who are not so sure of themselves. "Who's up and who's down" goes on a lot in our circle. Mostly it's friendly, but it feels good when you're more on top of your game than the others.

**Lou:** So there is some internal reward for succeeding at the demands of having a male ego: Good feelings inside, confidence, maybe even superiority, invincibility, and pride. And as well there are some external rewards too: You are looked up to, admired, envied?

**Gabe:** Yes, that's true. But I'm starting to feel "so what?" It's lost its juice to be the big guy. And on top of that it's gotten confusing around women

**Lou:** Yes. And to add to the confusion, we also know that the social expectations of how males and females are supposed to be and to act have been changing in recent decades.

**Liz:** I've known forever that my ego is a perfectionist. It demands I do everything right...no mistakes allowed!

**Lou:** Makes you strive but probably also tortures you?

**Liz:** Yes!

**Lou:** So when you do something perfectly, how do you feel?

**Liz:** I feel great! I've been super successful in my work life. I feel in control and competent. I like the compliments I get. I like it when people are amazed at how much I get done, and how well I do it. I like it when people look to me as the "go to" person. I guess there is a bit of superiority that goes with that. I am better than other people at getting certain things done.

**Lou:** Sounds like it is a fact that you are better at some stuff than other people. The good feelings and the facts are linked up, but they are different realities, aren't they? But at any rate, when you get it done perfectly, or close thereto, you get some good rewards, both in terms of how you feel inside and how others feel about you, how they see you. What happens if whatever you're doing doesn't get done perfectly?

**Liz:** I am merciless with myself. I really give myself a beating. I kind of yell at myself internally...sometimes out loud too. I've always felt this was how to stay on top of things. But I can also get real depressed and end up nonfunctional for stretches of time.

**Lou:** So there is a serious upside and a serious downside to the perfectionism you think your ego demands.

**Liz:** I don't know if it is me or my ego doing the demanding. I don't know if I can tell the difference. I guess I don't know if there is a difference. I do know that I'd like to find a way to perform really well without the downside. It takes the joy out of it all. And I find I am losing some friends along the way too.

**Lou:** Well that's precisely what we're up to here, isn't it? Asking and seeking to answer these questions: Is there a difference between me and my ego? If there is, what is it? And, is there a way to keep the upsides and lose the downsides of how we are currently operating?

**Mary:** As I said before, I was raised to believe that having an ego is bad. It meant you were prideful—one of the seven deadly sins, an offense to God. Being humble was good, being self-effacing, putting other people's needs ahead of mine was being good. This has often backfired in real life. But I still feel bad when I feel good about myself, or when my own needs jump up inside me.

**Lou:** So for you, having an ego, in the sense of feeling proud about yourself, is a bad thing. This dilemma is more common than we may realize. And yet we could still see it as a type of ego; that is, an ego that thinks having an ego is bad! So when you are acting in accordance with your belief, and not having an ego, what happens? How do you feel?

**Mary:** Well, I feel quietly good, maybe secretly good. I feel safe, too. Hmm. I hadn't noticed that feeling before until just now. Some people like it when I am focusing on them, making them feel okay, and that feels good and safe to me. But some people take advantage of me and then I get resentful. And when someone is obviously blowing his or her own horn I also feel angry and judgmental. And then I get on myself for being judgmental. Come to think of it, I feel best when I'm by myself.

**Lou:** So having an ego has some benefits, but living with the rule that feeling good about yourself is bad makes it really tough to ever feel all right with yourself.

**Mary:** That's for sure.

**Lou:** I believe as we continue our exploration you will see that creating the sense of safety you just spotted is one of the ego's major purposes. It desperately wants to create a sense of safety within groups of people who matter to us.

But let's take a moment and summarize the many different ways those of you who have spoken have used the word "ego" in describing your own personal experiences. I recognize that several of you are not sure there is any difference between you and an ego. But you all described some internal attitudes and beliefs that affect your behavior and feelings about yourself. For the sake of our discussion, I am going to put those descriptions all under the heading "ego." So far our examples hit on what egos do or demand or give you. We do not yet have a description of what an ego is. Let's see for now if there are any unifying themes in our examples.

We certainly have some divided points of view. Some of you see your egos as good and necessary—necessary for a sense of self, for motivation, and for self-esteem and respect. Others see the ego as both helpful and harmful. Others see your egos strictly as a problem. The ego is seen as blocking genuine self-realization, as getting in the way of being a good, or humble, or open, or authentic person. It is also seen as getting in the way of being a good team member. You see your egos as something that gets in the way.

There also remains the confusion around whether or not the ego is something separate and different from "me." After all, there's nobody else in my head, is there? It's just me in here doing this thinking and feeling...unless I have multiple personalities! Sometimes it feels like that, doesn't it?

One thing that seems to be common to your different views is the sense that whatever the word "ego" may point to, there always seems to be a self-evaluation involved—some sense of how it's good to be and how it's bad to be. This is true in my use of the word also. It seems to be in the nature of whatever an ego is that it is always concerned with judging and evaluating, pointing out what it considers good ways of being and what it considers bad ways of being. In fact, egos seem to me to be *compulsive evaluators*. And they appear equally dedicated to motivating us to do and be what gains our own and others' approval and acceptance, and to stopping us from doing or being what will bring disapproval and rejection.

This version of the ego could be described as our own personal public relations manager. This role seems to flow out of our deep need to belong and be valued by those people whose acceptance and approval matters to us. We could call these groups our "dependency groups" or our "tribes." Our first dependency group or tribe is of course our family. Later tribes might include peer, religious, social, business, sports, gender, and professional groups, amongst others. Each of these groups or tribes have their own conditions for maintaining membership and approval, don't they? You must be certain ways and do certain things to belong, and not do or be other things, right? Even amongst people who are into self-improvement or who are spiritual seekers. Good and bad ways of being seem to always exist, like Gabe was talking about the male tribe. You are a successful member of the male tribe if you...what?

**Gabe:** Don't show fear or need.

**Stew:** Don't ask for help...or directions!

**Frank:** Don't cry; don't be vulnerable.

**Gabe:** Dominate and have power; be competitive.

**Lou:** So those are some of the dos and don'ts of the male ego. What about the female ego?

**Mary:** Take care of everybody.

**Liz:** Don't be too aggressive.

**Tina:** Be good-looking.

**Liz:** Be the mom and be the professional...perfectly.

**Willa:** Make men feel good about themselves.

**Lou:** These are very different types of demands for each gender. What do they have in common? It's the "good/bad" thing again, isn't it? Each group has different "goods" and "bads," but always some acceptable and some unacceptable ways of being. And they also have in common the fact that how successful you are in meeting the expectations of the ego has consequences regarding how others feel about you and how you feel about yourself.

It turns out there are lots of types of egos, each with their own particular set of dos and don'ts. Just to point to a few of the many ego types, here is a partial list: saint, rebel, conformist, star, hermit, tough guy/gal, people pleaser, cynic, bully, know-it-all, martyr, entertainer, lover, hero, and dramatist.

I could go on, but you get the idea. Some of these will get fleshed out as we go along. But for the moment, let's stick with the male and female ego types. Here's a question for you: All of the qualities and behaviors that each of these egos finds acceptable are perfectly fine and useful in and of themselves, aren't they? Being fearless, stoic, independent, tough, dominant, competitive, powerful, or, on the other side, taking care of others, looking pretty, being an effective parent and professional, and making a man feel good—these are all useful and valuable traits or ways of being. So what's the problem? What makes the ego's favoring these traits problematical?

If you examine your experience closely, I think you will see that the problem is that the ego makes these ways of being and acting compulsory, mandatory, and good or bad. You *must be this way...and you must never be the opposite.* It is this rigidity and absoluteness of the ego, this black and whiteness, that makes it problematic. The male must always be tough and not need others or he will be rejected by his tribe (and probably hers). The female must always take care of others and not be concerned with her needs or she will be rejected by her tribe (and his). The ego says you can't have it both ways and remain acceptable.

Like I said before, the ego gives one thing but takes away another. It's always enforcing and reinforcing an inner split—"you can have this but you can't have that." The capacity to be tough is useful in certain challenging and threatening circumstances, but not at the cost of *never* being allowed to seek the comfort and protection of others. Likewise, caring for others is a blessing for those being cared for, and fulfilling for the caregiver. But the cost of not being allowed to be equally caring for oneself sabotages the benefits for all concerned in the long run. Is this discussion of ego types, of the ego's compulsive black and white demands, and its rewards and punishments, ringing some bells?

**Mary:** Wow! That list of ego types is an eye opener. I never thought of a saint as an ego type, but it can be, I can see that. Wow. If being a saint means you always have to be kind and gentle and loving and never angry, critical, or self-interested, then that's an ego at work, isn't it?

**Lou:** Yes. Compulsivity again. Rigidity. Black and white again.

**Mary:** So I may be really "good" to people, whatever "good" means, and still be seeking acceptance and approval, even though consciously I am telling myself I am just serving others. I do feel superior to people who are selfish and self-centered. I get off on judging them. Damn. I think I just told on myself.

**Lou:** Told on your ego, yes. But maybe not your "self." We'll see.

**Mary:** So there is a difference?

**Lou:** In my experience, yes. I think your self is showing up right now in being aware of how your ego operates. What I call the ego is not self-aware, self-reflective. It does not question its assumptions or motivations. And notice too that by being good you are not only seeking approval and acceptance, you are also avoiding disapproval and rejection. You are seeking safety, like you noticed before.

But first let's see if there are more questions about types.

**Matt:** I don't get the "hermit" as an ego type. If the ego is about being acceptable to your tribe or dependency group as you put it, the hermit seems to be saying, "I have no tribe"; "I am giving up seeking membership in any tribe."

**Lou:** Well remember, if it is an ego at work, there is a compulsive or compulsory quality to it. So you *have to be a hermit*. And contrariwise, it is bad, forbidden, dangerous to be social with other humans, and it *must* be avoided.

**Matt:** So my hermit ego feels good when it rejects membership in the human race. I am safe from rejection in my isolation, maybe even superior to everybody. I get it now. Hermits by definition don't hang out with a tribe of hermits, but if they did they'd all agree that all the other humans don't get it, that they're dangerous, or something like that! A hermit tribe would be like the self-help meeting for procrastinators, only worse. Procrastinators would all show up late. For the hermits, nobody would show up.

**Lou:** Precisely. And there is that experience of interpersonal safety and danger again being a part of the ego's function.

**Frank:** What I am getting is that each of these ego types is just a selection of certain human qualities, behaviors, and abilities that a particular person thinks are better or more acceptable than others, or safer. I don't see why we have to turn that into something called an "ego" or an ego type. To me it seems like just using your ability to discriminate between what behaviors you think are good or useful and what behaviors you think are bad or dangerous.

**Lou:** That ability to discriminate and select what behavior or ability to call on in any real life situation or challenge is critical to our being effective, safe, and wise, isn't it?

**Frank:** Obviously.

**Lou:** But what we are discovering is that this "thing" we are calling an "ego" loses that very ability to discriminate. What we are calling an ego is an internal "something" that compels us to select from a limited set of acceptable responses whether or not those responses are the ones that would best serve our needs, or the needs of others, in a given situation. The ego, it seems, is like the hammer that sees everything as a nail.

**Frank:** For example?

**Lou:** Let me respond in the form of some questions: Is it always good or useful to try to please people? Should we try to please those who are treating us badly? Is it always good or useful to dominate people? What about in a marriage or in teamwork? Is it always good or useful to be helpful? What about when someone needs to learn to do it for themselves? Likewise, is it always good to rebel, or always conform, or always seek attention, or always hide from it? Is it always good to be tough, or always be vulnerable?

**Frank:** Ah. It's the "always" that's the problem, not the behavior itself. It's what you call this "compulsory" quality that sets the workings of the ego against simple good judgment.

**Lou:** Yes; always this way, and never that way. Jamming our choices into categories that are "compulsory," "either/or," and "good or bad," seems to be the hallmark of a certain force or dynamism within us that I'm naming the "ego."

**Frank:** Would you say these are habits, like habitual ways of thinking and behaving?

**Lou:** I would say they are habitual in the sense that we automatically repeat them without thinking about them. But simple habits are not compulsory or compulsive in nature. We can choose to do something different from the simply habitual. I can change the route I habitually take to work, or go to bed earlier than has been my habit. "Compulsive" implies driven, out of control. It implies some kind of imperative, a feeling that "I must be or behave this way, "that "I don't have a choice" to respond differently. Have any of you had this experience? When you knew that the way you characteristically responded was not working but you couldn't stop yourself?

**Matt:** I am not a fighter, and I just lost an opportunity for a promotion because I didn't speak up for myself. I saw I needed to, but I didn't or couldn't speak up. I was afraid I'd sound too pushy or arrogant. But then I felt really bad about myself for being afraid and not pushing.

**Frank:** And I am a fighter and just lost a relationship with a good friend because I couldn't stop fighting with him over his religious beliefs. I knew he had a right to believe whatever he believed, but I wanted to save him from himself. I couldn't believe he couldn't see the errors in his thinking. I'm that way around politics too.

**Liz:** I'm coming back from a physical collapse because I couldn't take a break from working all the time. I'm also a compulsive exerciser. I don't like how I feel when I am not doing something productive. I was running in the park one evening a year ago and saw a light flash just behind one of my eyes. I ignored it and kept running. The next day I passed out in the office. The ER doctor said my blood pressure was acting like a roller coaster. There was nothing physically wrong, just stress.

**Mack:** I am a recovering addict/alcoholic. Eighteen years sober. What you're calling the ego we call "the disease talking to us" or "stinking thinking." So I relate to this. What I don't get is this: My drinking and drugging was compulsive for sure. Some of that was physical—my body craved my substances. But there was a mental, emotional part to it, too. My life is so much better now than it ever was. But I still don't know how to feel all right with myself, at least not in any steady way. I am never really comfortable in my own company. Alcohol and drugs took my uncomfortable feelings away, but eventually it all backfired, and my substances, or how they made me behave, made me feel worse about myself, not better. But I could not admit that to myself. I didn't know what I would do without the relief of alcohol and drugs, and yet they were killing me.

I really didn't know what to do until I crashed and burned and finally got some help. I remember how ashamed I felt for needing help and for not being able to handle drugs and alcohol. But I am not clear how all this relates to the description of the ego we are developing here. Oh, and also, in AA the ego is definitely seen as an enemy to getting and staying sober.

**Lou:** Thank you all for describing these experiences of compulsivity, of being out of control. Each of our egos is all about keeping us under its control, compulsively. For us to be out of the control of the ego, or for the ego to be out of control of us, if it results in damage to our self-image or to our standing in our tribe, is the worst failure possible from our ego's point of view.

In my experience we are an ego-driven society, and we are judged harshly as "failures" for any signs that the maintenance of our image and standing is not in our control. It is risky, socially and interpersonally, to admit to being out of control of whatever threatens our self-image, our standing, and our membership in our tribes. So I appreciate the risks being taken here and your courage in describing these experiences.

Let me say to Mack, who just spoke about his recovery from addiction, that I am also aware in AA that alcoholics self-describe as "egomaniacs with low self-esteem," right?

**Mack:** Yes.

**Lou:** Now that sounds on the face of it like a contradiction, right? How can you be an "egomaniac" and simultaneously have low self-esteem? In our simplistic, popular thinking about the ego we assume that the ego has nothing to do with low self-esteem. "Low self-esteem" is the opposite of "ego." Like someone said earlier, if we have an ego, it is our ego that gives us our self-esteem. I love that term, "egomaniacs with low self-esteem." I think it describes the human condition and the ego very accurately. Here's why:

The kind of self-esteem our egos demand that we generate (compulsively) flows out of the need to counter a deep and opposing belief that we are not all right to begin with—that we are unacceptable to begin with! This belief of a basic insufficiency and unacceptability makes it necessary for us to constantly compensate and counter this belief with proofs of our all-rightness and acceptability. No matter how hard or successfully we compensate, the secret feeling remains that our basic unacceptability is always in danger of being discovered or exposed. Thus, our compulsiveness, our reoccurring bouts of unease with ourselves, our getting and then losing our experiences of personal freedom and power, our feelings of being fraudulent, and our inability to rest and relax comfortably and consistently inside our own skins. I see all of us as egomaniacs with low self-esteem, at least to some degree.

At this time, I want to focus our attention on why the creation of an ego becomes necessary, and on how it is formed out of a split of our native selves into "acceptable" and "unacceptable" aspects. I want to describe how the ego then makes maintaining this split compulsory and compulsive. I want to clarify that the words "compulsive" and "compulsory" are pointing to felt, internal experiences and forces. They are not just concepts. This conditioned, rigid splitting is a major cause of being stuck in or sliding in and out of behaviors, beliefs, and attitudes that continue to cause us suffering.

I want to describe that experience of splitting our selves and talk about how it comes about. I think the best way to do this is to give you a document to read that lays out my understanding of what generates this need to split our selves, and then rigidly maintain that split. The document is a "job description" of the ego—of why it arises, where it comes from, what it does, and a first look at how it does it. You can read the document, formulate your thoughts and questions about it, and then we can continue our discussion about how this compulsive splitting shows up in *your* own experience when we meet again.

# chapter two

# A Job Description
# of the Ego

Here is what I've come to know. The ego is not just an intellectual concept but in fact something real that exists inside us. And we can come to "see" that "something" operating within us. The word "ego," as I use it, points to a real live recognizable experience—actually a bunch of experiences, inside us. The ego is a potent force to contend with on the "wake up trail." And, although many of you may not be clear on the difference between your "me" and your ego, or even if a difference exists, I am clear the ego is different from, and not the same as, our true self.

So if you will take my verbal description of the ego as a map for your own self-reflective use, then you can see if the map matches the direct internal experiences you have of your own ego.

*"Necessity Is the Mother of Invention"* (Plato)

To accomplish a full exposure of the ego, we need to start at the beginning. Although egos are real later in life, we know we are not born with one. Babies and toddlers don't have egos. An ego is something added on to our native selves a bit later in our development—or maybe mixed in with it. It is something that emerges or is created later on in our development. But what is the ego created for? Is it just a natural part of our development?

As human beings we have two basic tasks to accomplish. One is to make sure we sustain our connection with our tribe (family, peer group, etc.), and thus make sure we obtain from our tribe the safety and support that is necessary for survival and for becoming a fully empowered person. The other task is to be true to our own personal experience and fully realize our unique, true autonomous selves. The balance between meeting dependency needs and developing autonomy shifts back and forth continuously throughout our lives. A crucial understanding underpinning successfully executing this balancing act is that dependence and autonomy are two sides of the same coin; they are never completely separate in a human being.

So, some questions emerge:

- Why can't my native self keep my need for embrace safely met within my tribe while also making choices that develop and express my true nature?
- Why would I have to invent something like an ego to accomplish this balancing act?
- What makes adding an ego to the mix necessary?

To answer these questions adequately, we will have to take a look into the process of growing into full personhood. Yes, we are all human beings right from the start of our lives; but we are not fully developed human *persons* at birth. That development requires time and the right conditions. As so many of you know already, being safe and accepted within the tribe (be it family, peer group, organizations, etc.), while also being totally free to be and become your real self, is a very rare combination of circumstances in today's world.

## How does full personhood come about?

We are all born with a full set of human capacities (barring some physical disability). We all have amazing bodies that allow us to see, hear, taste, feel, grasp, and move. We all have intellects that allow us to think. We all have emotions that allow us to know what we feel, and through those feelings to know the meaning of any given experience for us. We all have the capacity to give and receive love. We all have creativity, which allows us to problem-solve and invent. We all have an "inner organ" that allows us to sense what is happening on an intimate level within us, and between us and others. This inner "sensing organ" empowers us to read whether someone is relating to us with pleasure, acceptance, easiness, closeness, and vitality, or with displeasure, fear, anger, tightness, distance, or numbness. This organ is the source of our capacity for empathy. This inner sensory organ is with us from birth.

## The Ideal

All of us are born as distinct and conscious beings. When our separate be-ing-ness is unconditionally respected, we are able to become free, whole human persons. When we are allowed to "be" and to "become" uncondi-tionally, then our native self will develop and emanate all its native qualities.

In a completely open, respectful, and consciously evolving family and human society, we would be allowed to have full access to all of our ca-pacities. We could use our intellects to figure stuff out and analyze differ-ent realms of reality. We could use all our emotions and feelings to know what we felt about different human experiences and what meaning they had for us. We could use our bodies and their senses to explore the nat-ural world and each other. Our curiosity about anything and everything, inside and outside ourselves, would be encouraged. We would be encour-aged to question our assumptions. The natural pleasure, joy, and challenge of learning would be nourished and sustained. Our creativity would be valued and nourished. We would be allowed to pursue our interests and our talents. The unfolding experience of our inner sensing organ would be honored and respected. Our uniqueness and autonomy would be fully embraced while our collective connections and dependence on each other were nourished and fulfilled. We could both be and become our full selves while simultaneously feeling secure about belonging within our tribes. But we all know that such families are at best rare, and that no such human society exists right now.

## The Reality

So instead we have societies that are more or less open to the full breadth and depth of human experience, and more or less closed. All our societies, our social groups or tribes, are closed in some particular ways and open in other particular ways regarding human experience and expression. I think about how an argument in public would be utterly humiliating in Japan but is considered street theater in Italy; or how our American culture places so much value and awareness on wealth, physical appearance, and social status and such little value and awareness on our inner lives.

Families within societies function similarly. That is, they are open to some stuff and closed to other stuff. We learn very early and very thoroughly, first within our families, what is okay to explore with our minds and our intellects and what is not; which feelings are okay to express and which feelings are not. We learn that there are some ways of moving and using our bodies that are considered okay and some that are not. And, in addition, tasks, accomplishments, and pursuits are all classified as worthy or unworthy, valued or degraded.

These rules about what's okay and what's not, what's good and what's bad, are carried within our early caregivers. These limits placed on our caregivers by their early caregivers make it impossible for them to achieve full personhood themselves. This in turn makes it impossible for them to foster full personhood in us. The limiting rules by which they are governed are communicated through them to us as children non-verbally and unconsciously, as well as in direct statements.

These interior rules and regulations within our caregivers restrict their capacity to respond in a fully attuned, open way to the expressions of our needs and to our moment to moment native experience. Our experience of finely tuned reception and acceptance by our early caregivers is disrupted regularly by the socially conditioned, tribal rules placed on their responsiveness. These rules include: "It is good to let babies cry themselves to sleep"; or the opposite, "You should never let a baby cry themselves to sleep"; or "Spare the rod and spoil the child" vs. "Punishing children is bad for their development." Every family and every tribe has its deeply codified rules and regulations regarding how we respond to each other. Some are supportive and others are harmful to our healthy development.

From birth on, we engage in a process of restricting the full use and expression of our inner human capacities and experiences in order to fit into what our caregivers have been conditioned to believe are acceptable or unacceptable ways of being. We are compelled to do so in order to preserve our sense of connectedness to them. *Connection equals survival. Connection equals safety.* As a result of these accommodations, we can end up like a car whose steering wheel has been set so you can only turn it to the left or right a very limited amount. This may work well enough on an absolutely straight road, but god forbid you have to deal with some serious curves. We all know that life's roads are full of those kinds of curves.

## Necessity's Invention = The Ego

I've been using the word "tribe" to point to any group of individuals whose acceptance and approval matters to us. The original tribe is our family, whatever form that may have taken. The tribe defines what is acceptable and what is not. The tribe decides whether you are to be embraced and protected or rejected, ostracized, and attacked. No currently existing tribe is safe enough for its members to be totally true to themselves. Because of the highly conditional acceptance of our original and later tribes it could be said that we end up always experiencing ourselves as continuously "in danger of being our selves." The ego takes on the job of making sure we never place ourselves in such danger, while it also works to preserve some jerry-rigged sense of self-respect and freedom of choice.

## Where It All Begins

We enter our tribal relationships at birth when our dependency on others for physical and "self" survival is at its maximum and our autonomy and choices are at their minimum. If left on our own as infants and very young children, we would not survive. The fact is there would be no, or very reduced, growth in autonomy and personal agency if our dependency needs were not adequately met when we were young. How well we are cared for as physical and human selves in our early years will determine the strength and flexibility of our autonomy and personal empowerment in our later years. The depth and genuineness of our tribe's acceptance of our true uniqueness will also determine the depth and authenticity of our own future self-respect and dignity.

We could make an analogy to a mighty tree: It starts as a seed in the earth. That seed depends on the right combinations of nutrients, water, temperature, and oxygen to sprout. Once sprouted above ground, it still depends on the supplies its roots gather from the earth, and now it also depends on the right amount of sunlight and oxygen above ground to continue to grow. If any of these needs are not met in the ways they need to be met, the tree falters and falls, or never gets off the ground to begin with. The tree's autonomy is expressed in its inherent urge to grow, to become itself, to climb to its full height, and to reach for its fullest bloom. The tree is not the sun, or the air, or the earth, or the water. It is its own self, its own creation, but not without all that it depends on to fully "self-express."

Our tribe's embrace and protection is just as critical for our physical survival, as well as for our full growth and bloom. We know this instinctively, and our body/minds never forget it, nor should they. The need for this embrace and protection endures from infancy to old age. Within the current state of human evolution, the highly conditional status of our ongoing acceptance within our tribes forces us to make some profound distortions of our true selves. Because of all the current tribal dividing of what's acceptable about us and what's not, we must bend and twist ourselves in order to fit in and to maintain safety, i.e. acceptability. *Thus the necessity for the "invention" of the ego.*

The ego becomes an inner manager that carries within, and carries out, all the lessons learned within our initial and later tribes regarding protecting our continued good standing. These tribes taught us what is acceptable about us and what is unacceptable about us; what ways of being or acting, what thoughts and beliefs, what feelings or desires, what traits or qualities, are safe to express within the tribe, and which ones threaten the continued embrace and protection of the tribe. The ego is created to compel us to stay safe within the tribe by editing and altering our native self. And, at the same time, the ego makes a noble, although disabled, effort to create within its host, i.e. you and me, a delusional experience of independence from the tribe and freedom of choice around self-expression. It finds creative and convincing ways to preserve within us a sense of dignity, self-respect, and freedom of choice, in spite of having to bend and twist ourselves away from our authentic self-expression in conformity to the will of the tribe.

## What The Ego Does

The simplest and clearest way to get a bead on the presence of the ego, and on what any ego is all about, is by watching what it actually does and how it does it, right inside your own experience, *by watching it at work*. This kind of close observation will lead us to greater clarity about the ego's existence, nature, purpose, and methods.

The ego has two jobs, both equally compelling.

> Job #1: The ego's first job is to maintain our *safety* within our tribe *by unfailingly compelling us* to behave in a tribally acceptable manner.

> Job #2: The ego's second job is to keep our *self-respect* intact *by unfailingly convincing us* that we are our own persons, completely free to make authentic and independent choices about being and expressing who we are, even though this is not true.

## What the Ego Does to Accomplish Job #1

*For this job, what the ego does is make sure you* **automatically, rigidly, and compulsively seek** *whatever makes you acceptable to those who matter most to you; and, vice versa, makes sure you* **automatically, rigidly, and compulsively avoid** *whatever makes you unacceptable to those same folks.*

So the ego is the maintainer of the division of our native selves imposed by our original tribes. The ego divides all of our native traits, capacities, and talents, and all the ways we might use them, into "acceptable" and "unacceptable." And it reinforces and enforces those divisions in a compelling manner. The ego divides "I" into an "acceptable me" and an "unacceptable me"; into a "good me" and a "bad me." The ego seeks to *guarantee* that we look good both to ourselves and to those who matter to us (our tribe), and to *guarantee* that the "bad me" never sees the light of day.

Of course, since we all come from different tribes, what *your* ego considers acceptable and unacceptable, its "goods and bads," if you will, may be quite different from what *my ego* considers acceptable or unacceptable. For example your ego might compel you to always place other people's comfort ahead of your own. And like all egos, it would reward you with feelings of being "good" if you do so, and punish you with feelings of being "bad" if you don't. Whereas my ego might compel me to always "watch out for number one," and, likewise, reward or punish me depending on my compliance or lack of it.

The list of different traits, capacities, and talents, and all the expressions of them, which the ego divides into good or bad, is endless. Take the intellect for example. Some egos have to know it all, all the time. While other egos compel their hosts to keep their smarts undercover. Or consider aggressiveness. Some egos compel their hosts to intimidate people continuously. Others compel their hosts to make sure they are never perceived as threatening. Some egos insist on trusting nobody; others insist on trusting everybody. Or sexuality. Some egos compel their hosts to seek sensuality obsessively. Other egos see sense pleasure as something to compel the host to always avoid. Even humor. Some egos make it so their hosts can't stop cracking jokes. Other egos compel their hosts to be serious all the time. Whatever is "good" in the eyes of the ego becomes not just good but *compulsory*. You can never not be that way. And for sure you better not ever be the opposite.

So any aspect of being human can be co-opted by the ego to fulfill its task of making certain that you remain acceptable and avoid being seen as unacceptable. Once the ego has taken up residence in its host, and once its particular "goods and bads" have been established, the ego is relentless in accomplishing a task which it sees as just as vital as the lungs' task to keep oxygen supplied to the body. It believes its task is necessary and compulsory for the host's survival. And it is accurate in this assessment, especially in our formative years, and often in our adult lives.

## What the Ego Does to Accomplish Job #2

*For this job, what the ego does is **rigidly, compulsively, and automatically** preserve a convincing belief in the existence of your autonomy, independence, and free will. It does this by maintaining the mental fiction within your conscious mind that "I am simply being who I am," and by maintaining complete unawareness of being coerced into an altered version of your native self.*

The ego's task is a complicated one. Yes, its first job is to manage the universal human need for the (relative) *safety* of the tribe's continued embrace and protection. However, every human being has an equally compelling need to *self-express;* to be and become the unique self that person is meant to be. The experience of being true to our essential nature and of freely making choices regarding self-expression is what gives us an authentic, self-generated sense of dignity, self-respect, personal power, and autonomy. Being forced to choose one of these fundamental needs over the other is a bit like being forced to choose between either inhaling or exhaling.

## The Problem Our Egos "Solve"

The uniquely human problem the ego attempts to solve is that most often our safety can be preserved only by acquiescing to the tribe's demands to suppress and repress certain vital expressions of our essential nature. Our dependency needs will be met only if we agree *not* to become the unique self we were meant to be—or to become only a very selective version of that self.

This demand to suppress our true selves is instinctively experienced as violent, hurtful, shaming, and frightening to the essential nature of our young beings. Having to treat the felt truth of what we experience as is if it was untrue or unworthy is exquisitely painful and enraging. The problem is that the expression of those feelings of hurt, fear, and shame, or any expression of angry protest against the demand to repress and suppress one's self, too often produces even more of a threat to our continued safety and protection within the tribe. Most often we are faced with a choice like the one faced by the wolf whose leg is caught in a trap: either chew it off or die. And, like the wolf, we make the decision to "chew off" vital pieces of ourselves in order to be safe and survive.

## Self-Delusion As A Solution

So how can the ego possibly take on the job of enforcing the demand to sever parts of its host's self, but at the same time do it in a way that leaves the emerging person with some sense of self esteem, freedom of choice, personal power, and autonomy?

Well, it takes some serious bending and twisting of the host's awareness and internal belief system. If our amazing human imagination was not capable of buying into delusional beliefs about ourselves and about "reality," and if we were not capable of covering up certain experiences in complete

unconsciousness, the ego could never exist. **The ego's existence and func-**
**tioning depends on these two uniquely human capacities: the ability to**
**push out of awareness and into unawareness, i.e.** *to repress*, **certain select-**
**ed inner experiences; and the capacity to believe what we** *imagine* **to be so**
**as if it were actually real. Of all living creatures, only humans have these**
**two capacities.**

I have a client who was repeatedly left in her crib to cry her eyes out because she was not "on schedule" for a feeding or diaper change. And this was
only the beginning. She learned very early her needs didn't matter and the
closest she could come to safety and care depended on never complaining
and on paying total attention to her parents' needs. So, as all children are
capable of doing, she gradually pushed her needs out of her own awareness
and became a "very good girl": polite, never angry, perfectly put together,
always looking to please and serve others.

She was rewarded for these behaviors with sparse praise, but, most importantly, by the avoidance of criticism and rejection by her parents. Her
ego established in her mind the belief that this "deal" was *her choice*. Her ego
repressed any conscious memory of her being terrorized and shamed into
this "choice" by her parents' insensitivity and neglect. It convinced her she
liked being a good girl; that it was a superior way to be...even saintly. The ego
dosed her with rewarding feelings of goodness, pride, and superiority. She
was also very smart and athletic, and doing well academically and athletical-
ly pleased her parents.

Later in life she married a man who believed his wife's job was to meet
his needs no matter the cost to her. Again, her ego rewarded her by convincing her that by giving up the expression and fulfillment of many of her
own needs she was taking the "high road," and would make her feel she was
being a better person. If she rebelled, her ego slammed her with inner guilt
and terror, on top of the fear and shame heaped on her by her husband's
wrath. When the relationship finally became unbearable, her ego tried to
convince her she couldn't survive separately, and would shame her for wanting to break out. Her ego still believed that living under the sway of the
self- destructive deal she had to make with her parents in order to be safe and
"cared for" was still the only way to survive. It took both gaining increased

clarity about the nature of her ego and great courage for her to accomplish leaving this relationship.

This is the division into "goods" and "bads" that the ego has to maintain, while also maintaining some sense of self-respect. Rewarding good behavior, and punishing with shame, fear, and guilt any slippage into "badness"... *while also finding a way* to preserve some sense of self-respect, autonomy, and free choice in its trapped host—it is an ongoing twofold management job. Unlike the wolf, what we chew off is not a limb that's now inert, just left behind somewhere, and forgotten. To suppress vital aspects of our essential selves, and keep them suppressed, takes a lot of aggressive repressing energy on the part of the ego. And it takes a lot of imaginative rationalizing and convincing on the part of the ego to keep its host a "true believer," and feeling rewarded and right for "choosing" acceptable behaviors.

## The Power of Believed Beliefs

The ego ultimately convinces the host that there is no suppressing or acquiescing going on, only good judgment. This capacity to convince ourselves that what we believe is actually true is truly awesome. It has its roots in the power of our imagination and in our capacity to believe that what we imagine is actually real—like the belief in Santa Claus as kids. We love the innocence and openness of kids believing beliefs we consider lovely or good. The completeness of their belief is quite stunning, and so vulnerable. We take it for granted that when we become adults we give up our "childish beliefs," convinced that what we believe as adults is "reality based."

Speaking of Santa, it is interesting to note how useful the Santa Claus myth is in the solidifying of our egos, at least in those of us who bought into it as kids.

> "You better watch out
> You better not cry
> Better not pout
> I'm telling you why
> Santa Claus is coming to town

He's making a list
And checking it twice
Gonna find out who's naughty and nice
Santa Claus is coming to town

He sees you when you're sleeping
He knows when you're awake
He knows if you've been bad or good
So be good for goodness sake!

O! You better watch out!
You better not cry
Better not pout
I'm telling you why
Santa Claus is coming to town
Santa Claus is coming to town."

It's kind of scary when you actually look at the lyrics, yes? The image of a "jolly" Santa and the cheerful melody accompanying the lyrics hide the dark side of the song's message. "You better watch out." "He sees you when you're sleeping/He knows when you're awake." "He knows if you've been bad or good." Wow. No escaping the eyes of this judge. Kind of like a disguised version of a wrathful God the Father. At least the belief in Santa Claus is a belief that the culture universally agrees must eventually be given up. At some point the child is "dis-illusioned." However, the "naughty and nice" rules stay in place within, but now under the ever-watchful internalized "eye" of the ego.

Some beliefs instilled in childhood are *never* given up—like the one in a wrathful god, or like the belief in prejudicial thought systems delivered by adults to innocent children and in turn carried on by those children into their adulthood. Every kid is taught that some version of an "other" is an inferior version of human, with no basis in fact. In our culture, kids are taught to believe that wealth and fame are measures of worth, and this belief is not given up. Rather, it persists into adulthood. We can become thoroughly, deeply, and passionately convinced of something that has no basis in reality. And we will even kill "the other" in the name of that conviction. That "other" can range from "someone who looked at me funny" to those seen as "infidels" to be beheaded by religious true believers. The most pernicious belief instilled by the tribe in our young minds is "I am not okay when I'm my true self." Out of that one fundamental belief all the other destructive beliefs emerge.

## Two Big Lies The Ego Uses To Do Its Job

The ego will do all it can to keep our "bad me" permanently buried in unconsciousness. And it will do everything in its power as well to maintain the belief that "I'm not hiding anything (unacceptable)" as the abiding conviction of the host. My "bad me" does not exist. This is, by the way, the root of all defensiveness. Egos can be more or less successful at this repressive aspect of their job. So we have some hosts who are incredibly well "defended" from any awareness of their "bad me" by their egos, and other hosts who are not so well-defended. But it is the ego's job nonetheless.

### Necessary Lies

Believed lies become necessary: lies that can simultaneously preserve both our sense of interpersonal safety within the tribe as well as preserve some illusion of dignity and autonomy; lies that manage to meet the tribal requirement to suppress our native selves while preserving some form of self-respect; a lie that manages to get our dependency needs met while skirting any conscious direct confrontation with the realities of our self-negating accommodations; lies that paper over the tribally-created conflict between our need for each other's embrace and our need to be our unique selves.

So instead of continuing to be angry at the tribal members who force us to violate our own integrity, to self-betray, we gradually learn it works better for our safety to hate and suppress the *feelings* of powerlessness, rage, hurt, shame, and fear generated when our need for the embrace of the tribe is met only if we deny essential aspects of who we are. We accommodate, and "smile," in order to preserve our safety. We act as if "chewing off pieces" of ourselves doesn't hurt, doesn't matter, or makes us better. We convince ourselves.

We become "well-adjusted." The acute pain and self-loathing that ac-companies self-betrayal is suppressed and replaced instead with feelings of inflation, rightness, goodness, and/or pride. (Here, by the way, we have the creation of the infamous "ego-maniac with low self-esteem.")

Our culture publicly endorses "individuality" and "autonomy" much more than it endorses our existential dependence on each other. Much of this endorsement, however, is lip service. It is in the service of an inau-thentic and highly conditional autonomy—an autonomy and self-respect "armored" against the recognition of our mutual dependence. This type of "rigged" autonomy and self-respect has many downsides, as we shall see. It usually collapses into shamefully experienced dependency when really put to the test.

So there are two profound repressions. The unacceptable aspect of the essential self is denied and repressed, and held there in the unconscious, bound in shame. And then the pain and self-loathing caused by that self-ne-gation is denied and repressed. We all seem to end up in this boat.

## The First of the Two Big Lies

So the first consciously held "big lie" the ego generates and maintains within its host is this: "I am aware of everything about myself, and I am not hiding anything (unacceptable) about myself from you or from me."

The more colloquial version of this lie is: "What you see is what you get."

For the ego, the ideal outcome is that we have no consciousness that this is a lie. It becomes a believed belief, a conviction, a delusion. "I'm just being who I am."

Our egos keep us convinced of the illusion that the altered version of me the ego maintains is "just who I am." The ego becomes the self. There is no experience of a separation or a difference between me and my ego. "What you see is what you get." In most of our current tribal/social groups, this would be considered well-adjusted.

Part of maintaining the belief in "what you see is what you get" is main-taining the delusion that "there is nothing about myself that *I* can't see," the delusion that we don't have an "unconscious"; don't have rich complex territories within us that we have no idea are there. Well over a century ago Freud introduced us to our "subconscious" and our "unconscious," two inner zones of unawareness that lay below the zone of our everyday awareness. These zones of unawareness hold vital information about our human needs and interpersonal vulnerabilities. These zones also hold our capacities for intuition, insight, creativity, emotional intelligence, compassion, and wisdom. This information and these capacities are hidden from our awareness unless we deliberately seek to access them.

So many years after Freud's revelations, it is stunning to me that the persistent denial of the existence of these zones of unawareness remains the rule. It has still not significantly penetrated our collective awareness that our egos, the guardians of what we must keep unconscious, are still editing and driving the content of what we can include in our most important conversations. Certainly we are not allowed by our egos to speak to our vulnerability to each other's judgment and rejection. This is a testament to the power of the ego's ability to keep us unaware of what it deems dangerous to our interpersonal safety.

Only when the strategies of the ego that are designed to keep us in the dark about the deal we have struck fail in some significant way are we then given the opportunity to begin questioning the accuracy and completeness of our enforced self-image, our "second nature," if you will—*but only if* we can find a way to get beyond the shame, fear, and self-doubt that arises when we fail to be, to do, or to have what our egos demand.

## The Second of the Two Big Lies

Here is the second big lie that the ego insists we believe within ourselves and in our interactions with others. Stated in the first person, the lie goes like this: "I do not feel frightened, hurt, or ashamed by your rejecting, disapproving, or disparaging me."

This second big lie is necessary in order to support the effectiveness of the first one. The ego seeks certainty—no leaks, no surprises. If I have *nothing* to hide that is unacceptable then I should *always* feel safe and secure in my own sense of self. I should always feel secure in my own acceptability of myself. This is the ego's version of self-respect, autonomy, and dignity—no felt shame, hurt, or fear caused by rejection or disapproval...*ever*.

It's the lie that is captured in that familiar sop: "Sticks and stones can break your bones, but names will never hurt you." This well-meaning verbal balm is always applied to someone who has already been wounded by "names." It is meant to convince the person that they don't have to feel the hurt they are already feeling. The lasting effect of this "balm" is to leave the injured party to carry the original hurt, *plus* the feeling that there is something wrong with them for feeling frightened, hurt, and shamed. And so going forward they live with an increased need to lie about the hurt in the future, both to themselves and to others.

## A Culturally-Driven Ego

This denial of vulnerability is one of the most fundamental "splits" or divisions within ourselves that the ego enforces in its compulsive, rigid, and automatic way. *This* "bad me" seems to be a universal one in the US. This shame about our vulnerability and about our need for approval is deeply embedded in our culture. It is culturally acceptable to show that you feel aggrieved, disrespected, misunderstood, mistreated, angered, and even enraged when rejected or disapproved of (a righteous defensiveness). *But never to show the feelings of hurt, fear, or shame that result.*

Many egos are very successful at blocking *all* awareness within their hosts of these feelings of hurt, shame, and fear as a result of rejection or disrespect. Most of our egos end up only being more or less successful, not completely so. Regardless of how successful, all egos are dedicated to lying about the presence of these feelings of vulnerability in any given moment.

As an example of this ego demand, think of the last time someone "got to you." When a rejecting remark, a criticism, or a joke at your expense hit that soft spot inside you and set off a twist in your chest or belly of hurt, fear, shame, or embarrassment. Think of how quickly and automatically "you" sought to control the look on your face, to make sure you didn't show any signs of being hurt or embarrassed, how quickly and automatically you sought to pass it off as meaningless or fun, or how quickly and automatically you looked for a smashing "comeback" or counterattack. It would never occur to you to say, "Hey, that hurt and embarrassed me." That would be shaming and shameful.

In truth, the other or the others who "got you" might indeed laugh, call you "too sensitive," or abandon you if you showed your hurt or embarrassment. None of us want to show that kind vulnerability, that kind of dependence on others. If someone spots your inner reaction and asks, "Did that hurt you?" your ego automatically compels you to deny it and to feel even more ashamed for having leaked enough of your hurt, fear, and shame so as to be seen by someone else.

These ego-enforced lies and splits within our experience of ourselves blunt or obliterate our *felt awareness* of the power of our primal need *for* connection with those who matter to us. If the *feelings* of hurt, fear, and shame that result from a severed connection to meaningful others are not admitted into awareness, then the awareness of our *need* for continued connection to others gets successfully suppressed along with them.

We know the *presence* of a need only by the feelings that arise when an *absence* of what is needed exists. Oxygen deprivation produces panic and gasping—and death if the deprivation continues. But if the need for clean air is met, we don't experience the need. Luckily we cannot suppress the feeling of panic, or the response of gasping, when air is in short supply, and we instinctively respond to protect our wellbeing. However, we *can* successfully suppress the feelings of hurt, fear, and shame that arise from rejection and disapproval, and so we can successfully suppress all awareness of the need for acceptance and approval itself.

## The Power of the Ego's Rule

The capacity of the ego to *compel* its host to do its bidding lies in how it both rewards and punishes its host, and in the unique power these rewards and punishments have over us. If you are being, doing, and having whatever your ego believes is necessary in order for you to be acceptable and valued, then it will reward you with some selection of pleasurable feelings such as rightness, belonging, superiority, pride, desirability, goodness, power, confidence, invincibility, excitement, happiness, and safety. If your ego thinks your choices are endangering your approval rating and your value, it will punish you with painful feelings of shame, humiliation, fear, self-doubt, depression, guilt, inferiority, weakness, and internal terrorizing threats of approaching rejection, abandonment, and ostracism.

The ego uses rewards that are intoxicating and irresistible, and punishments that are terrifying and deeply painful. The fact that our conditioned ways of thinking, feeling, and acting are tied to the intense need to belong and the terror of ostracism makes any challenging of those conditioned responses a daunting undertaking. This explains much of our difficulty changing the ways we think, feel, and behave in any significant way. It explains the persistence of behaviors and ways of being, even when we have come to see them in our current lives as now being ineffective, if not downright destructive.

The ego does not respond to evidence and feedback about the *current* effectiveness or destructiveness of its survival strategies. It experiences the strategies created in the past as still necessary for interpersonal safety, survival, and dignity in the present. Those strategies helped the ego's host survive the interpersonal minefields of the past and also maintain "self-esteem." This is what it knows to do to promote the host's value and safety within the tribe and within the host, and to ward off current perceived threats to membership and value. The ego does not self reflect. It is *convinced* of its perspective just as thoroughly as a young child is convinced that Santa Claus or the Boogeyman really exist. It reacts automatically and mechanically—and with great internal power—to determine our behavioral choices, as well as determining what we experience as safe to allow into our awareness about ourselves.

## Life Intrudes

In moments when the rigid grip of our egos is loosened by some external event, and greater openness and authenticity become permissible, we instinctively recognize how much we need each other's acceptance and cooperation, and how fearful we are of each other's rejection. We know that we can break, hurt, diminish, and even annihilate each other. A shocking eruption of a common physical threat often accomplishes this loosening of the ego's grip.

Being from New York City, I am reminded of how New Yorkers related differently to each other for several months after the events of September 11, 2001. For a while it was as if our collective denial was busted, and we knew in our hearts that we were all vulnerable and we were all in this together. The *felt* awareness of our vulnerability to others, and our need for each other's embrace, connected us. We were less embarrassed to let each other see that shared vulnerability and our need for each other's gentleness and cooperation...because we were *all* forced at the same time to *feel* that vulnerability, that blow to our collective safety.

Suddenly, tragically, it was acceptable, not shameful, to feel our fear, hurt, and pain over being treated as if we were worthless and unacceptable by the terrorists, to share it and to seek comfort for it publicly. For example, people would walk by a firehouse and see pictures displayed outside of the firefighters from that station who perished in the tragedy. They would become tearful. Some would go in the station and share the grief with the surviving firefighters, or share their grief with other passers-by crying openly with each other.

But as distance from the collective blow lengthened, our egos reasserted their control. Our egos reasserted their belief that showing our dependency on each other was too dangerous. Little of that collective emotional openness, gentleness, and connection remains amongst New Yorkers today.

## The Ego is a Workaholic

The ego is not passive. It is active and intentional. The ego runs a 24/7 monitoring operation. As noted earlier, eventually it becomes our "second nature." It operates unconsciously. We don't notice its presence. There is only "me." By the time we are seven or eight years old our egos have taken hold. The "goods" and "bads" may change when we shift attachments to different groups, but the ego just shape-shifts along with the changes. It never stops doing its job, i.e. compulsively keeping us acceptable to our (current) tribe, and keeping us mentally and emotionally deluded into believing that we are making smart and completely *free* choices regarding which aspects of our selves get expressed and which don't.

The difficulty for the ego, however, is that the behaviors, feelings, and thoughts we learned to suppress are not inert things but rather living, energized, and meaningful aspects of our native selves. They continue to press for expression. It's a bit like restricting our breathing to shallow breaths (which we do). We can get by, but the body is always pressing for a deeper breath. The body knows what it needs.

The ego must in effect stand guard at the borderline between awareness and unawareness of self. It must prevent any of these now shamed aspects from slipping over the border into awareness. If any slippage occurs, the ego launches attacks of shame, fear, and doubt at the host to convince him or her that repression is the only way to go.

## Signs of the Ego at Work

The signs that let you know that the ego is at work are always the same. Whatever the ego has decided is good and acceptable for its host to be, to do, or to have, it will make sure that its host *automatically, rigidly, and compulsively seeks* to be, to do, or to have exactly that. And likewise, whatever the ego has decided is bad and unacceptable to be, to do, or to have, it will make sure that its host *automatically, rigidly, and compulsively avoids* exactly that. *It is this automatic, rigid, and compulsory nature of the ego's operating system that is its hallmark.*

The ego doesn't believe in genuine free will or spontaneity. Those are too likely to cause the leakage of some unacceptable material that will only get you in trouble. So if the ego is doing its job well, what we will witness are folks who are totally locked into their "good" behaviors and their "right" beliefs, and totally driven to acquire their notion of "good" stuff. The ego actually removes choice from the equation. This is why the multi-millionaire can't stop seeking more money; the compulsive worker goes 24/7 without a break; the "good person" can't say no to any request for help; the battered person keeps trying to change their abuser; the compulsively suspicious person ends up isolated and alone; the student becomes suicidal over a "B"; the perfectionist is acutely embarrassed by any mistake; the know-it-all is ashamed of simple ignorance; or the "believer" denigrates or destroys non-believers. The examples are seemingly endless.

This is really the problem with ego. There is nothing inherently wrong with any of the human characteristics or capacities it chooses as its "goods." Take, for example, caring about other people's comfort—a lovely, generous trait. But if you *always have to* keep other people comfortable, then you *can never* be helpful to people in ways that might require them to suffer some pain or discomfort. Likewise, giving one's self-expression a high value is built into our DNA. Self-expression is necessary both for surviving and for thriving. However, if I *have to always* self-express, regardless of the consequences to others, then I will inevitably become insensitive, reckless, or abusive. As noted before, the ego is the epitome of the old saw, "To a hammer, everything looks like a nail."

Our egos helped us navigate and survive the interpersonal minefields of our early years as developing persons. The problem for us hosts is that the ego is acting as if we and our life circumstances have not changed since childhood and adolescence. It therefore believes that we hosts should not change any aspect of its rigid operating system. And it will penalize us for trying.

One of the biggest unacknowledged "elephants" in our common human living room is created by the culturally supported denial of our deep *need* for each other's acceptance, cooperation, approval, and good will—not simple preference...need. Without the collective presence of these qualities, in ourselves and in those around us, we are at real risk of being diminished, damaged, or destroyed by each other. This need for, and dependence on, each other, and the mutual vulnerability that it creates, is a fact, regardless of our denial. The elephant is in the living room even though, socially and privately, we may all be talking and walking around it as is if it wasn't there. At a deep emotional and instinctual level we are terrified of losing our membership, our status, or our value in the groups that matter to us; our continued existence feels endangered by such a loss.

> "*Power without love becomes reckless and abusive. Love without power becomes anemic and sentimental.*"—Martin Luther King

**King's quote captures what happens when we are forced into suppressing either our dependency or our autonomy by or egos. By not openly**

talking about our dependency on each other, we are in effect pretending this reality does not exist (the elephant). This denial disconnects us emotionally and spiritually from the possibility of experiencing each other's authentic and sensitively attuned embrace. It forces us away from *openly* seeking each other's cooperation, away from consciously and deliberately creating genuine mutual safety, satisfaction, and fulfillment.

Likewise, this denial forces us into a distorted and limited form of autonomy that is dependent on efforts to control each other's "cooperation" and "approval" through threats, enticements, and/or accommodations. These efforts at best create temporary illusions of personal power, safety, and fulfillment, not the real thing. They certainly do not create authentic autonomy or trustworthy interpersonal safety, both of which can only arise when grounded in the conscious acceptance of the primary reality of our dependence on each other. The need to deny that primary reality forces into the unfortunate extremes captured in King's quote.

# chapter three

# Does This Map Of The Ego Fit Your Experience?

## Workshop Dialogues Continued

**Lou:** Okay. You've had a chance to read the document. Let's talk through your questions and comments.

**Gabe:** You say this need for approval and acceptance is a "given," and so is our fear of disapproval and rejection. The power you give this need and fear, if it is accurate, makes *me* feel powerless. It makes me feel I would be ruled by these feelings if I had them; like I would be doomed to choose only what's acceptable even if I know I want or need to be some way that's not acceptable.

**Lou:** Is it my *description* of the power of these feelings and needs that makes you anticipate powerlessness? Or is it that the feelings and needs actually feel that powerful to you? Remember, I am using words and concepts but I really do mean to use them only to point to real experiences. So if my description doesn't fit your experience then please don't accept it as accurate for you.

**Gabe:** You mean have I ever not said or done something because I was afraid of rejection?

**Lou:** For example, yeah.

**Gabe:** I can't remember the last time I did that. I stopped worrying about approval a long time ago. I make a point of saying what I think and feel. I don't care what people think. Being myself is what matters. If I can't be me then what the hell am I doing here?

**Lou:** So what's true for you is that you don't *feel* the need for approval and acceptance and you don't *feel* the fear of disapproval. Is that accurate?

**Gabe:** Yup.

**Lou:** And it sounds like if you did feel those feelings they might have enough power within you to stop you from being yourself. Is that accurate?

**Gabe:** I couldn't tell you. I'd be speculating.

**Lou:** True. It would be a guess at what might happen until you actually had the experience of needing approval. So right now the need and the fear don't exist for you. Let me ask you what you do when someone actually does disapprove of you, when someone rejects you...someone meaningful to you.

**Gabe:** I figure that's their problem, not mine. I know what I think and I know what I feel. That's not going to change because someone else thinks I'm wrong or offensive or something. If I have to move on, I do. Look, I'll discuss anything with anybody and I'll debate with the best of them. I don't just shut the conversation down. But feelings are not the point. What's true is the point.

**Lou:** It sounds like you are someone who can be counted on to speak his mind. That can be a very useful quality. Sounds like you feel good about it too.

**Gabe:** It's a point of pride. I feel strong, self-reliant.

**Lou:** Leaving approval aside for the moment, have you experienced loving anybody recently, or being loved?

**Gabe:** Right now I'm not looking for love. I enjoy good company, a good time, and good work partners. But I like being free.

**Lou:** Remember the Martin Luther King quote? "Power without love is reckless and abusive, and love without power is anemic and sentimental." I love the dilemma that quote captures. His use of the word "power" was not limited to meaning "dominate." For him power meant the ability to self-express, to grow and evolve, to become fully oneself. And "love" meant the ability to maintain a connection, in a felt way, to others, in a loving, caring, authentic, and compassionate way. He was very aware of these two different needs—the need to self-express and the need to feel connected to others. He felt you had to fulfill both needs to be fully human and fully empowered. His belief was you needed to consciously balance back and forth between these two needs to create and maintain full personhood.

Under ideal interpersonal conditions these needs don't have to be in conflict with each other, do they? However, like I said in the "Job Description" piece you read, most human groups, including our families, don't create these ideal conditions. So, most often we are conditioned to believe we have to sacrifice one to have the other. Having both needs met feels impossible. It sounds like earlier in your life caring what others thought of you cost you too much in terms of the freedom to express yourself.

**Gabe:** That feels right.

**Lou:** If what you are sharing has a "compulsiveness" to it, then it sounds like that would be about avoiding the experience of needing approval. We might say your ego says you must absolutely do everything you can to avoid that experience, and that your ego rewards you with feelings of strength, independence, and personal freedom when you do.

**Gabe:** To me those are not rewards. They're the consequences or the results of a choice I've made: to give up needing other people's approval. So I guess I don't see the compulsiveness either. I don't feel compelled to not need approval. It feels like I chose to give it up.

**Lou:** That's good. That's clarifying. Let me ask you this: Have there been any downsides to giving up this need?

**Gabe:** My latest girlfriend thinks I'm a bully and a cold motherfucker, as she puts it. But I'm not sure that's a downside yet. I've lost a few friends over being what they considered contemptuous and arrogant, if that's what you mean by "downsides."

**Lou:** They're only downsides if they feel that way to you. Do you feel any loss in these results?

**Gabe:** One of those friends was my best buddy. He really got what I'm all about, and we shared a lot important experiences together. I miss him. But if he can't take me as I am, then I have to say "so long."

**Lou:** When you say, "I miss him," is that a feeling?

**Gabe:** Not really. Maybe it was at first but I put it away pretty quickly. Mostly I felt angry with him.

**Lou:** Sticking with an angry feeling is often one way to not feel the hurt, the sorrow, and the need. It might be worth checking inside yourself to see where you are in relation to those more vulnerable feelings.

But your experience raises a very central question: Is it possible to both really feel our need for each other's care and approval and still keep our freedom to self-express? If we allow ourselves to feel the full force of our need to belong, our need for approval and acceptance, are we then doomed to a life of what some call "pathological accommodations" to others expectations? Is suppressing our need for approval and our fear of rejection the only way we can have the full freedom to self-express, to be ourselves? And vice versa: Is shutting down the expression of essential and vital aspects of who we are the only way to fulfill our need to belong? Both choices seem necessary at least some of the time. This is a central dilemma we have all experienced.

**Gina:** I find myself very confused right now, and anxious too. This conflict between being myself and being acceptable is one I think I don't even want to look at. I found myself switching between not being able to sit still and falling asleep while you have been talking about this. My mind spins and then shuts down and then spins some more. I've done enough work on myself to know something important to me is being stirred up inside.

I was brought up by parents who very much believed "children should be seen but not heard." Good manners, being polite, and giving way to other's needs were cardinal rules. And I think they are good rules. But I wonder if they went overboard. But then I don't want to be self-centered. It's important we care about each other. And I am a spiritual person, too, and believe we are all one at some level. But I keep finding that people I thought were friends take me for granted or just plain treat me shabbily. And then I feel resentful and I want to say something to them, but I also feel guilty for not being able to rise above it and take the higher road. I mean, you can see can't you? I'm just going round and round here; you can see the spin I'm in.

**Lou:** Yes. You are right in the middle of the dilemma aren't you? You are living it right in this moment. It's like a terrible tear inside of us. There is no safe place, no place inside where you feel all right, no place you feel you can trust to get an answer to this dilemma, one that feels both true and safe enough to act on. You think one thing and something opposite invalidates that thought and so on and so on.

**Gina:** Exactly, but what do I do? I feel like I am going to fly into a hundred pieces. I am fifty-two years old and this has been the story of my life—only worse recently. I lost a daughter to a drug overdose a few years ago and my husband died shortly after. My only son has trouble being around me. He says he can't stand the anxiety. Anyway, I am going on again. I don't want to monopolize the time here. This is a workshop not a therapy session.

**Lou:** So what you are feeling has an "emergency" feel to it, yes?

**Gina:** Yes.

**Lou:** That is definitely the ego at work. It will terrorize you into some sort of submission if it feels that's the only way to keep you safe. So pause a moment and take a deep breath or two. Just for a moment feel into your legs and your feet, maybe press your feet a little bit into the ground. Good. Just recognize you are here now and not physically endangered.

What you are struggling with certainly has some urgency to it, but your life is not threatened right now; right here and right now you are safe enough. We are all in the same dilemma to one degree or another. I think it is a safe assumption to say that anybody in the room right now would not be here if they did not feel some of the same confusion and anxiety you are experiencing. Nobody is demanding that you solve this dilemma in this instant. And nobody else is going to solve their dilemma in this instant either. But we can share our search for some better way of living with the dilemma. Okay?

**Gina:** Yes. I can sit with that for the moment.

**Lou:** Let's look at your experience from the framework of what we have uncovered about the ego so far. The way your ego works seems particularly hard on you. Some egos will treat you well when you obey them, when you're doing and being "good," like Gabe's. We have seen they can reward you with feelings of safety, acceptability, even superiority, arrogance, and invincibility.

Your ego has you under continuous sniper fire. Right now there is no way of being or behaving that quiets your fear and anxiety. It almost seems as if it is not safe for you to feel safe, like it's dangerous to relax, even for a minute—kind of like the joke about the worry-wart who worries when he notices he's not worrying, or like the combat soldier who is not in a firefight in this moment but knows one could come in the next.

Depending on your personal history, an ego could conclude that it was "good" to never feel safe, never trust yourself, always be on the alert for a wrong thought or action. That type of ego could think it was smart, "safer," to keep you "compulsively" frightened that you are about to make a misstep or have a lapse in watchfulness all the time.

**Gina:** Sounds like me.

**Lou:** Every ego's goal is to create and preserve some sense of interpersonal safety by maintaining your acceptability and your perceived value, both to yourself and to those who matter to you. That is universally true of every ego. That's what it came into being to accomplish, first with your family of origin, and then later with your other dependency groups. The ego's intention is good—keep you safe. The methods it was forced to use, however, are brutal. There are two opposite strategies the ego uses to accomplish this, depending on what worked best to preserve a sense of safety in your family of origin. These two different strategies break egos down into two broad classes of ego types.

One class of ego types seeks to preserve the acceptability and safety of its host by presenting its host as having *higher* value, standing, power, centrality, etc. than that of the significant others in the host's tribe. These are what we might call self-enhancing egos. These are egos leaning in the direction of "power without love."

An opposite class of egos seeks to preserve the acceptability and interpersonal safety of its host by presenting its host as having *lower* value, importance, standing, power, centrality, etc. than the others in the host's tribe. And these we could call self-diminishing egos. These are egos leaning in the direction of "love without power."

Just to illustrate, let's take two obviously opposite ego types: the bully and the people-pleaser. The bully clearly fits into the first class of egos. The bully feels acceptable and safe by presenting its host as more powerful, superior, etc. than others in its tribe and by making the others in the tribe feel intimidated, unimportant, worthless, inferior, powerless, weaker, etc., and therefore less acceptable and chronically unsafe in the bully's presence. The tribe fears the bully.

The people-pleaser fits the other class. The people-pleaser feels acceptable and safe by diminishing his/her importance, value, power, etc., and making others in the tribe feel more important, valuable, powerful, central, etc. and therefore more acceptable and chronically safe in the people-pleaser's presence. The tribe feels safe with the people-pleaser.

The first class of ego types, the self-enhancers, includes what most people would think of when the word "ego" is used in popular parlance, e.g. the narcissist, the star, the hero, the know-it-all, the braggart, etc. The second class of ego types, the self-diminishers, would be considered by most to be examples of "'egolessness," e.g., the saint, the caretaker, the savior, the bumbler, the timid, etc. These egos are often seen as "weak egos." In my view this is a misunderstanding.

There are no "weak" egos. And every ego is by nature "self-centered." Every ego does what it does with determination and tenacity, with compulsivity and rigidity, in order to keep its host acceptable and safe. Just try to change an ego and see what happens. Egos always function with a rigid kind of "strength" and a basic self-preservative perspective. This includes the ego types that have learned that acceptance and interpersonal safety come from presenting their hosts in an image of weakness, subservience, helplessness, unworthiness "humility," incapacity, service to others, and/or "selflessness."

These types of egos can be more difficult to spot in ourselves because the rewards these egos dole out do not look like inflation or superiority. The admiration or status they seek to attain for their hosts has to be hidden and disguised as its opposite. I am reminded of the cartoon in which three rabbis are gathered at the "wailing wall" in Jerusalem. Two of them are huddled in a conversation about the third one, who is praying at the wall and is out of earshot. One of the twosome says to the other: "Look who thinks he's more unworthy than us." I am also reminded of the mother whose family is in chaos because she can't assert her needs or set boundaries if someone else in the family doesn't like it when she tries.

On a more humorous note, I have a good friend whose ego is of the self-enhancing type, whereas mine is of the self-diminishing type. We kid each other a lot about how these different ego types play out. He told me recently he had come up with a new diagnostic name for what he considers to be my mental illness – Self-Aggrandizement Deficit Disorder, or SADD for short.

Does this make sense to you guys?

**Frank:** Winners and losers. Superior and inferior. That's what I'd call your two groups of egos; or maybe dominant and submissive; or go-getters and do-gooders. To me the first group was always the only one to belong to. I never wanted to feel dependent. I just wanted—needed—to be on top, to be the one in control, the one with the power, the one that people feared and sought approval from, the one that made decisions, made things happen. That was exciting and energizing for me. When I pulled off another success, that was a rush. I could obsess about my winning strategies for days, months. I loved it.

Most of the people who worked for me were afraid of me. Many even worshipped me. I was a legend in my industry. Probably most of *them* had your group two type egos. They would do whatever I told them. They knew I was a visionary, a master at reading the trends, so they followed me; they were inspired by me. I turned people who probably would have lived second rate lives into winners, into success stories.

**Lou:**  Sounds thrilling. That kind of intimidating and effective power can be a high. A feeling of invincibility usually comes along with it. Certainly the heady feeling of superiority does. And there is your real talent and vision. These are capacities of your native self. Sounds like they may have gotten co-opted by your ego for its agenda. But I notice you're speaking in the past tense.

**Frank:**  Yeah, well, my wife divorced me and then I had a minor stroke. I don't know which was the greater shock. I went into a serious depression. I've recovered from both but I really lost my way. I felt humiliated by my physical and emotional weakness. I went from Superman to a scared little boy. I'm holding my own at work, but it no longer holds me. It's lost its meaning. Not completely. Maybe it's changed its meaning. This all happened a couple of years ago, just a couple of months apart. I've changed a lot but I am still finding my footing. I realize I need people in a lot of different ways now but I still hate it and feel a lot of embarrassment about it.

**Lou:**  Serious blows to you as a person, but also to your ego. Do you see the ego part of your experience?

**Frank:**  I do now. I didn't then. Then I just thought my life was over, that the "me" I thought I was had gone and was replaced with a failed, disabled human. But, yes, this split you describe the ego keeping in place, I got painfully introduced to the other side of that split. I had been living on the "reward" side of my ego for years, and not noticing or feeling any downside. I was riding high. Those "blows" knocked the shit out of me. I am definitely living with the punishing side of my ego now. I am plagued with feelings of shame and self doubt and fearfulness. I was never that way before. I never doubted myself. Now on bad days my ego lets me know all day what a wretch I am. It's awful.

**Lou:** It is awful; it's the worst. It totally sucks. Let's look at your experience a little more closely. It is natural for us to want to feel in control, to feel admired and listened to as an expert. It is also natural to enjoy being seen as a leader and to have others be willing to follow your lead. And autonomy feels good too, really good. To experience your personal power and independence is exhilarating.

Where your ego comes into play in your experience is that it made it *compulsory* for you to be independent and to lead. Your ego's rule was you had to be that way and *never* the opposite. Any sign of dependence, loss of control, or lack of leadership and your ego would hit you with those feelings of shame, fear, and doubt in order to compel you back into good behavior. When blows to your body and heart like you experienced a couple of years ago happen, it is natural to feel hurt, to feel some fear, to be sad, confused, and regretful...and to very directly get the frightening uncertainty of life, the impermanence of it.

What is not natural, but learned and conditioned, is the shame and pernicious self-doubt that the ego lays on top of these human realities. To feel like a worthless, failed human being because of a divorce or a stroke is *not* natural. It's very common, but not natural. To come out of those experiences with the kind of self-doubt that leaves you chronically questioning the very basis of your personal power and worth, that is very common also, but, again, *not* natural.

Our personal power actually rests in our natural capacities to respond to life's "blows"—our intelligence, creativity, will power, intuition, spirit, and love. Genuine personal power does not rest in position, status, or domination of others. That's the ego's belief.

For your ego, safety and acceptability can only be obtained if you are compulsively, i.e. always, independent and in a position of power and leadership and by having others be fearful and submissive to you. The ego's version of autonomy is *dependent* on creating those kinds of interpersonal relationships. It is a version of autonomy that is dependent on maintaining certain specified external circumstances, not on developing all your internal capacities. Actually, genuine safety flows both from our *autonomous* capacity to respond to challenges *and* from receiving the love, cooperation, and care of others.

Are you experiencing more clarity about these differences?

**Frank:** Intermittently. I get it and I lose it. When I lose it I am miserable to be around—angry, depressed, pathetic. When I get it I feel more at peace. I've been surprised by some people's love for me, even more surprised I've been able to let it in. But the shame is still big. The nasty feelings seem harder to deal with than the nasty thoughts.

**Lou:** That is so true. The feelings are even more convincing than the thoughts. Feelings make the thoughts feel really real. And "getting it and losing it," as you describe it, is actually the universal experience of what we might call the process of "waking up." We don't wake up once and for all. Everybody here has had some kind of experience of discovering they are not who they thought they were. For some, that involved a discovery that there was more that was positive about them than they thought. And for others, like yourself, that discovery involved seeing something about themselves their egos considered negative. In either case, coming to an abiding sense of your essential all-rightness is going to be a process of "getting it and losing it."

**Mary:** I am definitely on the other side of this coin from Frank. I was raised in one of the scariest versions of Catholicism. Like those Rabbis, the more unworthy we felt, the closer we were to God. The more ashamed we were of any sense of pride or confidence in our own thinking or our feelings, in our own inner voices, the better Catholics we were, the more "Christ-like" we were.

Christ was portrayed as this willing victim of God's wrath at us, that God was so angry with us humans that the only thing that would make him happy was if his own son suffered horrendous torture and a hideous death. And his son had to do it *willingly* if God the Father was to be appeased. I've been realizing how crazy that is recently. Right now I see that Christ was pictured like the ultimate people-pleaser, appeasing the ultimate bully, in your system. So the message to us kids was that we *made* God do this to his son for the sake of saving our skins from automatic eternal hellfire. So if we don't behave exactly like Christ, then we are making him, Jesus, suffer more and enraging God, too. So we were bad to begin with for making God have his only son tortured and killed. And the only way we were going to have any chance of getting to heaven was to always feel guilty and unworthy, and grateful to Christ for taking the big hit for us. And that debt could never be adequately repaid.

So if you get any ideas about feeling good about yourself, or proud, or like you have any say at all, then the devil has got hold of you and you're headed straight for hell. And hell was really scary. We were given graphic descriptions of our flesh burning forever. I was definitely conditioned into believing that being humble and submissive was the Christ-like way to be. I was taught to turn the other cheek, and all that stuff. It makes me feel guilty, resentful, and scared just thinking about it. Maybe I'll go to hell. I'm all mixed up inside.

**Lou:** So for your ego, the only safe and acceptable way to be and act is as if you are unworthy. Kind of like you were convicted as a small child and you've been on some kind of eternal probation or parole. Only now you've got an internal probation officer you have to report to every day to make sure you're feeling unworthy enough.

**Mary:** More like every minute. But, you know, it's still hard to believe that my unworthiness is not true, that it is just a belief.

**Lou:** I hear you. And again like Frank said, the feelings of shame, fear, and doubt make it all seem so true! That will be a continuing piece of your work, of your self-recovery process. I mean finding out that the feelings are not accurate. They are real, but not accurate assessments or predictors. And you'll learn that it is permissible and natural to feel good about who you really are, the whole you.

**Matt:** My ego is like Mary's but it didn't come from being in a religion—although in my late twenties and early thirties I fell into a spiritual cult. My mother was like Mary's God, and I was the son chosen to be her appeasing sacrifice. She had a lot of trouble with people who had minds of their own, who disagreed with her, and who didn't depend utterly on her approval. She had ways of making sure I was always uncertain, insecure about myself and of her acceptance of me. She seemed to need me to need her.

Looking back, it was like she wanted me to be a "good dog"—"sit, stay, and fetch," as she wished, and to always be overjoyed to see her, like a happy puppy. If I wanted to be with my friends, or just by myself, she would get hurt and make me feel guilty. If I didn't immediately respond to her wishes, she would tell me how disappointed she was in me and how that behavior "was not the boy she knew."

And she would also fly into these terrifying rages about how me and my brothers and sisters didn't appreciate what she does for us and how much she sacrifices. Or she would fall into week-long dark periods in bed. I was a very good boy. I learned to be very compliant, polite, and attentive to other people's needs. When I was good, my mother—and her friends—would praise me and tell me what a special boy I was. In fact I ended up being a very nice ghost of a person.

**Lou:** You mentioned you got involved with a cult. In some sense our families are the original cults. The cult experience is defined as one in which a person is dependent on another person, or a group, for their sense of self and safety to such a great degree that the dependent person gives complete power and authority over his/her behavior and significant life decisions to that other person or group. It is kind of an ultimate version of what might be Gabe's nightmare of dependence on the approval of others.

But this is the interpersonal state in which we all start out within our families of origin. We don't give up our independence and sense of separate self like adults may do in the cults we've all read about. We start out as kids with no independence or developed sense of self to begin with. We are utterly dependent, physically and psychologically, on our original caregivers. They don't have to brainwash *away* a sense of self and replace it with a new submissive version. They just have to brainwash *in* who and how we are supposed to be in order to be safe and acceptable.

Under the right conditions we can grow more independent, autonomous, and self-authorizing over time within our families. If those conditions are right we grow into a full version of personhood. If the right conditions for this growth are missing, then we are left vulnerable to the pull of cults in our later years. In this sense, your family experience set you up for joining the cult later in your life.

**Matt:** I see that so clearly now. Being in that cult, realizing we were all being held hostage and abused emotionally and spiritually by our leader, and finally leaving, was a defining experience in my life. Finding my own voice and learning how to respect my own feelings, and then keeping that inner connection to myself has been a long pull for me. I still have serious bouts of doubts.

**Lou:** Thank you for that phrase: "bouts of doubts!" I am going to use that one going forward. In my book, self-doubt is the most destructive of the negative inner forces we must deal with as humans. We'll talk more of this later. So you, like Mary, found it safer to doubt and distrust your own feelings, safer to be a good cult member. If you trusted your own feelings you would naturally express them, and that was a dangerous proposition with your mother, and then with the cult leader. It meant being rejected, attacked, and ostracized, which was much too threatening for a child and similarly for an adult with not enough inner sense of validity and value. Mom and the leader had the power to make you okay, make you acceptable, make you valuable, and therefore make you safe in your belonging.

**Matt:** That power to make me feel okay and safe was a huge thing. I had found a source of hope in much of the spiritual reading I was doing in my twenties. By that time I had a sense that I was lost. Spiritual practices promised I could find my "True Self." I had begun meditating and I'd had some experiences of peacefulness that were new for me. My wife had heard about this teacher who was described as a "meditation master," so we went to one of his workshops. He would talk about the "True Self" and we would meditate for long periods and also chant. He was an American who pulled from some of the Eastern spiritual traditions. He was like a wild man. It was all very exotic and intense.

He was someone who could do "transmission" of spiritual energy by touching you. I had never heard of this and was skeptical. But people I knew well who were sane, successful, well-known people were flocking to him. So in this workshop he came around while we were meditating and touched me with his thumb right in the spot between my eyes, and it was like I had been given a drug or something. The only way I can describe what happened is that my heart broke open and it was gushing love, gratefulness, and joy. I thought of everybody in my life one at a time and just felt these enormous surges of love for each one. I was weeping with joy. When we moved from meditating to chanting, the singing would fill me with this blissful feeling. It was all literally mind-blowing. It was the first time ever in my life that I had felt that good. I think I was hooked from the start. I mean, if this guy could "give" me that experience, why wouldn't I follow him? If that experience was somehow a part of my true self, for sure I wanted more of that!

**Lou:** Naturally.

**Matt:** So I began going to a lot of workshops, and then volunteering to help set them up, and spreading the word, so to speak. I became a part of his organization and eventually worked fulltime for a number of years. Unfortunately that original "high" was not sustainable. An occasional shot of it kept me going, but looking back I can see that I was feeling like me and many of my fellow volunteers were faking it. We were not as happy and loving as we acted. There was precious little authenticity and honesty. And the closer I got to central people in his organization, the more I saw the power trips going down under the guise of spiritually training those below them. There was a lot of public shaming of people, with the rationale that it was a good way to "bust their egos."

And then it got around that the leader was sexually active with many of the really young girl volunteers, again calling it part of their spiritual training, part of their "awakening process." He was in his sixties...and he espoused celibacy! Anyway, that was the downside. The draw was those early experiences. I think a lot of people look at former cult members as if we are just crazy or weak. They don't understand that what you are "given" that can pull you in. It's a lot like drugs or alcohol really. That taste of not only being all right, but of being really fine, is compelling. This teacher kept telling us that what he "gave" us was inside us already. He also said we could find it only by following his way, that meeting an "awakened being" was a very special gift and an opportunity, and you waste it at your own peril. The possibility that that feeling was the real me was too compelling to turn down. And then to find a community of people that support the hope that you can live in that feeling continuously, wow.

**Lou:** I couldn't agree with you more. You know, there is a great book called *The Wrong Way Home* written by a psychiatrist named Arthur Deikman. His thesis is that we are all members of cults, just that some are considered acceptable and others not. The extreme ones we hear about. The ones that end in some form of violence or other horror are just one end of a continuum. He points out how business and social organizations function like cults. I believe what I call our tribes are cults. It seems to me we are all either participating as cult members or as cult creators, and often both. And what draws us into these "cults" is not only what they give us—an experience (or the hope) of being fully acceptable, fully all right and safe—but also what they promise to relieve us of, i.e. our painful feelings of not being acceptable, of being outsiders, of insufficiency, and a lack of safety. It is this double whammy of good feelings replacing bad ones that gives any our *seeking* its compulsive quality.

**Matt:** I had to let go of that seeking to finally find a true version of me. But I had to crash pretty badly as a result of that seeking before I was forced to look in a different direction—inside instead of outside. And the biggest change was I had to stop avoiding experiencing what was inside me that frightened me and caused me pain. I've had to keep moving into it and go where it leads me—that's included experiencing my own self-hatred, my own internal attacks on my self.

**Lou:** That too seems to be an unavoidable part of the work of waking up from our ego's version of who we are, part of the work of an authentic self-discovery, and self-recovery, process. The ego is a nasty ruler and uses feelings of self-hatred for the host as one of its tools to keep us in line.

**Stew:** A few years ago I would have thought you were all wackos—especially Matt. Joining a cult! Forget it. I was a cult. I know some of you know me from my public life. Well being a huge rock and roll star is a lot like being the leader of a cult. I had tens of thousands of people around the world worshipping me, loving me. My music, my singing, and my dancing made them feel good, alive, and outrageous, like me. I was Mr. Outrageous. I did the most drugs, had the most sex, and did the baddest behavior. When I was performing I felt supremely confident. I was a god. My fans couldn't get enough of me. The women would throw their panties at me on stage, and then later, after the show, their bodies. That feeling of being the baddest and the best was what I craved. That was intoxicating. I couldn't get enough of that.

I'd have to say my ego was certainly in the self-enhancing group, but, you know what, it also fits in the self-diminishing group in the sense that I really felt I was giving love to my fans, that I was performing for them to feel good, and that what I gave them was a real gift. I've even had fans tell me that some song of mine changed their lives, helped them get through some bad times, feel like they could be who they really are. It was like I was giving them permission to be really alive! So my ego seems to be in both camps.

**Lou:** Well maybe your ego was not at work. Maybe what you're describing was simply your native self being creative and having a good time, and really providing pleasure and release and permission for your fans. The hallmarks of the ego being involved are the "good/bad" split, the rigidity, and the compulsivity. So were you aware that it was compulsory for you to be the "baddest and the best" as you put it? That you *had* to be the star and have that love affair with your fans if you were to be acceptable? Would you experience some sense of worthlessness or unacceptability if you weren't the star and the lover? Was it a "have to?"

**Stew:** Hey, I've always been the center of attention. I can't stop it. It never really has felt like a choice I'm making. But it also never felt like I was out of control. My drug use was intense, but I could also leave it alone for stretches. But no matter where I go or who I'm with somehow the energy swirls around me. Stuff seems to just fly through me—thoughts, feelings, impulses, movements, whatever. My mind is really fast, my body too. And I am really smart and really intuitive and really creative and really outrageous. What comes in my mind goes out. I'm a big personality. I know this.

I don't think my energy ever really stops completely, but the closest it came to shutting down was when I finally realized I couldn't stop my former girlfriend from continuing to cheat on me and shit on me in public and private. I had left my wife for this girl ten years before. I thought she was the love of my life. She turned out to be an unbelievably destructive experience for me. She was the one person I couldn't please, couldn't entertain, if you will, couldn't keep happy. No matter what I did for her, what I accomplished, or what I gave her, she'd find a way to knock it, question the value or my motive, or just take it like it was coming to her.

She kept telling me that I was the problem in our relationship. I knew I could be difficult to live with. My ex-wife had cited my self-absorption in my career and in my own mind as a reason for divorcing me. Of course she found out about my sexual exploits too. That didn't go over well. But with, let's call her Wanda, I was different. I really fell hard for her. I was really preoccupied with her. Really focused on pleasing her. I didn't want anybody else. It was all okay for the first year or so, but then she started taking me down. When we were out she would drink and she'd get drunk and she'd make fun of me in front of my friends, tell them stuff like my dick was too small. Or she'd ignore me and flirt with other guys. Or she'd say something offensive or embarrassing to someone we were partying with, or wonder out loud how anyone could be friends with someone as wacko as me.

At first I chalked it up to her being drunk. But it started happening when she was sober too. I found out she was having sex with other guys. And yet she didn't leave me. And I couldn't leave her. I kept trying and hoping I could bring her around, make her happy. I took her on expensive trips, bought her shit. She was really miserable. She was a miserable person. It was like she needed me like some kind of dumping grounds for her misery.

My bandmates and friends saw what was happening to me way before I did. Anyway, it's a long and sordid, miserable story and I ended up having a kind of breakdown. I tried to kill myself. Took a bunch of Ambien. Not many people know this. A friend saved my ass. When I came to in the hospital it was like the wheels in my mind were jammed. They just wouldn't turn over. I could feel the wheels trying to get going again. My creativity was gone, too, and had been for a while. I was kind of frozen I guess.

This is a long way around to answering your question. But yes, there was a "have to" in it with her. Looking back I can see the addiction in it. She was my drug. I needed a fix and I needed her to fix me, too. I didn't really realize it when I was in it. I just thought I was in love. And I can see the connection to my choice of career now. I was so good at what I did, how I got what I needed, or what my ego needed, that it all just seemed natural and fine. I was just being me—outrageous, amazing me with thousands of fans who adored me—until being "me" failed disastrously with the one "fan" who mattered most to me.

**Lou:** What you describe seems to be universally true. That is: when your ego's program is working, when you are successfully doing what your ego thinks is the way to be and the way to get your needs for approval met, then it does seem natural and fine, as you put it. It feels like I am just being me and I am fine. Whether it's being in love or your career really humming along. It's great. You feel in control and acceptable, even superior and invincible. You really *feel* that way! The rewards are powerful. Like Gabe said, they don't feel like rewards, rather just the natural consequences of being on the right track. You're actually experiencing the best that any ego has to offer, and it's pretty damn good stuff!

**Stew:** Yeah, until the crash.

**Lou:** Tell me what kept you in.

**Stew:** The relationship?

**Lou:** Yes.

**Stew:** Well I didn't know then what I know now. It's embarrassing. I was a fool. I let myself be humiliated time and time again. And I kept coming back for more. People knew me as someone with a lot of confidence, even arrogance. They couldn't believe what they were witnessing. Some of them were glad—the ones that were envious of me in the past, or the ones I treated with contempt of my own. But the friends who cared kept trying to warn me to get out.

Looking back I see I had moments of real clarity about the destructiveness, dysfunction, and out-of-control-ness of it all. But I couldn't follow through. I couldn't step away and stay away. Looking back I can see that I was compelled to seek her approval, to make her happy, to make her see I was a good guy. And I was convinced I could if I tried hard enough. That was my pride. And I couldn't face the "failure." That was my shame and fear of being alone and worthless.

When I began letting in how she had been beating the shit out of me, I became compelled to make her see how badly she had treated me, that she had hurt me and humiliated me. I couldn't believe she couldn't see it—or wouldn't see it. I felt this burning need for justice, to be vindicated, to be acknowledged as the good guy and not the bad guy. But she was, and probably still is, totally committed to the version of the story in which I was the bad guy—to the point of lying spectacularly to herself and whoever would listen. It was stunning, shocking. I just couldn't believe it. Where I am now is I've accepted the hopelessness of reaching her. Any hope now seems delusional, and, come to think of it, I guess the hope was kind of compulsive too.

**Lou:** Your egos were a perfect fit for each other. Your ego believed the way to acceptability and approval was by pleasing her and trying to meet her needs for approval and acceptability. Her ego believed the way to acceptability and approval was by dominating you and diminishing your sense of acceptability and approval. You needed to be the good guy in her eyes. She needed to be superior and the "needed one" in your eyes. Your ego needed to believe you could win her over and believed you *had to* in order to be safe and acceptable. You could not at that point step away and claim your own worthiness and refuse to submit to her abuse of you. "Love without power is anemic and sentimental" and self-destructive. Her ego needed to believe she didn't need your approval and had to aggressively deny her need in order to feel safe and acceptable. "Power without love is reckless and abusive" and also self-destructive, although not as obviously in the short term

**Stew:** I felt like a gigantic wimp. I felt worthy of nothing but contempt. That feeling still takes me over.

**Lou:** I know how you feel. I can't tell you the number of times I "wimped" out on standing up for myself because of fear of disapproval, rejection, or somebody's anger with me. My ego was convinced, and had me convinced for a long time, that taking any action that threatened the ego of someone who mattered to me would result in something that felt like death...literally terrifying. My ego was definitely on the "love without power" side of King's equation. For my ego, if having a self meant being rejected, then not having a self was the only course of action. Self-suppression meant survival. Self-expression meant personal extinction, abandonment, and ostracism.

**Stew:** Seems terribly "needy."

**Lou:** Yes, it does. And it is. And we have a lot of contempt for our neediness, don't we? We hate it for what it makes us do, for making us sell ourselves out, making us weak in the face of others, like Gabe was saying early on in our discussion.

**Stew:** Yes, yes, and yes.

**Lou:** We are in a terrible dilemma. The need for approval and connection is primal, and so is our need for autonomy and self-expression, what King called "love and power." When these needs conflict we are forced into horrible choices—like the analogy of the wolf caught in the trap chewing its leg off in order to survive. We may get to choose which leg we chew off—the "power" leg or the "love" leg—but we lose a leg either way. And actually, when we're forced to make this life-denying choice we lose both legs. The power I gain if I have to "chew off" my capacity to love and connect is a dependent power, not an autonomous one. It depends on my suppressing *my* need for connection and on suppressing *your* need for full self-expression. I must make sure your self-expression never exposes my hidden need for connection and approval.

And If I have to "chew off" my capacity for autonomy and self-expression, the "love" I may gain is also dependent, not genuine, not free. It depends on suppressing my self-expression and making sure you never see my power. I must protect your image of being the one who is needed and dominant, and not the needy one, so you will continue to accept me.

**Stew:** Still, in this moment the "power without love" position looks better. At least I wouldn't be feeling the shame I feel.

**Lou:** Yes. It's a bit like taking a drink or a drug. It works to put the shame down and to create more ease and confidence within you, even superiority.

**Stew:** Yes!

**Lou:** The trouble is it's a lie. You are not free. You are not autonomous. In either position you are dependent on successfully manipulating some individual or some group into buying a lie about yourself. In the one, the lie is "I am safe in this world only if I don't ever need *anyone's* approval and acceptance." And in the other, the lie is "I am safe in this world only if I keep my personal power and need for autonomy hidden from those who matter to me."

These self-beliefs create states of emergency when their rigid rules are not met. There is no internal, autonomous, self-authorized safety zone for our own personhood. Our safety and all-right-ness must continuously be re-established, defended, buttressed, and protected in all our relationships. There can be no sustainable relaxation, no real rest, no real "safety inside my own skin." Any rest we may get is like the brief R and R periods soldiers are allowed from the active combat arena—nice, but in the back of their minds they know they have to go back to the battlefield.

**Stew:** I can *feel* that's true. I was not aware of that stress before, of that tension in me. I had enough going for me in my career that was positive that I could ignore those feelings. Ignore is not the right word. Those feelings just weren't on my radar. I was riding high. When you're winning on the battlefield it can feel really exciting.

**Lou:** Absolutely! Our egos love to find ways of suppressing any awareness of the fear and humiliation caused by both our physical and personal vulnerability. Their goal is invincibility. That is what they were originally created to do—to protect us from the unbearably painful feelings of shame and humiliation arising from having aspects of ourselves chronically disapproved of and rejected as youngsters. We had to find ways to suppress those feelings or our budding sense of personhood would have been completely overwhelmed by them.

The best that some folks' egos can do is to keep their hosts living just outside of, or in and out of, that sense of overwhelm all the time, like Gina was describing. But if there are ways of being and acting that your ego thinks are good and you find ways to really maximize those ways, your ego is going to reward you with feelings of excitement, superiority, invincibility, pleasure, pride, confidence, etc. It's like a "high." It's intoxicating. And it can last a long time.

**Stew:** It did. And the drugs, drinking, sex, fame, money, power, and success really helped keep the high going. You know, if I got a bad review or my band got compared to some other big band in a negative way, I could always say, "Fuck it," and snort a line, buy a house, or get laid. It could be as simple as going to a restaurant and being recognized and I was on top again.

**Lou:** In a way, when you become famous, become a public figure, your tribe or dependency group expands in scope and size. For some the expansion even becomes global. The numbers of people whose opinion matters to you can grow to enormous proportions depending on how large a public role you play.

If your public loves you, thinks well of you, finds you acceptable, and approves of you, this "quantity" of approval can be gloriously inflating to the ego. I can only imagine what it is like to fill a stadium with tens of thousands of adoring fans and have them screaming and yelling in excitement and joy during your performances.

And likewise, if your public turns on you, rejects you, it can be devastatingly deflating. Fame is a powerful social phenomenon in this country, and worldwide. Most of the intense feelings associated with being famous, as well as the intense feelings that come with being *associated* with those who are famous, are all ego-driven. The highs and lows of public acceptance and rejection are like a rollercoaster for our egos.

Since all our egos, across all levels of society, are hooked on being and doing what is acceptable and approved by our tribes, it figures that we are all hooked on fame--either obtaining it, being connected to people who have it, or vicariously living through those who are famous by watching and reading about their ups and downs. Everyone has had the experience of unexpectedly being in the presence of someone who is famous, or infamous. There is a kind of freeze and excitement, and a furtive gaping or outright gawking—and a kind of a creepy feeling, too, if you look deeply beyond the surface excitement.

It is as if something special and/or threatening is happening. You are in the presence of someone who either has "it" or has lost "it." And that "it" is, or might be, contagious. And that "it" has something to do with being acceptable and approved of...or not. And if I'm not famous, then I don't have "it" so I feel "less than" the famous one. And if the "famous one" has taken a hard fall and become publicly diminished, then I feel "better than" the formerly admired one.

**Stew:** Tell me about it. I think I've experienced the whole gamut. But it still gets me. I still get pulled into the vortex of reading reviews and gossip and thinking about our earlier successes, getting back on the emotional rollercoaster. Besides the downside of the deflation, there is also creepiness to some of the upside, to the adoring way people look at you. You get a bad feeling they are not seeing you, but some image they/you have created.

It feels like they are feeding off of you, filling some hole, sucking your life juices out of you, like you're being used. And they think somehow just because you're a public figure you belong to them and you owe them and they can just walk right up to you and talk to you like they actually know you, like you're their friend or something. Sometimes it's a high, don't get me wrong, but it creeps me out a lot, too.

**Lou:** It is creepy. And I'm sure you have experienced being in a fan's shoes and had the same reaction to some person who was famous or infamous in your world.

**Stew:** You're right! I've met some of the greats, and I'm sure I didn't relate to them like people. I was nervous and star-struck, even fawning, now looking back on it. I was giddy, too, like somehow now I was as special or cool as they are because I got to hang with them. I was bouncing all over the place. But it really is so momentary. There's nothing reliable about it.

**Lou:** I don't think we can help it. It's cultural, social ego programming. We are more an ego-driven culture than we are a personhood-centered culture. Being famous and acclaimed is considered a great thing by the entire culture.

You know I'm thinking that this might be a good point in our conversation to share with you more specifically how the ego works, how it does its job. You remember I said earlier that there are two sides to the ego—a side that rewards for "good" behavior and a side that punishes for "bad" behavior. This seems like a good time to focus in on the rewarding side. So I am going to give you a document that describes this part of the ego, which has a set of inner "host-managers," I call the "Seeker, the Inflator, and the Convincer." It is hard to separate the two sides because they really work in concert, but for the sake of clarity this document takes a shot at describing the reward side first. So read it and then we'll pick up our dialogue again.

# chapter four

# The Ego's Reinforcement/ Reward Team

## The Seeker/Inflator/Convincer

This document is about the reinforcing and rewarding side of the ego. The punishing/enforcement side of the ego will be addressed in a separate document later. This document spells out what our internal experience of ourselves looks like when we are acting in accordance with what *your or my* particular ego thinks is good." It will describe all the rewards, reinforcements, and perks that go with that circumstance. The three internal "managers" responsible for this reinforcement/reward side of the ego are called the Seeker, Inflator, and Convincer.

## The Seeker

The member of this threesome called the "Seeker" is responsible for focusing the ego's host, i.e. you or me, on continuously and compulsively seeking whatever your ego considers "good." The Seeker's driving belief about what the ego considers good is simple: "I must have it, and more of it is better." If you are not driven by the Seeker to acquire the most that you can of whatever is considered good by your ego, then the Seeker is failing at its job. If, for example, your ego believes that certain *ways of being* make you more acceptable, then you *must be* more and more that way. That could require you to be more heroic, tougher, kinder, wiser, smarter, prouder, humbler, gentler, funnier, more aggressive, more peaceful, more dominant, more entertaining, more stylish, more knowledgeable, more sophisticated, and so on. Whatever your ego thinks is the good way to be or behave, the Seeker will *compel* you to be the best, or at least better than most, at being that way.

And, if your ego believes that *having* something makes you more acceptable, the Seeker will also make you *compulsively seek* more of that, for example, it may be money, good looks, fame, power, success, muscles, endurance, status, wisdom, enlightenment, self-awareness, good deeds, people's gratitude, followers, sexual conquests, lovers, friends, influence, control over others, and so on.

The Seeker's belief is not just "it would be nice, useful, helpful, fun, or challenging to be or to have "more." For the Seeker there is no such experience as simple curiosity, passion. pleasure, or interest in "being" and "having." No, it *must* have more and *must* be better. There is no "okay" or "good enough," or experiences of the simple pleasures of being and becoming. In the ego's world there is only "more" and "perfection." The Seeker creates a sense of urgency, importance, or priority to keep you compulsively seeking what "you must have" and compulsively being "the way you must be." There is no choice. The Seeker seeks what it considers essential to the host's self-survival and safety within the tribe.

Of course the "good" that is compulsively being sought by the Seeker is what you and those that matter to you have been socially conditioned to *believe* is good. And since your ego operates out of the belief that acceptance within your dependency group/tribe is absolutely critical to your interpersonal safety and survival, this acceptance and approval must be compulsively sought and maintained.

## Upsides and Downsides

The upside of this single mindedness on the part of the Seeker is probably pretty obvious. When you are *compelled* to acquire something or to be some way, chances go way up that you will succeed. When your "life" depends on you getting something done or appearing a certain way, you are highly motivated to make it happen. To meet your ego's demands, your Seeker will use any and all of your inherent capacities. It will use your unique native gifts and talents, say for being funny, public speaking, sexual attraction, writing, dancing, singing, or working with numbers, etc. It will use your intelligence, creativity, will, intuition, personality, senses, athleticism, awareness, heart, emotions, looks, memory, whatever works, to accomplish its ego-driven purpose. Great accomplishments, art, inventions, organizations, good works, products, and discoveries have come from the efforts of ego-driven Seekers. So too have all the great evil inventions, the untold numbers of brutal, sadistic, evil works and the actions of our many destructive leaders and organizations, as well as countless destructive products. When the ego considers harmful beliefs, as well as destructive ways of being and acting, as "good" for its host...look out.

This *compulsivity or rigidity* on the part of the ego is precisely what makes the Seeker's methods problematic, and so often destructive, even when seeking "good" rather than "evil." It is obviously problematic when what the ego considers "good" for one individual or one group is detrimental or destructive to others. Look at the Christian Crusades, China's Cultural Revolution, Hitler's Nazism, and ISIS's jihad as gross examples of individual and group egos doing extraordinary damage to millions and millions of people in the service of what they were all convinced was the "greater good."

The problematic side of compulsivity and rigidity is not as clear when what the ego considers "good" is also generally considered good by others. Most of the possible "goods" that egos may incorporate as their own are not inherently good *or* bad; they simply are what they are. But when ego-driven seeking rules your behavior, you *cannot stop* seeking or acquiring what the ego chooses. You have no choice. There is no such thing as "enough" or "another way." And you cannot ever "be" or behave the opposite of your ego's choice, even if it is clearly called for by your current situation or is clearly causing harm to you and others. It's the ego's way or the highway.

It is this fact—that the ego's "goods" become compulsive and then are rigidly acted out—that turns our continuous seeking (even for "good stuff") into a negative, even a destructive and dangerous force. Physical fitness is taken to the point of exhaustion and damage to the body. Or the time and energy necessary to create and sustain nourishing relationships is consumed by the ego in its single-minded purpose of acquiring more and more wealth. Helping someone else is pushed to the point when the one you are "helping" turns on you with rage, demanding to be left alone. Protecting your reputation as honest and good turns you into a liar about the harm you cause. The need to sustain your dominance over others leads them to resist you or abandon your cause. The Seeker behaves like the aforementioned "hammer that sees everything as a nail." It operates within a narrow response repertoire and forces us to respond with a "hammer" to situations that are not "nails."

Another downside to compulsive seeking is this: While the Seeker may leave you, its host, *some* internal room to experience personal pleasure in the process of getting its job done, pleasure is by no means considered an essential part of its process. Outcomes are everything. And the overriding outcome sought is continued acceptability and interpersonal safety. There may be momentary pleasure in some particular approved acquisition, accomplishment, or self-image improvement. But then that outcome must be continuously maintained and maximized. There is no rest and relaxation for the Seeker. The Seeker is pretty much on the job 24/7. No wonder so many of us feel so "stressed out" and energy-depleted.

## The Inflator

When you are behaving, acquiring, thinking, feeling, and believing in the ways your ego wants you to, then the Inflator member of this threesome rewards you with the glow of such momentary feelings as excitement, happiness, superiority, goodness, adequacy, righteousness, control, power, invincibility, security, and belonging; of having status and influence; of being admired, valued, and desired; of being entitled, successful, a winner; of confidence about being "on top of it" whether physically, materially, intellectually, emotionally, or spiritually.

The Inflator is selective with the feelings it doses you with. It chooses the right one for the particular moment and for the host's particular ego type. So if it is some aspect of "saintliness" the ego seeks and the host, in a given moment, successfully acquires or manifests that aspect, the Inflator will dose and inflate that host with feelings of "humble" goodness and worthiness. If it is some form of dominance over others that the ego seeks and the host successfully acquires that dominance, then the Inflator will dose and inflate that host with feelings of power, strength, and superiority. If it is some form of conformity the ego seeks and successfully acquires, then the Inflator will dose that host with feelings of rightness, control, correctness, and security, and so on with specific rewards tailored to each of the different types of egos.

It is significant that the Inflator uses feelings, and not just thoughts, to control its host's thinking and behavior. Thoughts by themselves, once exposed to evidence and reason, are more readily dismissed or changed, or at least questioned. However, combine thoughts with feelings and you have a much more potent inner force to deal with. A particular thought, matched with the right feelings, turns that thought into an internal "truth," not just a concept, an idea, or an opinion. That thought is no longer simply accurate or inaccurate; it is a believed belief. It is "true." It is "the Truth." It is a "must." There is no other way that could possibly be more right.

Let's say, for example, that your ego thinks that frightening people should always be your "go-to" interpersonal strategy (powerful, safe, effective, etc.). When the Inflator combines that *thought* with *feelings* of superiority, power, and excitement whenever you successfully frighten people, those feelings combine with the thought and result in a powerful self-reinforcing experience. "Every time I frighten people I feel superior and powerful, and people do what I say (and my fellow bullies admire me more). *Of course* it's always a 'good' idea to keep people afraid of me."

Or let's say your ego thinks pleasing people should be your "go-to" interpersonal strategy. When the Seeker compulsively and successfully focuses you on pleasing someone, and the Inflator then adds feelings of goodness, safety, and the warm inner glow of being admired or "loved" to the experience when you do so, of course you are going to believe that pleasing people should always be your default interpersonal strategy. Especially if your fellow "people-pleasers," as well as the people you please, accept and praise you more when you do.

The feelings the Inflator uses to reward successful seeking are not good or bad in themselves; they are just feelings. It is when pleasurable feelings are *used* to reinforce compulsive, driven behavior, behavior that has become automatic, unconscious, reactive, and beyond our choice, that those feelings become problematic.

The good feelings we feel when obeying the ego can blind us to the negative consequences of our ego-driven actions. Being rewarded with good feelings for obeying the dictates of your ego when the cost of obeying is sacrificing your dignity, compassion, autonomy, and self-development is poisonous and self-destructive. Compulsively pursuing pleasing feelings, such as arrogance and superiority, in order to avoid being aware of your own self-hatred is poisonous and self-destructive. Receiving the "blessings" of praise and esteem from "good people" is poisonous and self-destructive when the cost of receiving those blessings is your subjugation and the suppression of your self-development. Receiving the promise of God's love at the cost of being required to hate yourself and forever feel unworthy is poisonous and self-destructive. These are all forms of drinking the Inflator's brand of "Kool-Aid."

## The Convincer

The Convincer member of this threesome of reinforcers/rewarders chimes in to convince you that whatever your ego tells you is correct or right, and that contrary points of view are wrong or simply ignorant. The Convincer also uses feelings to reward and reinforce. It will dose you with *feelings* of certainty and confidence that your ego's way is the best and the only way. These are feelings, not facts. The felt experience of certainty and confidence is not dependent on anything factual. Think of the certainty and confidence we feel in our prejudices. Listen to a politician or pundit bloviate about their opinions as if they were facts. When the ego has the host successfully seeking and acquiring everything it thinks is required for acceptability, the Convincer's job is easy. It just keeps dosing its host with those wonderfully reassuring feelings of certainty and confidence, and, even better, arrogance and righteousness.

It is also the Convincer that creates the believed illusion that the host is making autonomous choices and acting on free will. The Convincer is the one primarily responsible for preserving the host's sense of personal autonomy, power, and self-respect by creating the illusion of choice and rationality, while in fact what's really happening is that the dictates of the ego are being obeyed. It does this by infiltrating the intellect of the host and using "reason" and argument to delude the host into believing he/she is acting out of rational deliberation and choice, is being "realistic." It blinds the host to the compulsive, automatic, and rigid quality of the host's ego-driven thinking, behavior, and feelings.

The arguments and reasons the Convincer uses can be full of holes obvious to any outside observer, but the ego does not care. Through the Convincer's gift at creating a righteous and believed sense of truth, the ego keeps the host within its sway. One sign of the Convincer at work shows up when the host is challenged and gets heated and rigid about his or her "case" for the rightness of their "choices." The Convincer is in fact frequently wrong, but never in doubt.

This power to convince is impressive. It will convince you that you have not made a mistake when you have (or that it is someone else's fault); that you really know what you are talking about when you don't; that you know the real story about someone when you don't; that other people's points of view are stupid and inferior when they are not; that your prejudices are not prejudices, but the truth; that your arrogance is earned; and that your beliefs are the truth, not just beliefs.

It seems our early innocence and dependence on others, joined with our capacity for imagining, leaves us vulnerable to beliefs that have no basis in reality. Think again of my earlier examples of belief in Santa Claus or the Boogey Man. We don't know enough about "reality" as children to know that what we are being told by the "gods" of our childhood may be complete fiction. We identify with our parents. We are naturally inclined to believe them, wholeheartedly. The groundwork for prejudices, fundamentalist beliefs, black-and-white thinking, and distorted world views is laid down early in our development. This early pliability also makes it possible for us to be convinced as kids that the truth of what we directly feel in our own hearts and bodies about frightening and harmful interactions with elders is "wrong" or "bad" to feel, and not to be trusted, or convinced that our native thoughts and intuitions about what is actually going on with others are crazy, dangerous, or sinful. We can be and often are "convinced" out of believing our own true experiences.

Every type of ego is fundamentally seeking the experience of an inner sense of interpersonal safety for its host. To create this inner sense, every ego seeks to protect and maintain the host's self-image in accordance with tribal rules and regulations. However, egos do not allow their hosts to be conscious or openly acknowledge that this is the ego's most fundamental goal. To acknowledge this would be an implicit admission that the acceptability of the host's selfhood *could* come into question—an admission that there *might* be something to prove or correct. The Convincer's job is to maintain an inner sense and an outer appearance that everything is just fine with its host's self. Approval must be assumed, not sought. So when the Convincer is in control it never allows interpersonal safety and acceptability to be *a public or conscious* concern. If the Convincer is successful, the experiences of interpersonal and internal safety and acceptability should already be established and never in doubt.

So successfully seeking, acquiring, and being what your ego demands is pretty seductive, right? This is what life is all about, right? Who wouldn't want to feel the ways the Inflator makes you feel, or the kind of conviction and confidence the Convincer creates within you. And so what if we *compulsively* seek what the ego thinks is good? It's still "good," right? There is no need or motivation to question how or what you're doing when it is all happening successfully according to your ego. Why would you?

## Challenges To The Convincer

The Convincer's job only becomes harder, and changes, when the Seeker and the Inflator are not able to drive the host into meeting the ego's demands. When this happens, the Convincer shifts gears and performs a failsafe operation.

A client comes to mind who is a good example of riding high when meeting the ego's demands and tumbling low when life situations call for acting in ways our egos won't allow. Her story illustrates how the Convincer does its job when all is going well, as far as the ego is concerned, and then how it works when circumstances in the host's life have created the threat of a disillusionment breaking through the walls of "protection" the ego throws up around the host's acceptable self-image.

The client is a woman who had been raised in a wealthy, high status, but emotionally cold and neglectful family. She had also suffered a severe rejection by her peer group as she was entering adolescence. She basically raised herself emotionally and socially. In her later teens, and very precocious, she sought connections in the New York club scene of the late '70s and early '80s. She made friends with older patrons who became her tutors in how to "win friends and influence people." She learned quickly that feeling or showing social vulnerability and fear was not the way to succeed. She had already gotten a powerful dose of this lesson in her family and in her early peer group experience.

As she "grew up" in this scene, she became extremely popular amongst the people who were regulars in the scene. If you sought her friendship she could be charming and warm. If you crossed her she would cut you dead— publicly, if necessary, for full effect. She connected with people who had power and influence in the world of finance and high society. She was very attractive physically and took pleasure in her sexuality. Men found her attractive, exciting, and intimidating. If you were her lover, besides the enjoyment of the sexual connection, you automatically gained status and entrée into circles of people with power, influence, and social standing. If the break up was messy on the man's part, she would make sure that those open doors slammed shut. She was gifted with high intelligence, a powerfully creative mind, and strong will. She became a very successful entrepreneur and businessperson in her own right.

This woman's ego—let's call her Jane—was a refined version of the bully ego—a charming bully. She was dominant, in control, and would be ferociously critical and intimidating when it seemed useful to her. But she was also charming, warm, attentive, generous, sexually open, and ego-boosting to the man she was currently attached to. What her ego considered "good" (i.e. the "must haves") included the following characteristics:

- Control and power over others
- Invincibility
- Physical attractiveness
- Social status and admiration
- Financial wealth
- Extravagant entertaining
- Independence and autonomy

None of these characteristics are inherently "good" or "bad." They are what they are. But, as we are witnessing, when each "good" must be compulsively sought and maintained to the exclusion of their opposites, trouble eventually ensues.

But, of course, before it does, the ride can be really great, even ecstatic. Great success and significant accomplishments can be created—and sometimes for a long time. For Jane, from the time she got the hang of the club scene, say around age eighteen years old, until she was just beyond forty, she had an amazing run. She was never without a lover, was sought after for her parties, charities, and business ventures, and had plenty of good press and financial success. She felt invincible, happy, and on top of her world. Her Inflator pumped her up with feelings of superiority, safety, power, confidence, entitlement, excitement, and rightness. And the Convincer had an easy time of reinforcing her belief that her way was the best way, especially with all the social agreement surrounding her. Certainty reigned—certainty that she was making all the right choices, certainty that she knew who she was, and certainty she wasn't hiding anything about herself from either herself or others. It was totally intoxicating—better than drugs and alcohol, although those helped fuel the high and quickly extinguish awareness of any moments of emptiness or uneasiness.

Shortly after turning forty, she fell in love for the first time in her life. Up until this man, we'll call him Jeff, she had always liked men but saw them primarily as sources of company, opportunity, excitement, fresh experiences, and hopefully entertaining and interesting conversations. She would attach but not deeply. This was true of friendships too. Her feelings for Jeff were different. Before him, she had never really missed anybody if they were absent. Now, when Jeff was not around she found herself filled with a mixture of anxiety and longing that could only be quelled by his presence. This dependency on him for her sense of "all-rightness" troubled her, frightened her.

Her ego made her feel ashamed of her "weakness" and vulnerability, but her Convincer could not suppress the awareness of her need for him. She tried moving away from him for stretches of time. Jeff was pretty self-possessed and autonomous. He'd been married once before and had learned a lot about himself and what he wanted in a relationship. He loved her, but, because of the deeper self acceptance he had gained from his experience of loving and losing once before, he knew it would hurt but that he would be all right if this didn't work out. So when Jane would pull away, he would express his dismay and tell her how much he missed her. But he wouldn't chase her down.

All of this was totally new for Jane. She was always the one pursued. Her Seeker and Convincer doubled down. They needed to get her back in the grove of feeling in control. The man was supposed to depend on her, not the other way around. She was supposed to be independent. She didn't know what to do with her powerful need for his love and approval. She, her Convincer, had learned to hate those feelings, to really believe they were weak and dangerous. Since the Convincer could not suppress the awareness of her need for him, the Convincer switched tactics in order to protect her image of herself. It got her to believe that Jeff was the problem. Blaming is a favorite strategy of the Convincer when there is a chink in the ego's ability to sustain an acceptable image. She began criticizing and putting Jeff down for his distance and lack of attentiveness when he was engaged in his own life and his separate interests. He was a successful journalist and he loved to write and to travel for his work. Writing was a solo occupation, and of course traveling also took him away from Jane. He would call her every day when away but this was not enough. He would invite her to travel with him, but she had projects of her own. And besides, according to her ego, she could not appear to "belong" to him or depend on him. Her Convincer convinced her to forget about him, to dive into a new financial project, and to increase her social entertaining. The Convincer called on the Inflator to pump her up with feelings of independence and power while engaged in these extra efforts.

But something happened that blew a hole in Jane's ego's operating system. Jeff saw that he could not satisfy her enough to make the relationship sustainable, despite their love for each other. So, ten months in, he ended it. Jane was devastated. She became obsessed with him and anxiety ridden. This crisis overran her Convincer's (and Inflator's) best efforts and forced her to face her need for love and connection, and to become more conscious of just how much trouble she had with the feelings of vulnerability those needs created. This was her "I'm not who I thought I was" moment. That was the point at which she knew she needed some kind of help. Her initial understanding of "help" was, of course, controlled by her Convincer. So she believed she needed help "getting over" her weakness and dependency, i.e. to conform better to her ego's demands. This is where we began our work together, which led to her discovering, much to her initial disbelief, that her strength and safety did not require the complete suppression of her "shameful feelings" of needing approval, acceptance, and love.

Now I'll move on to a different client. His moment of disillusionment, when the Convincer's power to convince collapsed, his moment of "I'm not who I thought I was," wasn't about realizing and accepting his need for connection and love. He was familiar and comfortable with those feelings. His wake-up moment was about recognizing and accepting his need to exercise his personal power, and to respect and act on his inner truth. His "wake up" moment was about his need to be true to his own experience, and to accept the interpersonal risks that went with acting in ways that *threatened* his connections to others.

We'll call him Johnny. He was a musician, a member of a very successful rock and roll band. Johnny was the "good guy" in the band. He was the diplomat to the other more self-involved members of the band. In terms of his ego type, he may sound unusual for a rock and roller, but, in my experience, having worked with many bands, there is always a band member with his type of ego. In a real sense, Johnny was the "interpersonal glue" that had kept the band together for the past twelve years. The ego types of the other band members ranged from "Star/Bully," to "Hermit," to "Joker." Johnny's ego could be labeled "Saint." Add to this mix the fact that all of them had strong strains of "rebel" running through their egos.

Every member of this band was highly creative and highly skilled instrumentally and vocally. They complemented each other and together created a genuinely unique sound and style. Their "whole" was definitely greater than the sum of its parts. While there were a few moments in their history when a couple of the members thought they could succeed on their own, mediocre or failed solo projects brought them back to the reality that the band was their most powerful and satisfying vehicle. So they knew they were very dependent on each other both for success and for satisfaction.

Their success surfaced several issues that were predictable points of conflict between the members of any band. Money, credit for songwriting, and the process of putting songs together and practicing them as a band became the most "radioactive" interpersonal arenas. Whenever these topics came up in a conversation, that conversation quickly devolved into a frustrating argument.

The two songwriters in the band were Johnny and the member with the Joker ego type. We'll call him Zeke. Zeke plays lead guitar and Johnny plays bass. The other two members are Joey (Star/Bully), the lead singer, and

Benny ('Hermit'), the drummer. They enlist side musicians to fill in different sounds when necessary, but they are the core members of the band.

Johnny and Zeke make a great songwriting team, with Zeke doing the lion's share of writing melodies and Johnny writing lyrics. The biggest problem for Johnny is dealing with Joey, the lead singer. Joey has a good ear for when a song really works, the ones that are likely to be hits, so he has a lot to say about Johnny and Zeke's writing. But having a Star/Bully ego, combined with a nasty addiction to OxyContin, he has had some very disruptive effects on Johnny and Zeke's creative process. A common experience is that Johnny and Zeke have the beginnings of a song and Joey, being stoned and inclined towards arrogance, jumps too early into their creative process and says the song "sucks," or some other contemptuous criticism. Zeke tends to joke off Joey's comments, but Johnny, having a Saint-type ego, avoids getting angry and swallows the shame induced by Joey's bullying and contempt.

When Johnny attempts to back Joey off by asking for more time to work the song out, Joey feels disrespected and that his talent for calling the hits is being challenged. He then goes into drug-addled/ego-driven overdrive and will rage about not being listened to, going through all the hits he's picked, and on and on. He comes around later, when he sobers up a bit, and makes some half-hearted apology for blowing up. In those "saner" moments, Johnny would explain to Joey how destructive his outbursts were. Joey would promise to be better.

But the pattern persisted and the damage to the creative process was accumulating. Johnny and Zeke were getting less and less productive and much less adventurous with their creativity. Joey was getting less and less reliable himself. Depression hung over the band. The band's manager and the record label folks were getting anxious and frustrated. Everybody was afraid of losing their lead singer, a unique talent and an essential part of the band's "sound." He'd walked out before and gone on dangerous benders. The manager, his bandmates, and the record label folks all told Johnny they didn't want him to rock the boat.

Johnny knew he had to do what nobody else was willing to do because of their fear of Joey's reaction. He knew he had to speak his anger and frustration with Joey, as well as his fear for the band's future. And do it in a way that might have real impact, it would have to be done in an all-hands-present band meeting. He had to be willing to risk the band blowing up. He loved the band, his bandmates, and his career. He loved making music with his buddies. They had worked so hard for their success. But Johnny realized the band was going down the tubes anyway—and so was he. He was becoming more and more unhappy with and ashamed of himself for stuffing down what his intuition was telling him was necessary to do: to speak up; to risk rejection, even ostracism from the band.

But Johnny's Seeker and Convincer kept pushing him to find a peaceful, "loving" (non-assertive) solution, convincing him that that was the "right" way. The Convincer made him feel like a "bad guy" for thinking about confronting Joey publicly in a meeting and ruining everything for everybody. He knew it would shame Joey. His Seeker kept pushing him to "take the high road." The Inflator joined in and rewarded him with feelings of "goodness" and safe superiority whenever he would back away from considering speaking up.

Johnny had debilitating bouts of terror, shame, and depression about taking action. It was at the moment of realizing that "who he thought he was," who he thought he *had* to be, wasn't working for him that he sought me out for some help. He didn't realize it at the time, but he really needed to discover that this challenge to who he thought he had to be contained some good news. He needed to challenge the beliefs of the Seeker, Inflator, and the Convincer that his safety and wellbeing depended absolutely on his suppression of the "shameful and dangerous" aggressive/assertive side of himself, so powerfully forbidden by his Saint ego. He needed to claim his personal power and authority, and see it as a form of loving his mates, which he did, to the band's great long term benefit, although the short term was pretty miserable for everybody.

## When All Is Good With The Ego…
## And When It's Not

It stands to reason that if you are doing what your ego says is good to do, and you are being rewarded for doing so, then it would make no sense for you to question the rule of your ego. It's working! No need to fix it or seek an alternative way of being and living. No need for awareness that there is more to you than what your ego tells you, and deeper still that you are not your ego. When they're working, we are happy to be identified with our egos.

And there is normally a strong social reinforcement of our "good me's." Within our own particular dependency groups everybody is in agreement as to what are the right ways to think, behave, and feel. Everybody is in agreement about what are the correct beliefs to hold. In a particular dependency group or tribe everybody is trying to maintain their membership and their standing by following the interpersonal rules operating collectively within that group. It is very unusual for anybody to step outside of the rules of their particular dependency group and their particular ego.

So our conversations stay within those zones that are safe and acceptable. These may be zones that are very pleasant, very "loving," very interesting, very useful, even very creative, but they are limited by the rigidity and compulsiveness of the egos involved. Real open dialogues that push the edges of the parties' limited awareness are rare. Most of our conversations are affirmations of what we already know, what we already think, and what it is acceptable to feel and believe. Only in a rare conversation do we reveal some aspect of ourselves that we are not sure is acceptable. Sounds a bit like a cult, doesn't it? Very often it takes a crisis of some sort to open us to these more meaningful and deeper conversations.

It is only when this upside of the ego stops working that questioning arises. Even when we do experience a breakdown in compliance with the ego's demands, we usually do not question the demands; we simply try harder to meet them. But sometimes the breakdown is big enough or persistent enough that we can't get back in the ego's good graces. These are hard times—times of confusion, feeling lost, feelings of failure and inadequacy. At their worst such breakdowns can produce deep depressions and suicides, or spirals into destructive drinking, drug use, and other self-destructive behaviors. These crises in confidence, self-esteem, and belief can be devastating. But it takes some form of breakdown in meeting the demands of the ego, or breakthrough beyond them, to open the ego's owner into seeking a different formula for living than the one the ego has made *compulsory*.

## When The Host Can't or Won't Do
## The Ego's Bidding Anymore

The reinforcing/rewarding side of the ego rarely succeeds to unfailingly keep the host interpersonally safe and on the "straight and narrow." Glitches in maintaining and strengthening inflation and conviction occur for everyone. For example, some important member of your current dependency group publicly slights you or moves to higher status; or like Jane, a lover rejects you, and your ego can no longer hide your dependency on someone else for approval and interpersonal safety; or like Johnny, the bass player, when the continued membership in your dependency group is threatened by your need to act on behalf of your wellbeing in a way that your ego forbids and also threatens rejection by the group.

Or contrariwise, as many folks on a self-development or spiritual seeking path have experienced, a breakthrough into an experience of a larger, freer, more alive sense of self arises within, to great relief and pleasure. Even if that experience disappears and you are plunged back into the old experience of a constricted and oppressed sense of self, the Seeker/Inflator/Convincer's grip on its host in these instances has suffered a mortal blow. This reinforcing/rewarding threesome's compulsive efforts to keep the host's awareness and behavior operating within a limited edition of a "self" have failed, temporarily, but often fatally. Awareness of there being "something more to me" has broken through within the host.

Of course the ego doesn't go quietly away. So the "something more to me" that has pushed into awareness is labeled as "something wrong with me" or "something bad about me." Or, when the something more is seen as positive by the host but is lost, the ego will label the host as "bad for having lost it," or seek to convince the host it was all a fluke or a one-time anomaly anyway.

So despite these types of image management crises that every ego encounters in the course of living a human life, the ego does not change its ways. The ego doesn't change its fundamental beliefs. The ego has a mind of its own and is not interested in feedback or experiences that call its operating principles into question. If we think of the ego as a fortress of delusional beliefs, then the Convincer is the one that mans the barricades against an invasion by reality (positive or negative), and will fight, sometimes to the death of the host, to ward off any disillusionment of the ego's belief system. The possibility of disillusionment is experienced as an emergency by the ego.

## The Native Self's Push for Wholeness: Another Threat to the Ego's Control

We have to remember that the ego was formed by splitting our native self in two, into a "good me" and a "bad me." This means that the ego can never really relax. We can only *truly* relax if it is all right to be who we are *completely*. When we can fully accept who we are, then we can move with ease, peace, connectedness, and personal power. This is our natural, unconditioned state of being. Unfortunately, it is not our normal state. When our acceptance is based on suppressing a "bad me" and selectively presenting a "good me," a chronic internal tension is created. What was whole has been forcibly pulled apart. The native self never stops seeking to regain wholeness. As I said in an earlier book I wrote with my wife, we end up feeling "constantly in danger of being ourselves" (*A Conscious Life*, 1996).

However, the inherent tension of that split can become so normalized that we don't even notice it. If we do, we call it "stress," "tension," or "chronic anxiety." Maintaining this split becomes so automatic, we become so skillful at it, that, like good actors, we are so believable that we believe our act ourselves. We become our act—just like good method actors. Our inner Convincer works hard to convince us that we are autonomous beings making our own choices. This is a valiant but disabled attempt at creating and maintaining a sense of dignity and self-esteem. We need to believe we are being our own independent selves. We start acting when we are so young that after a while we no longer remember that we are acting. My act is now "me."

Still, as good as we get at the act, there is an inner tension. Since my membership and my standing in my dependency groups is always conditional on how well I present my "good me" and hide my "bad me," then I can never truly rest within in the knowledge that my membership and good standing are givens. And as well as I may have blotted out "my bad me" from my own awareness, it still lives inside me. It still wants to self-express;

it wants to "become." It wants to be re-membered. It pushes for recognition and re-integration. My real, whole self needs to be and become; needs to grow and self-express. *Needs to.* There is an inner howl of pain and outrage at being violently split in two and forced to betray our true selves—to deny our true inner state. Most often that howl stays on "mute."

So there is a kind of vigilance required of the ego to watch out for leaks in the system of suppression. And there is a pressure that is always building within the Seeker to seek more and more of what is considered "good." There is often chronic performance anxiety running just below the surface of our day-to-day encounters and actions. "How am I doing?" is a question that always seems to be hanging in the ego's interpersonal air. And you'd better be doing "great." "Good enough" is in the neighborhood of failing. There is no "good enough."

# chapter five

# How Are You Doing In Your Ego's Eyes?
## Dialogues Continued

**Lou:** I hope the document on the Seeker/Inflator/Convincer was helpful as a pointer to and a clarifier of your own experience. I don't think of these three names as just concepts. In my own experience, and the experience of hundreds of clients, what has evolved is not so much the development of an abstract theory. Rather this is a description of the experiential equivalent of an actual internal "entity," or set of entities. Others have called them "mind parasites" or "mental complexes." These entities are like implanted computer chips that have taken over the running of our thoughts, beliefs, emotions, feelings, choices, and behavior. They are not who we are. They are not our native selves. They create a facsimile of ourselves—an "as if" self; a conditioned and conditional self; a self created in an image beheld in someone else's eyes, not our own. Like I said before, I know this sounds like we're all schizophrenics. And in a real sense we are. We are deluded, and we are being bullied and seduced by the alien voices (of the ego) in our heads and hearts into thinking, feeling, and believing we are a very slim and distorted version of who we really are. I know that sounds psychotic. It is not. It is what we take for "normal," meaning "okay," "acceptable."

But then I'm describing *my* experience. Some of you have already described the experience of a split inside yourselves. But let's see how this more detailed description of these rewarding/reinforcing ego entities fits or doesn't fit in your own experiences. And let's see how these entities impact your efforts to change.

**Mack:** I come back to what I said about "the disease" talking to me—my "addict" talking to me inside my own head. I really connected to your description of the Convincer. I was completely convinced I was not an alcoholic, and nobody could tell me otherwise! I was a hard partier, not an alcoholic. I was in control, man. Don't fucking tell me I'm outta control. You know what I mean? If I was out of control it was because I wanted to be out of control. I liked being out of control. I liked being dangerous. I liked not caring what happened, being reckless. Drinking helped me get there. If you didn't like how I was when I was drunk then "see you around."

I can remember fights with my younger brother because he called me a "drunk." He'd warn me I was headed for a fall and I'd blow him off, even when he bailed me out of jail for punching a waiter out in a restaurant. I blamed it on the asshole waiter—and another time on an asshole cop. I mean I was convinced! It took me getting shot to finally wake up.

**Lou:** "Denial" is not a river in Egypt, right?

**Mack:** You said it. Looking back is amazing. I was truly delusional. In almost every one of the really bad experiences in my life, alcohol and drugs were major players. I lost my first marriage, two businesses, and was almost killed. And those were just the highlights. I just could not believe I was out of control of my drinking and drugging. The drinking was the worst of it. I just could not see it that way. I mean, after a while I couldn't deny I had a "drinking problem," that I drank too much. There was just too much evidence. But that I could not control my drinking!?! Impossible. No way. That meant I was out of control! I just could not let that in. I was all about being in control. I was the top dog, the alpha male, the leader of the pack. One of the biggest hits to my image was when I realized my good drinking buddies were starting to avoid partying with me. One of them got honest with me and told me I was too much trouble and too dangerous to be around when I drank—and he was a guy who never backed away from a fight.

**Lou:** "Denial" is not like lying, is it? It's not like you know something is true and then say it isn't. You really believe that what you think is accurate, is fact. People close to an alcoholic who is spiraling out of control as a result of drinking can't believe the alcoholic doesn't see that drinking is what is causing the problems! They think he or she is lying.

**Mack:** I know. I mean, we do lie. But we really believe we're in control of our drinking, or can get there. Looking back I can hardly believe it myself. It's all so obvious in hindsight.

**Lou:** "Denial" is not limited to alcoholism or addiction. I don't believe it is caused by those diseases. I believe those diseases are caused by it...or made possible by it. I believe we are born with the capacity to repress and suppress the experience of reality when it is too much to bear. And I believe we all enhance the capacity to "deny" reality or delude ourselves when we emphasize *believing what we think* rather than paying attention to our senses and to what we feel directly.

Our unawareness and disbelief of the reality of unconscious forces, feelings, and conditioning is also a major block to seeing the full reality of being human. One of the major difficulties I run into working with people who are stuck in patterns of behavior that harm them and those around them is the *conviction* that they are conscious of, aware of, everything there is to know about themselves and whatever reality they are dealing with. It is simply unbelievable to them that they may be having and communicating feelings they are not aware of, or holding onto beliefs and judgments that are *unconsciously* determining their reactions and their choices.

The realization "I am not aware of every aspect of myself" is a revolutionary and transformational moment. It is the beginning of the crumbling of the Convincer's power and of the return to connection with our native selves.

**Frank:** I was convinced that the only way to be all right in this world was to dominate, to be superior, to put people down, and to intimidate. It was crucial to never be a "loser." My mother taught me this. I remember walking down Fifth Avenue on many weekends with my mother and she would be whispering in my ear judgments of people we passed. She'd say things like:

"Look at this one. Who does she thinks she is!? Look at the colors she put on!" or "Look at him with his ugly face!" Constantly judging. I felt superior and special when she did that with me, like we were these special conspirators who knew everyone else were losers. It felt exciting, exhilarating. I ran my relationships and my business with that same attitude. Being "nice" or kind was for weaklings and sissies. I was convinced that being contemptuous was the way to win in life. I still can feel a creepy shame feeling when someone compliments me for being kind.

**Willa:** Well, given that I have lost an experience of my "self" that I considered really good, that I really liked, and that I felt to blame for losing it, I feel reassured by your description of these entities, like even though it was a good experience, maybe there was some reason my ego didn't want me to have it or keep it. So the way you describe these guys it's like I can blame them and take it off me. And it gives me hope of retrieving the experience. So I'd like to believe that your description of them being separate from "me," from my real native self, is accurate, but I am having trouble really seeing that separation inside my own experience. It still feels mostly like it's all me in here.

**Lou:** If what I am describing is going to make a difference for you in how you live inside your own skin, then what I describe will have to shine your light on something inside you that maybe you didn't see or feel before, or maybe couldn't see so clearly. So thank you for staying accurate and authentic about your own internal experience right in this moment of our conversation. I really appreciate that, because your doing that keeps us in this exploration in a way that guarantees we won't end up traipsing around in a field of conceptual bullshit; it guarantees that we won't stay stuck in some map of a territory but never get down into the experience of the territory itself. I am always so relieved when someone is willing and able to do that with me. I feel connected, like we're standing on the ground together, the same ground, and looking out from there at each other, and talking to each other from there. Then it's a real exploration, not an abstract discussion. You know what I mean?

**Willa:** Yes. I can feel the pull to go into some kind of "belief" or wish, but I know I'm sick of believing and wishing. I want to *know*.

**Lou:** That's so cool. Even if it means feeling frustrated, lost, despairing or frightened in a given moment?

**Willa:** Maybe not always. No, not always.

**Lou:** Good. To me, that's a part of this experience of discovering ourselves. Sometimes our frustration, confusion, despair, or fear over ever being inside our own skin in an authentic way overwhelms us. We lose trust that there is any value or good outcome possible from only following our own experience.

**Willa:** Totally.

**Lou:** Let's take a moment and look into your experience of this loss of sense of self. You, Lucas, and Matt had what we might call pleasurable disillusionments. You both discovered by direct personal experience that there was more to yourself than you thought—and that the "more" was a really good thing, something you would naturally want to keep. Right?

**Willa:** Absolutely.

**Lou:** That's different from what Mack and Frank are describing. The Seeker/Inflator/Convincer side of their egos worked well for them for a stretch of time. They got all the rewards for being "good" or "right" according to their egos. Then they had experiences that crashed the fortress walls of the Convincer and disillusioned them in painful ways. The crashed walls revealed their buried "bad me's." In contrast, your disillusionment felt good. Nothing about a "bad me" was revealed in your discovery that there was more to you than you realized.

Let me ask you a few questions. Did the "more to yourself" you experienced feel unnatural in the moment of experiencing it?

**Willa:** No. It was a surprise, and really unfamiliar. But when I was in it I felt that this was my true nature. If I look back into the experience of that blissful year it did not feel unnatural at all. This sounds contradictory to what I just said, but in an unfamiliar way it also felt familiar. It felt kind of like when you take a deep breath after a stretch of uptight breathing. It was like remembering something natural that you forgot and didn't notice you'd forgot—like you forget how good it feels to breathe easily and fully. It was like that, only more profound of a discovery. It was only after the emotional fallout of my failed love affair that all the doubt came up about what's real and what's not.

**Lou:** So you went from knowing something in the way you wanted to know, and not settling for wishing or believing. You went from that "knowing," that certainty of your own direct experience, into truly doubting that direct experience. The experience of falling into the pain and suffering brought up by your broken heart certainly obliterated your contact with those good blissful feelings and replaced them with "bad" feelings. But not only that, that painful experience of yourself also made you doubt the reality, the truth, of your earlier blissful experience of yourself—I would guess not only because you lost that blissful experience, but also because you couldn't make the blissful experience come back. True?

**Willa:** Yes. Yes. Looking at it in this moment I guess that breathing analogy applies here too. I can remember to breathe deeply and then I can actually do it. I could remember the experience of my blissful self but I couldn't "do it." I couldn't make it come back—like I couldn't get my romantic relationship back to being loving again, come to think of it. That inability to recapture those experiences made me question their validity, their reality. It made me doubt that they were ever valid or real. You know I never noticed that assumption until just now.

**Lou:** Interesting. What do you make of it?

**Willa:** I'm not sure.

**Lou:** Take a moment and see what comes up.

**Willa:** Well, looking at the assumption from its logical implications, it would mean that any experience I can't make happen again or keep alive would be considered invalid, not real—like if it is not reliable, predictable, controllable, I guess, then the experience doesn't count...or I am a failure. That's in there too—that I should be able to repeat and control my experience of myself, of my insides. If I can't, then there is something wrong with me, or whatever I am supposed to be doing I'm doing wrong.

You know the whole fall from grace also felt like an emergency to me, too. It really panicked me. I felt really bad about myself—like I'd gotten myself thrown out of two paradises at the same time, and like I'd never be allowed back in to either. I felt like an untouchable.

**Lou:** Wow. Nasty stuff. From the heaven of belonging and being all right to the hell of rejection and unacceptability.

**Willa:** You got it.

**Lou:** And you feel you did all that to yourself?

**Willa:** I'd like to think otherwise, but there's nobody else in here.

**Lou:** So you feel that you decided to take away your bliss experience and ruin your relationship?

**Willa:** Maybe more like I let it happen and should have been able to hold onto the good stuff, or get it back.

**Lou:** So it's not that you caused the two paradises to go away, but you should have been able to prevent them from going away, and you're bad for letting it happen. It seems that in this assumption there is the belief that you were doing something or not doing something that you should have been able to stop doing or start doing that would have allowed you to stay in these paradises. So it seems you caused it. Yes?

**Willa:** That is where I've landed. Yes.

**Lou:** Did you know what to stop doing or start doing?

**Willa:** I've tried everything I know to do and stop doing and it hasn't worked. I changed my diet, stopped drinking the little alcohol I did drink, tried being more generous and loving, meditated more, tried to let go of seeking, and on and on. Nothing has connected me to that experience again.

**Lou:** Could you consider the possibility that you're not defective or bad but that you may be missing something; that you may be blind to something?

**Willa:** Possible.

**Lou:** If you were blind to something, genuinely ignorant, would you be unacceptable because that was true?

**Willa:** Hmm. I know this sounds irrational, but yes. It's like I am supposed to know already. I am supposed to know how to "do" relationships. And if I found my true self I should know how not to lose it again.

**Lou:** So at least in these very personal matters, ignorance and blindness are not acceptable; they make you unacceptable, make you a failure.

**Willa:** I feel awful right now—like I'm trapped in some horrible maze that has no exit.

**Lou:** The way the ego works means there is no learning allowed. You're not allowed to make mistakes, to not know. The ego sees that as too dangerous to your interpersonal safety. You could slip up and get rejected, lose your membership, your status.

Let me ask you another question. Even though you're not sure you have an ego, given how we have been talking about different types, if you had to type yourself what would your type be like? What would some of the operating rules of your type be if you had one?

**Willa:** The rules are easier to get to. I know I have some pretty intense rules about what's okay and what is not. One big rule is that it is bad to complain; it is bad to be angry, bad to criticize.

**Lou:** Ever?

**Willa:** Yes.

**Lou:** So never ever complain, be angry, or criticize?

**Willa:** Saying it out loud seems crazy, but yes that's the rule.

**Lou:** So you're being "bad" right now according to that rule.

**Willa:** Yes. I can feel the embarrassment right now, the shame.

**Lou:** So I figure the opposite side of that rule, the "be good" side, is something like, "Always be satisfied with what you've got; always be happy, cheerful, and positive." Does that fit?

**Willa:** Yeah—especially the second part.

**Lou:** So always be happy, cheerful, and positive?

**Willa:** Yeah.

**Lou:** And I figure when you're being "good" you feel good; you feel acceptable and right, maybe even proud of yourself? And when you're being "bad" you're hit with shame and anxiety and doubt.

**Willa:** Yes, although I've got Mary's rule about it being bad to feel good about yourself. But for sure the shame part.

**Lou:** It's starting to sound something like a "saint" ego. Do you remember choosing these rules?

**Willa:** No.

**Lou:** So what you've got is a rule that is an "always" and "never" kind of rule, which makes it compulsive, gives you no choice. And it's an "either/or," a "good/bad," kind of rule also. And it happens automatically. So does that fit your experience?

**Willa:** Yes.

**Lou:** So far that fits our description of what we're using the word "ego" to point to. Your experience of this rule would fit what we're taking as a sign of the ego at work, the ego being a conglomeration of these kinds of automatic, rigid, compulsive rules. So maybe in this sense you could say you have an ego, yes?

But, you know, I think the difficulty you're facing is the doubt that there really is anything more to you than what we are now calling your ego. The "you" who experienced the two paradises no longer seems real. That "you" was not only less familiar than this "you" we are now talking about, but it was also certainly less "reliable" than this one. That one disappeared and can't be retrieved. This one always shows up, right? Automatically. You don't have to work to experience this one, right? It's always at the ready, if not always present. Is this your experience?

**Willa:** Absolutely accurate! I also didn't realize until right now how sad I am about the loss of that other self. I could fall down weeping about that right now if I let myself. I loved that self. I feel like my best "me" died when I lost that self and couldn't get her back. I didn't realize it, but since I lost it I have been in a kind of suppressed mourning. And I've experienced a lot of fear too—fear that it's over for me, that the good self is gone for good. (Weeping softly) Despairing. I'm sorry for breaking down here.

**Lou:** I guess you're complaining again, huh?

**Willa:** (Laughing/crying) Crazy, eh?

**Lou:** Your grief is not crazy. You lost a loved one. What's crazy is that rigid compulsive rule about never complaining or being angry and always being cheerful. It makes it impossible to feel your pain and frustration, so then you can't investigate those feelings, learn from them, hear their message to you and then respond accordingly. There is no evolution of your experience; it stays stuck, cycling over and over, keeping you in place. Life gets flattened. Really feeling your grief is part of life moving through you, and moving you along your own evolutionary trail—*grief*, not shame and blame. Sometimes it's really hard to separate them.

When we lose something or someone and we have some belief that we should have had the power to prevent that loss that becomes an invitation to the internal shamer to have a field day. And that stops the grieving. How can you weep with any semblance of release over losing something or someone when you feel ashamed or guilt-ridden for losing it? If there are tears, they will be tears of despair and self-loathing, not simple profound sadness, acceptance, and letting go. When you're taking a beating you can't let go. In your ego's operating system you will automatically take a beating for any loss that happens to you. You will always be to blame for it.

What are you experiencing right now?

**Willa:** Sad and grateful.

**Lou:** Say more.

**Willa:** I don't think I'm done weeping over my loss. But right now that feels just true, not good or bad. And I feel like I just got home again, like I was lost and just got found...by myself. I'm inside myself again. It's hard to describe—bittersweet. I think without knowing it I had abandoned myself. (Weeping again.)

**Lou:** It is truly sad when we have to do that to ourselves, and such a relief to reclaim ourselves. What you are experiencing is one of the signs of actually having a moment of the freedom to be yourself outside of the grip of the ego. It feels precisely like coming home. But you can't return to your inner home if you can't feel your sadness, pain, anger, and fear over losing it. If you can't feel those feelings you will never even know you're lost. You'll just be numb, or high, depressed, self-hating, endlessly trying, giving up, or whatever—anything but feeling what it actually feels like to feel the loss of your self directly, the loss of your inner home. I truly thank you for letting us all travel with you back home. I'll bet that many in the room were walking right there with you in their own experience. Thank you.

**Lucas:** I've been sitting here crying to myself. God, I feel like I walked the same trail Willa just walked. It was like she was doing the work for me. Thank you Willa. I feel more at peace with myself right now than I have in long time. But damn, I'm still confused. What did my wife not getting my experience have to do with my losing it? And if my ego was in on the act, why wouldn't it want me to feel free, feel good?

**Lou:** I just want to make a note here: The power of a group that collectively chooses to move, however incrementally, toward more openness, authenticity, and awareness is awesome. Every individual's experience when it is openly and consciously allowed to unfold organically and be "felt through" in the moment has the effect of moving everybody else's experience along in their own individual unfolding. It's a great blessing. And I am going to answer your questions about your experience in a general way first, and then we'll come back to your particular experience.

First of all, no ego feels safe with unplanned spontaneity. Egos don't like surprises. They are frightened and ashamed of being out of control, unless it is planned. No surprises please. Nothing unexpected please. And especially not if the surprising or unexpected experience is a radical departure from the image of myself that my ego is compulsively maintaining. And this is true whether that experience is felt as positive or negative *by the host.* If it is outside the limits of experience set by the ego then it is feared. It is seen as dangerous to the future acceptance of the host in his/her tribe *by the ego.*

The ego does not have the capacity to embrace spontaneous, unplanned, uncontrolled positive personal changes, revelations, or unfoldings as potentially a good thing, even though those changes may produce some pleasurable feelings in the host. Even discoveries of unknown positive qualities within the host, if those same qualities are considered unacceptable by the ego, will be fought by the ego. Crazy, yes?

And of course, if only unpleasant, uncomfortable feelings are produced in the host by the changes or revelations, then the ego and its host are typically on the same page regarding getting rid of those feelings as quickly as possible. It's counterintuitive to the host, and anathema to the ego, to think of looking into painful feelings for their message and meaning rather than looking to swiftly remove them.

Any emotional or feeling experience that is outside of what the ego expects and plans for is considered too risky to allow because of the ego's deep fear of losing control altogether. Remember, the ego deals in "either/or's," and "blacks and whites." So in regard to managing its host, the ego's experience is that it is either in complete control or completely out of control—or in danger of being so. So in a universal way, no matter what the internal experience may be—a thought, an insight, a feeling, a sensation—if it threatens the control of the ego, the ego will seek to quash it, be it pleasant or unpleasant to the host. That is a universal operating principle of every ego. When you look deeply into the experience of your ego controlling you in any given moment, you can actually feel the compulsiveness of its grip, feel the tension of that effort to remain unfailingly in control, especially when control is being threatened. The problem is that not much of life is actually in our control.

That general rule being said, the ego also has reasons particular to its host for choosing to shut down an experience the host may find pleasurable, liberating, fulfilling, or enlightening. Maybe now we could look a little more closely at your experience, Lucas.

**Lucas:** Sure.

**Lou:** Actually, before we go there, I think we need to be clear when we are talking about these positive experiences of self that the "good" feelings they can produce are not the same as the "reward" feelings the ego produces for what it considers good behavior. The pleasurable feelings that Willa and Lucas, and also Matt, are describing are feelings that are inherent to certain natural states of being. These states of being are reflections of our essential nature, our essence.

As an example, some of you have had the occasional experience of being in the "flow," or being in the zone. Certainly the performers and artists in the group have had that experience. And anyone here seriously into a sport has probably experienced those moments where you feel "on" or in the zone. The experience is beautiful. There is a sense of ease, even in the midst of intense physical exertion or mental concentration. It feels like there are no blocks, no wrong moves. It's joyous but not excited, not agitated, not an engineered "high." It can be very quiet and very intense at the same time. Some people reach this state while meditating, chanting, or praying.

These feelings are not created by the ego. They are not controlled. They are not designed to control you. They are the result of a letting-go that is also not in the ego's control. They are in fact the result of the ego's grip being released for one reason or another. And the ego has no say about that happening either. If the ego does have a say, this will never happen.

What we're looking at here is why the ego wouldn't want to allow— even want to reward—the appearance of these natural states of being. And why are these natural states so rare, so fleeting, typically so out of reach? So often discovered and then lost? What's the problem with them for the ego? This is the source of much of our suffering along the path of waking up, which I alluded to in my opening remarks. It's the source of our "getting it and losing it."

**Stew:** I've been chasing those feelings my whole life! When that happens in the band it's like a fucking miracle is happening. It's way better than drugs— even sex...well, maybe.

**Mack:** There is a feeling like that which happens in certain AA meetings, where the sharing has been really open and authentic, painful and joyous and real. It feels like some kind of special love, muscular and gentle at the same time.

**Frank:** You know, just the other day I was heading home in my usual rushing "you better get off my sidewalk" way, and I passed this shaky old woman with a walker trying to cross Sixth Avenue. I went right by her; barely noticed her. But a little ways down the street a voice inside me said, "She needs help." I brushed it off at first but then I remembered I'm trying to find my heart these days. So I went back and asked if I could help. She gave me such a smile. I melted. I had never felt such a sweet moment before. It stayed with me for most of the evening, kind of like I was floating in some sweet fluid. That's not ego reward right?

**Lou:** No. If I've got it right, what you did was actually *against* your ego's rules. But no, even beyond the fact that your ego would typically have given you shit for any kind of "sentimental" or "soft" behavior. What you're describing is a state of being and the flowing feeling that emanates from that state. That's not the ego at work—although your ego can take possession of the experience later and whack you around either for valuing it or for losing it.

**Liz:** The last time I remember feeling something like you're describing was when I was playing tennis competitively in college. There was one big match where something shifted inside me. From that moment on that game was this intensely pleasurable experience—joyful really. I was taking so much pleasure in my body, in my movements, in the feel of the racquet, in the sun and the air on my skin, even in a feeling of connection with the girl I was playing against. It was like a high but with none of the edge and anxiety that have come with drug highs for me. I didn't really care if I won or lost, and yet I played with such focus, intensity, and energy that it was almost like I couldn't lose. I remember after that game I wept. Everybody thought I was crying for joy over winning. Winning was cool, but that wasn't what it was about. To this day I don't really understand those tears. But now, listening to the others speak, maybe they were tears of joy coming from that state I dropped into. I don't know. It was embarrassing at the time to be crying. I did feel out of control then and that was not okay.

**Lou:** This is always powerful for me. I've experienced this in so many, many groups before. It seems that when we get the opportunity, when it is safe enough, to talk openly about our egos, it automatically follows that people start remembering and being in touch with something in themselves radically different from the experience of their egos. To me this validates the importance of owning our egos consciously, compassionately, and honestly moment to moment, of "de-criminalizing" having one. When we do, it seems to open us up to contact with what we might call our essential selves. Later in our discussion we will focus on opening our access to our essential selves more deliberately.

But I have found if we're not aware of what keeps us disconnected from ourselves, and don't take responsibility for it, we may have a few fortunate experiences of contact with our essential selves, but we will never find a way to incrementally clear the barriers to greater access to the felt truth of who we are. It seems to me the ego never goes away. It is always ready to move its delusional view of you into your "home" and make you convinced that it is who you are. It puts us back in trance. We need to find ways of continuously waking up, but first we need ways to notice when we've been put back into trance, and see the trance state for what it is. That's both the beginning of waking up, and that's the work of staying awake more consistently. The process of waking up more and more fully and more and more quickly includes the experiences of waking up, falling asleep, waking up again, falling asleep again, waking up again, etc.; or getting it, losing it, getting it again, losing it again, getting it again, and so on.

This has been a bit of a detour, but I think what you've spoken about is an important piece of walking the path to recovering our full selves. It is important we share with each other our glimpses of experiences outside the sway of the ego, and notice the real difference in the quality of those experiences. But we've come a long way around to circle back to Lucas and his experience. Let's revisit your "twenty-four hours of freedom," as you put it. It sounds like it was similar to some of the positive experiences the others were just describing.

**Lucas:** Yes, it does. It didn't feel engineered. And it did feel completely natural, although completely unfamiliar at the same time. There was a quiet joy inside me. I felt full, not empty. I felt safe inside me, like I could trust myself. I didn't have to be on guard all the time. I could be at ease with myself. It was quite amazing.

**Lou:** Another description of that "natural but unfamiliar" aspect of your experience that I quite like is that it "feels like a miracle and no big deal at the same time."

**Lucas:** I like that. And you're right; that feeling or state was really different from the feelings I got when I was rewarded, as you put it, by my ego. My ego is a bit like Frank's and Liz's—not so much a bully, but a tough guy. I loved being competitive and beating other people. My specialties were basketball and poker. I played both really well in college. I was so good at poker I didn't have to work for my tuition. I played in some pretty high stakes games.

After college I got into the financial markets and I've played that game really well too. Hitting it big in the market is the same kind of high I got from being the high-scorer on the basketball team or winning a big pot in poker. I felt superior. I liked being looked up to. I had a lot of swagger. I had a posse in college that I was the leader of. We partied big and got the pretty girls. That carried through my twenties. Making financial bets that paid off big, cocaine, drinking, strip clubs—I was a "master of the universe."

I just turned thirty-seven and things have changed. Looking back those highs did have a kind of thin, frenzied feel to them. I wouldn't have said that then. And after a while there was also some serious hell to pay the mornings after. Ultimately my state of mind got messed up enough that I made some pretty bad judgments and then tried to cover them and made it worse. It's what brought my partners to the point of forcing me to accept a buyout. I made a lot of money, but the ouster blew my self-esteem all to hell.

I was pretty down when I did that workshop—and my wife was pretty fed up with me too. This feels a little like that workshop. People are talking about stuff you just don't talk about in normal life. A lot of it is embarrassing. But then it's not. I remember when somebody in my group at the workshop described this really humiliating experience she had had as teenager, and then being ridiculed by her classmates on top of it. I remember cringing inside and remembered feeling shame and humiliation at blowing a basketball game, or when I lost in this big poker competition. And then I realized how much humiliation I felt about fucking up at work. I couldn't believe this woman was talking about it, and that she was willing to do a psychodrama about it, relive it with us! She asked me to play the role of one of the boys who humiliated her. She saw I could play that role for real. That was a wake-up call—one of many. I got into it. When we were re-playing the scene with her, I could feel the anger inside me and the coldness of my decision that it was better to be a "humiliator" than "humiliatee."

Later on she was given the opportunity to express some of the rage she couldn't let out back then. Boy, did she let it fly. I was playing the boy she hated most, so a ton of that rage was directed at me. I wasn't scared. It's all done in very safe way. What surprised me was how much I felt her pain and her rage and her need to reclaim her dignity. That really set me up for my work with someone playing my father. He was always humiliating me, putting me down—my older brother put me down, too. Once the rage was finished the sadness came. I bawled. I wanted my father to love me really bad, but he couldn't. And then he died.

**Lou:** I figure as a result of that experience you can see better why you needed to develop a "tough guy" ego.

**Lucas:** I didn't think of it as my ego until recently, but yeah. My father hated what he called "wusses."

**Lou:** So let's imagine that you brought the "self" that came out of the workshop to your father, and that you were able to hold onto it in his presence. If you're willing, imagine that experience as for real as you can right now. How would you be different with him than usual? And what do you think your father's reactions would include?

**Lucas:** Hmm. Let me think a minute.

**Lou:** And feel, in your body.

**Lucas:** Okay. I'm imagining being with him and feeling like I know I'm all right. I'm getting that feeling back in my body. First of all, I would be standing a little differently. I feel straighter, more erect. That's different right there. Usually I'm sort of stooped. Also I don't feel afraid of him. I'm just looking at him, looking in his eyes. I'm in no hurry. I guess cause there's no emergency feeling. He doesn't usually keep his eyes on mine. He looks, looks away, says something, looks, looks away, says something. Like that. I'm imagining him noticing I'm not looking away, that I'm looking at him. He braces a bit, and says, "What?" in a challenging kind of way, like I'm threatening him or challenging him by not looking away and standing straight. I imagine myself saying, "What 'what'?" back to him, kind of playfully. This is way away from normal.

**Lou:** Let it be. Keep going.

**Lucas:** Now I see him getting really pissed and using his scary voice and saying, "What the hell are you looking at!?" You know what I want to say to him? I want to say, "I see you. I'm not afraid of you anymore." So I imagine I do. He gets red in the face, like he's about to blow. It feels scary now, like he's gonna come at me. But I put my hand up, and I say, "Stop...don't!" loud, like a command. And he stops. The juice goes out of him. He looks away. And then he walks away.

**Lou:** Powerful moment, even though an imagined one.

**Lucas:** It felt very real to me. I can also see why I couldn't do that as a kid, or even an adult, until now. He was scary, and he didn't want me to be strong, be as strong as him. He needed to be top dog, boss, bigger, you know?

**Lou:** Yes. This is precisely why for your own safety and some semblance of belonging with him you had to suppress your sense of being really okay, of being equal.

**Lucas:** Yes. That's it really. We could never be equal as persons. It was never safe for me to feel that.

**Lou:** It was never safe for you to really know that, on your own authority, not his. *Knowing* it is a different experience from thinking it, from just knowing it rationally, logically, or even objectively. It's different from "acting" it, also. Knowing it, in the sense that we are talking about it, is more akin to feeling it. We will talk more about this difference later on.

Your ego still thinks it's not safe, it's forbidden to feel equal, to feel ok. So it guarded and guards against you feeling that way. It took that feeling away from you and replaced it with the old one, put you back to being stooped and feeling defensive, angry, blaming, like him. It seems like your wife's cold reaction to you was like taking away permission for you to stand straight. Your ego doesn't know or care that you discovered who you really are. Actually it cares only in the sense that that discovery threatens to break your ego's rules for interpersonal safety.

**Lucas:** I see. Hmm. Looks like I may be schizophrenic for a while.

**Lou:** Yes. You'll be going back and forth between getting it and losing it—again, not intellectually, but the feeling knowledge of it. But you will lose this "knowing experience" less and less, and have it more and more, both qualitatively and quantitatively, over time. There'll be a coexistence, but the felt experience of the real you will keep expanding the space it occupies inside of you alongside the space your ego occupies.

You know how at night when you're dreaming you are completely in the dream? It feels completely real. You don't know it's a dream. And then you wake up and you know it was a dream. It loses its reality. That is usually a very black-and-white experience. One minute we are in the dream and feel it as real. In the next minute we are awake and feel it as unreal. The kind of "waking up" we are talking about here is sometimes that black and white. Sometimes we have the experience of feeling "how could I have believed *that?!*"—whatever the belief was.

But in the experience of waking up from a dream in the morning, when we are up and moving around, we don't go back into the unconsciousness of the nighttime sleep state and return to dreaming. No, we stay awake. We don't go back to sleep. But in the wakeful waking up we are dealing with, it is entirely possible, and indeed the norm, to "wake up" to some true experience of yourself and then in the next minute go back "to sleep" regarding that experience while still walking around in a conscious, not-sleeping, state.

**Lucas:** The "having it more and more" part sounds like good news, but I'm not sure I like, or even understand, the rest of it.

**Lou:** I know. There is actually a lot embedded in what I just said, but I'm going to save a fuller description of what I'm pointing to for later in our dialogue. For now I want to continue to talk about these highs and get some of the others' experiences.

**Liz:** So you remember I said my ego was a perfectionist type, if indeed that was my ego and not me?

**Lou:** Yes.

**Liz:** Well, listening to everyone talking, and reading your documents, as you call them, sounds kind of "Mormonesque," or like Scientology, you know.... "*The Documents!*" (Laughter.) But anyway, something clicked inside me in the last few minutes about the difference between my ego rewards and the simple personal satisfaction of accomplishment. I felt the difference. The words that came to me about the personal satisfaction were that it feels "wider" and "calmer." Maybe these are weird words to use. And the public satisfaction, the ego rewards, feel more "narrow" and "jittery" to me.

That experience reminded me that there is a real difference, or, as you were saying, a *felt* difference. The one is not fraught with all the highs and lows. It isn't so dependent on the reaction from the "public." It's a less dramatic version of what I felt on the tennis court that day that I described. And it's real tentative right now, but the difference is there. Only this time there are no tears. Instead, I'm *pissed* that I wasn't in on this possibility earlier in my life *and* I want to make sure I *don't* lose it! Getting it and losing it over and over again sounds like some version of torture to me, like emotional waterboarding or like some sadistic tease.

**Lou:** Good.

**Liz:** Good!! "Good!??" Fuck you.

**Lou:** I didn't mean to be insensitive. For me what's good about how you are being with yourself right now, where you are speaking from, is that you're listening to your *own* experience very intimately right now. You've "paused," in a sense. You're not just charging ahead or falling down in a collapse. You've stopped for a moment, this moment, and you're looking inside and listening inside to what *your own* true experience is telling you. You're pissed. To me that's trustworthy.

That's also self-respectful. That's you saying, "My experience matters. What *my* insides are telling me matters." You may not know in this moment how your experience is going to play out. And maybe you're also pissed you can't control how this self-discovery thing is going to play out for you. And your ego will feel really threatened by that and will get really judgmental about you for not knowing what to do about holding onto the good "wider and calmer" feeling, right?

**Liz:** Ego schmego. I'm pissed. I want to know what the hell you would suggest I do.

**Lou:** What I am going to say is not a joke. I would suggest that you go as deeply and fully as you can into your feeling of "pissed off."

**Liz:** Oh great!

**Lou:** Stay with me a moment. What you're calling "pissed off" is not a concept, right? It is an experience that is happening right now inside your body and your mind, right?

**Liz:** Yeesss.

**Lou:** And I'm sure you would much prefer feeling "wider and calmer" to feeling pissed off.

**Liz:** Where are you going here? This all seems pretty fucking obvious.

**Lou:** Yes. Obvious, but not *fully* felt through yet. Try something out. Do you still feel some of the pissed off feeling?

**Liz:** Yes.

**Lou:** Take some of your attention off of me and put it in your body and see if you can feel inside where the pissed-off feeling is actually happening. Scan around in your body and see if you can locate the area.

**Liz:** Easy—it's in my chest and my belly. And, oh, it's in my shoulders too... and my neck...and my hands...and my thighs....and my breathing. It feels like my breath is kind of pushing up and out of me. Hmm. You're right in one regard. There was more there than I was aware of. I wasn't really feeling the full physical experience. But so what?

**Lou:** Do you feel any differently or anything else since having looked more intimately at the experience of being pissed off? Look inside again and see.

**Liz:** Huh. I feel less pissed, calmer. Jesus, some of that "wider" feeling is there too. How the hell did that happen!?

**Lou:** Would you be willing to look a little more deeply?

**Liz:** I guess.

**Lou:** You really don't have to.

**Liz:** No. Some part of me wants to. I'll go with that.

**Lou:** You know, for what it's worth, you have a very developed capacity to go inside yourself and look around. Many, many people can't do what you're doing. It's probably been both a blessing and curse in your life.

**Liz:** Jesus. Will you get out of my head, please?

**Lou:** So go inside again. Close your eyes if that feels okay to do. Focus your attention, your awareness, on your chest and diaphragm. Just feel around in that area and notice what sensations are connected to the pissed-off feeling. If the pissed-off feeling disappears don't worry, just notice what else is there.

**Liz:** (Crying quietly.)

**Lou:** Take your time.

**Liz:** Damn. That was a surprise. The pissed-off feeling was gone and this lonely feeling was there. I felt so alone, so lost, so isolated—like being in some kind of solitary confinement and not having a clue what I did to get there.

**Lou:** Maybe...maybe all it took to get there was being yourself. Maybe being yourself was the crime.

**Liz:** (Crying again)....Jesus. Fuck. There's a big anger in there. I want to scream and shout, "Fuck you! Fuck all you white people! Fuck all you black people! Fuck all you ugly people! Fuck all you men! I'm supposed to feel *bad* because I've got white and black and Chinese in me!!!?; because I'm a woman!!!?; because I'm smart!!!?; because I'm beautiful and sexy as hell!!!? Fuck you!....Fuck you....Shit....Motherfuckers. (Starts laughing).....(hysterically)....whew! What the hell is going on here? Hey, you know what, I don't care. I don't give a shit. I'm all right again. I've got a big, wide, easy feeling inside me, powerful too.

**Lou:** Surprising, eh?

**Liz:** Yes sir. And so am I gonna fucking lose this again?

**Lou:** I can't know for sure. But my bet would be on "yes." Your ego, my ego, doesn't fold its tent and sneak off into the desert just because you loosened its grip for a moment. Look, Liz, the only thing you did different in this moment of your life was instead of going with your ego's conditioned, automatic, compulsive need to control your experience and get rid of "bad" feelings, you did the opposite. You looked right into them, you moved your awareness right into them. You might say you got intimate with them instead of rejecting them. And look what you discovered, what you uncovered, and look where it took you.

What we need to discover for ourselves, each of us, through our own direct experience, is that we're all right even when we don't *feel* all right, even when we don't think we're all right, and even when we're convinced we're not all right. But we have to stop running from those feelings of not-all-right if we are to really know they are not the truth of who we are—if we are to know the true nature and meaning of whatever feelings we may be experiencing in any given moment of our lives.

If there is anything "to do" when you've lost a "state of grace," it is to look fully and deeply into the intimate, felt details of your experience. Right in the very moment of having lost that state of grace, what sensations are you experiencing? What emotions? What thoughts? What assumptions? What judgments? What beliefs? Don't try to change them; simply know them. It seems very counterintuitive.

Are you are all right with this for the moment, Liz?

**Liz:** Yes. Let's leave it here for the moment. Thank you.

**Mary:** What about those of us who have not experienced the kind of good feelings or ego highs that it sounds like Liz, Stew, Frank, and Gabe all seem to have experienced. Me, Matt, and Gina all seem to have egos that have no rewards, only punishments—or at least they don't give us any good feelings because those are bad, or dangerous, or something not good for you. What are the rewards?? I already feel like I'm complaining.

**Lou:** And we know that's bad, right?

**Mary:** Right, but I'm serious. I mean, I think I'm getting where we're headed here. The gist of this seems to be that our egos keep us from contacting some truer, more real version of our own personal experience. I get the part of where the ego keeps me away from that by calling it "bad," but you're also saying it keeps me away from that by kind of seducing me with rewards and with feelings of certainty when I'm being "good," doing what my Seeker says to do. I can't speak for the others, but if for me feeling bad about myself, or at least never feeling good about myself, is "good," then how could the Inflator and the Convincer possibly reward me?

**Lou:** Doesn't make sense.

**Mary:** Right.

**Lou:** In a certain sense, none of this makes sense. In a certain sense this is all really "crazy" when you start looking into it. It's certainly not logical, and it's certainly not rational, is it? But it's also not ir-rational. It's just non-rational. The *experiences* we are looking into have nothing to do with the rational domain of logic, reason, and analytic thinking. They are in what we could call the non-rational domain—the domain of sensations, feelings, emotions, intuitions, insights, perspectives, beliefs, etc. Some of those experiences are spontaneous and in the moment. And some of them are conditioned and automatic. But none of them have to do with reason or logic. I say this because looking into your question of how your ego can reward you if good feelings are bad is going to mean not looking to rational logic for the answer. We will have to look into the non-rational domain to discover how your ego rewards you, to discover what your particular ego uses to reward you, and to discover what felt experiences it uses to reward you with. Okay?

**Mary:** I'm nervous about this right now. I feel like I'm about to go to confession to some priest I don't know—not that I'd want to know the priest. Part of what made confession work for me was that the priest couldn't see me and I couldn't see the priest. I've never fully trusted priests. But okay, how do we do what you're proposing?

**Lou:** Just so you know, my ego is a lot like yours. But let's take a moment here. So in my role here, I'm like a priest, I'm an authority, and you've been conditioned to believe me—at least your ego says you should. And you believe I have something you want that you also believe you don't have. Let me ask you this: If you wanted to in this moment, if it didn't feel right in your gut, if it was really too scary right now for you to follow my suggestion, could you choose in this moment to say, "No, I think I'll pass"? This question, by the way, is for everybody in the room, not just you.

**Mary:** I'd like to believe I could. But I don't know. Thinking about saying, "No, I won't" feels scary. It feels like I would be being willful, or maybe unwilling to do what is the good thing to do—what would be good for me to do. It feels a little like disobeying, too. It also feels like everybody in here would be judging me as being weak.

**Lou:** Forgive me for diverting away form the question of how your ego rewards you, but this is so important—important for all of us. So what you're saying, Mary, is that even if you felt it wasn't interpersonally safe for you right now to explore these issues with me, it would also not feel safe or permissible to refuse, that it is not a given in your operating system that you can say no just for the simple reason that you feel afraid of what you're signing up for if you say yes. Is that an accurate description?

**Mary:** It is definitely not a "given."

**Lou:** So pushing this a little more, even if you felt I might be suggesting that you answer some questions that you knew would be shaming to you, you would still feel some pressure to follow my lead and answer the questions because it would feel shaming and embarrassing not to?

**Mary:** Yes.

**Lou:** Then we are not in a safe relationship with each other—at least not in this moment. If you feel you can't refuse, then you are not safe inside your own skin and you are not safe out here. You are trapped in a set of rules that make it impossible for you to safely protect your own emotional skin. Do you get the sense of that?

**Mary:** I have never felt the right to feel safe. I didn't even consider the notion until this moment. It's like I learned I couldn't trust that my own fear was telling me something I should listen to, that there was something real to be afraid of.

**Lou:** Yes. So early on, not just for you but for all of us, our fear becomes disqualified as a source of trustable information in our relationships with one another. If we feel afraid of someone or some interpersonal situation, then something is wrong with us, or we shouldn't be, or we're overreacting, or we're imagining things, etc. Maybe it's legitimate to be afraid if someone is holding a gun to your head (for some tough guys, maybe not) or if a bear is running straight at you. Most of us are embarrassed by our fear. At most we will admit to being "a little nervous" when we may actually be feeling something akin to terror in an interpersonal or social encounter. We can't be safe if we can't feel and listen to our fear. We will ignore or underestimate danger and risk. We will enter into and/or stay in situations too long that are harmful and dangerous to our emotional wellbeing because we ignore the wise prompting of our feeling of fear. This is especially true in intimate relationships. So our experience of our feelings of fear becomes ungrounded. It becomes disconnected, "free floating anxiety," dissociated from any identifiable, knowable cause. And then it does seem "unreal" and "unnecessary," some trick our minds are playing on us, a "condition," a "mental disorder" that requires medication.

What we are doing here is a very intimate, "close in" exploration. We are exploring areas of great personal vulnerability. We are sharing and opening ourselves to each other from internal places that can be hurt by the insensitive or cruel "touch" of others. We each are talking about matters that expose us to a keenly felt likelihood of harsh judgment, and to the painful experiences of rejection, shame, and to our possible disqualification as acceptable members in the eyes of the human race, of our specific tribes, and of the members of this group right here, right now. A most important set of questions arises: How do we have these kinds of conversations *safely*? What does "safety" mean in the context of these questions? And what would a safe space look like in which to hold this kind of conversation, the kind we're having right here?

I am going to share with you later one of my infamous "documents" that goes into this territory more broadly, that looks not only at how we relate to our experience of interpersonal safety and danger, but also to that of interpersonal pain and pleasure. But for right now, I want to come back to Mary here and to her particular experience of risk and safety. Where we left off a moment ago with your experience of your own feelings of fear is that your not sure they have any validity or that you have any right to the feeling of fear in a given moment.

**Mary:** Yes. Right. But I must say I feel much safer in this moment since you actually described what has happened to me with regard to my fear and made it sound acceptable. At least I don't feel crazy for having this craziness about my fear!

**Lou:** That's really important. That's the beginning of feeling safe for you right now, or for anybody considering what you're considering doing in a conversation—being allowed to be right where you are as you begin, being allowed to start the conversation, any intimate conversational exploration with someone, from exactly where you are, and then being able and being allowed to move along that conversational path while staying exactly where you are emotionally each step of the way, moment to moment, *including being afraid each step of the way, including deciding not to go forward in a given moment because it feels too risky.*

You know, if you are required by your ego to *ignore* your fear, then you are in the most dangerous of all interpersonal circumstances. The most dangerous ones are not the ones that actually include some danger, risk, or fear. The most dangerous ones of all are the interpersonal moments that *do* include some felt sense of emotional danger, risk, or fear, which provides us with a warning, but instead of listening to this warning we are forced by the rules of the ego to ignore or dismiss our feeling of fear, *before* being allowed to *have* it, *before* taking any time to really look into it, *before* consciously listening to it. Given those conditions there is no free, conscious choosing of our response to the risk or danger. There are only automatic, conditioned, non-conscious responses to our fear available to us.

When this is the case, we are truly at the mercy of others. Instead of trusting, relying on, and using the warning signal of our own feeling of fear, we are instead compelled to hope for and rely on the good intentions of others, even when those good intentions are not there, or when the good intentions of others are shadowed by their own unacknowledged and harmful interpersonal ego strategies. So we were looking into the possibility of exploring how your ego rewards you, and you felt some fear about doing that. As you put it so well, it felt like you were about to make a confession to a strange priest in public.

**Mary:** I want to get something out of the way...another confession of sorts. I'm a Catholic nun. I often feel weird "admitting" that. I anticipate a lot of pigeonholing. Once it's out there it's like I'm no longer a person, a woman, a regular human being. The saint thing comes down pretty quick. And then there is all the abuse people have suffered at the hands of nuns as kids. So it's complicated. But I'm getting fed up with hiding.

**Lou:** Good for you. Where are you about looking for rewards?

**Mary:** I'm nervous about it, about the shame I am probably going to feel. But I feel like I want to bust the shame, tell it to "get thee hence" (laughing). Funny I never thought of it as kind of a devil, but it is, isn't it? The shame, I mean.

**Lou:** Yes. It acts like one. So you're making a thoughtful choice to take the risk of bumping into the devil.

**Mary:** Yes. I feel kind of brave right now. Whoops! That's feeling good about myself! The devil will get me for that! (Group laughs.)

**Lou:** A question: When you really are being good and not feeling good about yourself, feeling unworthy, and sinful, those are painful feelings, right?

**Mary:** Yes.

**Lou:** And when you confess your sins of feeling good, when you admit them to a priest or someone else, what do you feel? Do you just feel bad? Just shame and guilt? Or are there other feelings?

**Mary:** Relief. It's like I'm giving into being a bad person—stopping fighting it. Like the worst is over. And I know God likes this. God will think I'm good for admitting I'm bad. I feel safe again, like I won't be condemned to hell now, like I'm back to being a member of his tribe—the only correct tribe. It's not so much I'm forgiven for being a bad person. Being a bad person is a permanent condition. But by admitting my sin of feeling good now I'm accepted again by God and my fellow believers. I belong again. I'm safe. I feel comforted. And it feels right to feel I'm a bad person, like this is a good way to be. There's conviction—I guess in both senses of that word. There is a kind of certainty about it all that feels good.

**Lou:** So feelings of relief, being liked by God and others, safety, acceptability, belonging, comfort, certainty, and rightness seem like pretty powerful rewards to me; pretty seductive.

**Mary:** You're right! Very seductive. But, you know, like others have said, they don't feel like rewards as much as they feel like laws of nature. You know what I mean? Like if you eat well you'll be well, or like breathing feels good. It's just the way it is. Maybe just simple cause and effect, not some manipulation or a seduction by the ego. You know?

**Lou:** Yes, I do know. That's how embedded our identification with our ego is. Egos don't feel unnatural. They don't feel like alien entities inside us manipulating us. They feel like "me." This makes me think of the position many Black Americans were in before the Civil War. There was a category of slavery called the "house slave." This role was familiar from the "mammies" or butlers portrayed in the movies of the '30s, '40s, and '50s. The slaves put in this role were "beloved" by their masters and their master's children. They often lived in the master's house and enjoyed many material privileges and benefits. Trouble is they were still slaves—persons with no rights, no real autonomy, and no freedom of expression, certainly no right to be who they really were, to become all they could be. If they got "uppity" the reaction of the master was swift and brutal. It became very clear who had the power and who didn't, who determined what was allowed and what wasn't. On the other hand, if they submitted to the rules of the master, all went smoothly, comfortably, safely. Harriet Tubman, one of the most heroic and famous "conductors" in the Underground Railroad system used to free slaves, is quoted as saying, "I freed a thousand slaves and could have freed a thousand more if only they knew they were slaves."

It is kind of the same with your ego and you. Your ego is the "kind" master as long as you obey the rules and don't get uppity, don't start thinking you have any right to feel good about yourself. You're allowed to live in the "master's" house and feel safe, comfortable, even loved, although at the price of giving up your autonomy. Those are powerful feelings connected to powerful needs—needs to belong and feel safe. If you get "uppity," then you risk the loss of all that is available to you to meet those needs. And, in addition, your ego will become the brutal master and give you a shaming whipping, or possibly even the death sentence by being thrown out of the congregation of the ones acceptable to God.

In a very real sense, "being a slave" to the ego gets normalized. The pain and constriction of it gets pushed out of consciousness. It's only if the "bad you" slips out and you remember there is more to you than your ego wants you to know that there may be an awakening that you are being held captive—that is, if the "brutal master" doesn't beat you into submission and subjugation again.

**Mary:** You make it sound like there is a civil war going on inside me, and, you know what, sometimes it feels that way. Although, I think I've been siding with the bad guys without really knowing it, actually thinking they're the good guys! I've been a house slave thinking I'm lucky.

**Lou:** I've been there. My ego still sucks me back into that deal, still tries to fool me into believing that's who I am.

**Mary:** How do you fight this fight?

**Lou:** Well, we have to know what we're fighting and what we're fighting for before we can fight effectively. Many of us, myself included, didn't even know we were in a fight, or what we were fighting, or that we could fight, let alone how to fight. It actually takes some very particular skills and inner resources to disempower the ego. We can all develop them. Some you already possess. Some you will have to learn. Some you will invent on our own.

But first we need more clarity about what we are fighting. Actually the clarity we need right now is about how the ego fights against our connecting to our essence, to who we really are. And for that we will first need to share the information contained in another "document." We have already looked at a document about the rewarding/reinforcing side of the ego—the Seeker/Inflator/Convincer trio. This next document looks at the punishing/enforcing side of the ego. There is another trio that is responsible for the work of this side. They are called the Critic/Terrorist/Doubter. I'll give you the document and then we'll pick up our discussion after you've had a chance to read it.

# chapter six

# The Ego's Enforcement and Punishment Team

## The Critic / Terrorist / Doubter

This side of the ego uses highly uncomfortable feelings to do its job. The reinforcement/rewarding side of the ego used very pleasurable and comforting feelings as rewards to *seduce and compel* you to think and behave in certain ways. This enforcing/punishing side of the ego uses very painful and frightening feelings to *discourage* you from thinking and behaving in certain ways, and to compellingly whip you back in line with the ego's program of acceptability as it is laid out by the Seeker/Inflator/Convincer.

As with the ego's rewarding side, there are also three inner entities in charge of carrying out the goals of the ego. These three are in charge of enforcing the rules and regulations of the ego. They dole out the punishment for any misbehavior on the part of the ego's host. These three entities are called the Critic, the Terrorist, and the Doubter. They always work in concert, but in any given moment one may be more active than another. As implied in their names, they use feelings of shame, fear, and self-doubt to punish and frighten the host both for failing to live up to any of the ego's demands, and, even more so, for any move on the host's part that dares to challenge the rule and authority of the ego.

As I write this document, I am experiencing these three at work within me. By describing the inner workings of all egos, and by "telling on" my own ego, I am violating a cardinal rule of the ego's operating system, i.e. "Do not see me and do not talk about me." This rule allows it to remain in power over its host. Egos always work undercover, in stealth mode. Egos always want to remain hidden from view and to do their work in the shadows of the host's unawareness. So my exposing the inner workings of the ego has the punitive side of *my* ego jumping into action by dosing me with feelings of fear, shame, and doubt about what I am saying. And you too may well experience uncomfortable feelings as you read this document.

If the ego is seen for what it really is, a false "second self," a maintainer of a highly edited image of the host's true self, then the ego's tyrannical rule is in danger of collapsing. In *The Wizard of Oz*, after Dorothy's dog Todo has pulled aside the curtain covering his control booth and exposed the wizard as "just a man," the wizard tries to distract their gaze by threatening Dorothy and her friends with loud and frightening sounds and visuals. He shouts at them through loudspeakers, "Don't pay any attention to that man in the booth!"

The ego, like the wizard, fears the exposure of the falseness of the image it works so compulsively to keep presenting as real. At least the wizard had the grace to let the image go and accept being "just" a man. Apparently he never got brainwashed into believing he really *was* his wizard image. He was not identified with his image; he just used it. So his image did not have a life and a mind of its own inside his psyche. He could just stop pretending, and let it all go.

This is not the case with our egos. We, the hosts, aren't sure we are not our egos; we *are* too mixed up with them, merged with them. Our egos hate and fear being exposed as something separate from our native self. That awareness disempowers the ego just like the curtain being pulled did for the Wizard. The ego believes this exposure is too great a risk to its host's interpersonal safety. Egos will do whatever they can to stop their hosts from pulling the curtain back. And they will punish their hosts severely for any attempts to move in that direction.

When someone (like me) does something that is strictly forbidden by the ego, the ego's Critic/Terrorist/Doubter trio goes to work to prevent it from happening. Exposing the ego is a fundamental challenge to its continued rule. As an example of how this trio works inside somebody who is not playing by the rules, I want to share with you what I experience as I write about this relentless inner triad. I do so not to depress or frighten you but to describe what a moment on the battlefront with the ego can look and feel like.

We need to support each other on the front lines of this inner battle. But if we don't know the nature of the "incoming" that will be thrown at us, we will be at a great disadvantage. Below is a description of what the "incoming" being delivered by my C/T/D (with the support of my S/I/C) looks like inside of me in the moment of writing about them. I will be giving more explicit separate job descriptions of the Critic, the Terrorist, and the Doubter a little further on, but I believe the following description of my encounter with them will give you a live action preview of how this fearsome threesome does its job.

## A  Live  Report  from  Hell

As I take on this piece of writing, I am feeling completely uninspired. I am feeling depressed, despairing, and afraid. I feel like I have nothing to say. Right in this moment I am in the nasty grip of my Critic/Terrorist/Doubter. At the moment there are no thoughts involved; there is just a feeling combination of fear, shame, and doubt. That combination of feelings exists inside my chest and my belly. That's where I feel those feelings, like a painful, swirling mass of energy, a "clump" of discomfort. Right now those feelings are coloring my entire emotional experience. In the moment of this writing, those feelings are very convincing. I really feel/believe I have nothing worthwhile to say, and that I don't even want to speak. I am afraid of exposing myself as inadequate and as a fraud. I'm afraid everything I am saying is a lie, some kind of self-serving lie. In this moment I really doubt that I can write about the ego in any way that ends up being useful to anybody. These feelings are the ones that so many times in the past have made me avoid sitting down and spending the time that it takes to do the writing. These feelings make me not want to write at all. In this moment I am not even clear about what's my ego and what's me.

That confusion is part of the deep doubt that the Doubter has put me in. When that deep feeling of self-doubt is implanted in my heart and my gut, as it is in the moment of writing this, I feel disabled, completely disempowered internally. I have lost my inner compass. I have lost access to any source of felt inner truth. I no longer trust what I knew before this attack. I no longer trust my own capacity to know. I don't believe that I will ever he able to figure anything out. I am lost.

After the Doubter has pulled the rug out from under me, then the Critic and the Terrorist deliver shame and fear, and I have no power to counter them. I have no ground to stand on to face them. It is like my capacity to know or trust anything I know with which to fight the shame and the fear has been buried in some kind of thick, writhing, energy-sucking mud. In this state, if I receive encouraging words from someone, I can't feel any belief in them. Kindness causes a cringe of shame inside. Objective facts or truths have no weight when I am in the grip of self-doubt. That self-doubt joins with a feeling that there is something wrong with me (Critic). I feel a kind of internal sickness. I feel not well. I feel that my very being has been contaminated with some poisonous gas. I feel weakened. This opens the ground inside me for the critic to pile on feelings of shame, inadequacy, failure, and revulsion. It also opens my insides to the terrorist shooting his bolts of fear into my body about being attacked, abandoned, and ostracized by whoever reads what I am writing. So now the self-doubt is compounded with both fear and shame. At bottom I already feel ostracized, alone, isolated, shameful, terrorized, and powerless to change anything that I am experiencing. I feel like a pariah.

This internal combination of feelings, this emotional state, makes what I know about the ego no longer accessible to me in any way I can use it for my own benefit. It's just a bunch of worthless concepts and ideas that have no juice, no power, to release me from my ego's grip. It makes me feel like I can't speak any living truth. It makes me feel like everything I am saying is a lie, a fiction, something I made up.

The self-doubt that the Doubter creates seems to me to be the most insidious and harmful of the evil triad's ways of working on me. This self-doubt is not comprised simply of thoughts; it shows up inside my body/mind as a set of feelings that result in what I call a "fearful, shameful maybe." These feelings include a sinking feeling in my stomach, an empty feeling in my chest, fear, a feeling of weakness and a loss of core energy, a sapping of motivation and will, a deep sense of helplessness and powerlessness. And of course the experience of self-doubt is dosed with a deep feeling of shame about my sense of inability and incompetence.

I know there will be more moments like this. Moments like this are not about who I really am. Moments like this are about being in the grip of the punitive side of my ego.

## The Part of Me That Knows

I am grateful I have an ever-increasing access to another part of me that remembers that this effect is exactly what the ego wants to create within me in order to stop me from exposing it. My ego does not want me to be in touch with the part of me that knows. I will describe this "knowing" part of my native self in more detail later. In the ego's eyes, that place of knowing within me, and the intuitive truths that emerge from it, represent the possible overthrowing of the ego's rule. The ego does not want me to listen to the unfolding of the truths from that inner truth place—truths like the felt knowing that I am safe inside my own skin or that I am *already* just fine as a person. Those are revolutionary and heretical notions as far as my ego is concerned.

In moments like the ones I described above, the Critic/Terrorist/ Doubter swarm the place of truth and knowing inside me with feelings of being endangered and unworthy. At times they make it impossible for me to reconnect with the part of me that knows. In dark moments like that I have to reach outside myself for release. I find music helps me enormously. And making some contact with nature also helps release the negative state.

Knowing what I know and trusting that knowledge are considered dangerous and forbidden by my ego. It is the Critic/Terrorist/Doubter's job to suppress my inner source of knowing, to make me doubt my intuition and instincts, to make me afraid of my truth of the moment. And it is the job of the S/I/C to make me settle for the compensatory pleasures and comforts it provides. It is the S/I/C's job to make me forget about the pain that the suppression of my personal knowing and awareness creates, and replace it with some kind of pleasurable sensation or, short of that, some sort of numbing so I don't feel it—for example, watch TV, or go to sleep, or have a drink. It is the Critic/Terrorist/Doubter's job to surround my inner truth place with terrible feelings of shame, fear, and doubt. Going anywhere near the source of my inner truth arouses the C/T/D, and that triad then pumps an array of toxic feelings into my heart and my belly to distract me and to disguise my place of knowing. It hides it from me.

The Critic/Terrorist/Doubter lives right next to and around my inner truth place. It presents itself and its feelings *as* the truth. It feels so close to my inner place of felt truth that I can confuse it with the truth. When the pure experience of "I am here now and all right" arises as my autonomous, separate, real self and as a source of inner knowing and strength, too often the first experience that personal presence encounters is a dosing of shame, fear, and doubt by the C/T/D. Then "I am" identifies with shame, fear, and self-doubt—so then I am shameful, I am afraid, I am self-doubtful.

I want my truth place. I love my truth place. The truth place is pure and open, and completely trustworthy, a source of both becoming and responding. But to reach it, to access it directly inside me, in my own direct experience, I often first have to move through the confusing and distorting feelings of shame, fear, and self-doubt.

## Some of My Evolution

In the past, I had been ruled by those feelings created by the Critic/Terrorist/Doubter. And as a result I gave up access and ownership of my true experience. Now there is an inner part of me that knows very deeply that I no longer want to ally myself with that self-abandonment, that knows that life without deep access to my own true inner experience is empty, that life without that access is meaningless. Life without that access is without genuine connection to others. Life without that access is to live in fear of others. Life without that access is to navigate interpersonal relationships, and life in general, without a trustable personal compass.

For a long time I did not have any access to my inner compass and was not conscious of it as something to be trusted. When I woke up and realized that there was much more going on inside of me than I was aware of, that was the beginning of seeking to experience my own experience. That was the beginning of stopping suppressing, repressing, and looking away from my own inner experience. That was the beginning of trusting myself. At first I was very frightened, hesitant, and shameful, but gradually I have more and more courageously, proudly, and confidently followed the guidance of my own inner experience. Thank God for that turn, that inner turn. That was the beginning of listening to the wisdom, strength, and clarity of my own inner compass.

## The Ghost In The Machinery

I am now going to separately describe the mechanics of each of the members of this punitive trio. I want to describe how they each do their different but interrelated jobs, to give you a graphic description of each, which you can then use to shine a light on your own inner experience and see if it fits. But before I do that, I must say something here, which I said, but perhaps not clearly enough, in my description of the Seeker/Inflator/Convincer.

As before, I will be speaking from what I've learned from my own experience and the experience of hundreds and hundreds of clients. That said, *you* will have to determine if my experience, and theirs, fits yours. My words may be interesting (or not) but they will have no value beyond mental entertainment if they don't connect you more clearly with a direct experience of your own inner realities in a way that frees you, in a felt way, from the limitations and destructive patterns you have felt plagued by and stuck in.

So what I want to make clear is this: Every one of these inner "entities" is a real, autonomous, active, "alive" member of the altered state of consciousness within you that I am naming the "ego." The ego is what one writer/researcher calls a "mind parasite." Here is how he puts it:

> "....the critical point to bear in mind is that most people are quite literally "not themselves." Rather they are inhabited by other 'selves' internalized during childhood, which, like viruses, commandeer the machinery of the host (in this case the mind)."

He goes on to say:

> "One of the reasons for the failure to appreciate mind parasites has to do with their very nature: their most basic 'trick,' as it were—no different from any virus—is to hijack the machinery of the mind in such a way that the mind does not recognize what has

happened....While it is possible as an adult to develop a psychological 'immune system' that can detect and minimize the workings of
these parasites, it is impossible to do so as an infant, before we have
any idea of what is happening to us. Therefore the most troubling
parasites are precisely the ones that feel most familiar to us—indeed,
that we mistakenly identify as 'I'....Like parasites that inadvertently
kill their host, these mechanical patterns do cause insanity, paral-
ysis, and even death. Thus, until one has systematically identified
and eliminated (or at least learned to control) these viral specters of
childhood from the mind, one will continue to unwittingly do their
bidding, even if it means making oneself miserable in the process."
                    (Godwin, R. W. *One Cosmos Under God*, 2004)

Godwin's is a dramatic description, and far more accurate than we
would like to believe. These inner entities, or mind parasites, these "ghosts
in the machinery," have an agenda of their own, a very rigid one. We are not
in control of them. They do what they are programmed to do, automatically,
compulsively, and regardless of whether or not they are serving their hosts'
*current* wellbeing. That we have them is not our fault. As Godwin points
out, our mind, and sense of self, was hijacked before we could say "no."

Godwin's point about our identification with these parasites emphasiz-
es a critically important truth repeated regularly throughout this book. We
are so merged with these parasites, they have so fully infiltrated our day-to-
day sense of self, that we actually think and feel like we are thinking what
they are thinking. We feel and believe that those ways of thinking, feeling,
and behaving that are dosed with feelings of certainty and confidence by the
S/I/C are all ways we are choosing; we are just being ourselves. And we feel
and believe that the self-hating, self-doubting, and self-terrorizing thoughts
created by the C/T/D are our thoughts—that *we* are thinking them. We
believe the shameful, fearful, and self-doubtful feelings are accurate and de-
served if we are failing to do our ego's bidding.

In fact, what's happening is the reverse. If you watch the arising of these
thoughts closely you will see that *you* never think them up. You don't sit
down with yourself and choose to hate yourself, scare yourself, and doubt
yourself. You don't sit there with yourself and consciously say to yourself,

"You know what, right now I am going to decide to hate myself, scare the shit out of myself, and doubt that there is anything inside of me that might be valuable or useful." No, these thoughts and feelings just *happen* inside, like a tape recorder got turned on. The trouble is they happen in your own head, and there is nobody else in there, so naturally you say, "I think..." or "I feel...."

When I first point this out to someone who is not aware of these parasites as *separate internal entities* with "minds" of their own, they either think I'm crazy, that I am calling them crazy, or both. We believe we are "of one mind" inside ourselves. We believe we are not split up inside; that would be "crazy." That's schizophrenic. "I'm normal so I can't be that way." And upon first becoming truly aware of these parasites as separate internal entities, people feel scarily out of control, like they are victims of some alien invasion of mind snatchers who stuck a thought-controlling implant in the base of their skulls.

It is absolutely critical that we come to see our egos, and their inner self-image managers, as separate, as not "me," as imagined and believed illusions of self. But it is also critical that we come to see that our egos, and their self-image managers, are energized and active, rather than inert and passive. In some sense they are "alive" within us. This may initially feel unbelievable, weird, crazy, frightening, or "all of the above." But we will never separate from them if our "I" remains naive. We will never separate from our ego's grip if we don't understand that it is actively invested in maintaining its grip, and that the existence of our ego and the strength of its grip are not our fault. We need to de-criminalize the possession of an ego. Having one is simply part of being human. It is necessary for our early safety and survival. The problem is not so much that we possess an ego, but that our ego possesses us, and we don't know it.

So now let me give you those separate job descriptions of these entities—the Critic, the Terrorist, and the Doubter—despite the fight they put up to stop me at the moment of writing this.

### The Critic

The Critic (as well as the other two) is called on by the ego to go into attack mode in two different circumstances. The first circumstance is when the host fails to live up to the demands of the ego to behave, think, and feel in a manner acceptable to the ego (and to the ego's current dependency group/tribe). If the host fails to "seek" successfully whatever the Seeker says is "good," the Critic hits the host with anything from a hint to a solid dose of shame in order to shock the host back into acceptability. Most people who have experienced some "failure," loss, or mistake are familiar with this inner voice or entity, and many people have written about some version of the "inner critic."

In this first category of cases, the host is still completely bought into the ego as no different from his or her "self" and into the "rightness" of the ego's rules and regulations as well. In this state of mind, the only option the host has is to try harder to meet the ego's demands, as if they were simply his/ her own demands. If the host "gets it together," then the Inflator will reward the host with many good feelings and the tribe will find him/her acceptable again.

If, for one reason or another, the host keeps falling short of the ego's demands, the Critic will intensify the doses of shame and feelings of humiliation. When continuous failure happens, a variety of image-protective reactions swing into high gear (more about these a little further on). But, if all efforts at correction fail, then depression, panic attacks, and withdrawal can follow. Even suicide can begin to make more and more "sense" to the ego-controlled host.

The second category of cases that call the Critic into action are completely different. In this second category, the host has discovered through directly felt personal experiences that he/she is not his or her ego. He or she has discovered that there is much more within him or her of interest and value than was formerly known or was conscious of. The host has discovered, uncovered, found some way to access what has been given many names—the true self, the real self, the authentic self, essence, essential being, etc. I have been referring to it as the native self. Whatever we call it, the discovery is always caused by some undeniable experience. In the best of scenarios, following such an experience, the host becomes committed to a process of separating the real self from the false one, i.e. the ego. Of course this is the worst case scenario for the ego, the ego's nightmare, and it will fight to put the genie back in the bottle with every tool in its formidable toolkit.

So in this category of cases, the Critic will hit the host with doses of shame, embarrassment, and humiliation at every discovery and expression of the true self. The Critic will do its best to shut down the inner exploration and discovery of the differences between ego-self and real self.

## The Critic and Shame

The feeling of shame is the main tool of the Critic, so we need to spend a little time getting clearer about what "shame" is. (I will come back to finishing the description of the other two members of the enforcing/punishing team after clarifying the experience of shame.)

I have come to understand that the *need to avoid* consciously *feeling* this frightening, exquisitely painful, and complex feeling is the root cause of all our intra- and inter-personal stuck places. If we did not feel so completely *compelled* to avoid feeling and showing our experiences of shame, we would relate to one another very differently—more genuinely, more openly, more compassionately, more humbly, more respectfully of our need for each other's acceptance and approval, etc. We are ashamed of the experience of shame. Avoiding the experience of shame is the life's work of the ego, and if the experience cannot be avoided in the host, then it must absolutely hide it from others' view.

## Shame — What Is It?

Like the word "ego," the experience to which the word "shame" directs our attention is not clear. Many of us "kind of" know what it feels like. Many of us think it might be a form of guilt. Many of us don't consider the feeling of shame as part of their experience at all. Everybody seems to be aware of the experience of embarrassment. Everybody also seems to have had at least one experience of humiliation. But shame? Not clear.

A major reason for this lack of clarity is that the felt experience of shame is devastating to our sense of being an acceptable person or having an acceptable "self." Who wouldn't try to avoid such an experience? When shame is acute and alive in the moment, it annihilates our sense of acceptability and therefore raises the terrifying specter of ostracism from the tribe. If some circumstance happens to trigger the feeling of shame within you, you can experience an internal emotional free fall from acceptable, respected member to worthless fraud and outcast in a second. I am not referring to the external perception of you by others (although it may match the internal one) but to the internal experience of your own sense of self.

And here is the real kicker regarding shame: to *feel it* feels shameful. And to have your shame "seen" by others is even more shameful. It is like it doubles down on itself, intensifying the feelings like a nuclear explosion. It even feels shameful to simply acknowledge you *know* of the inner feeling of shame; that would mean you felt it on some shameful occasion. So generally this feeling is never spoken of. It works in the shadows of our awareness. Looking directly into it feels like staring into the eyes of some voracious self-hating and self-annihilating demon.

## The Experience of Shame

The experience of being shamed is so uniquely painful and frightening for us as children (and later as adults) that it creates an internal state of emergency. It is not just an uncomfortable feeling; it is a feeling that signals a serious and frightening threat to the safety and reliability of our connection to those who as kids we depended on for our physical survival. And what makes it doubly threatening is that shame includes the belief that it is something about us that has caused this severed connection. We are to blame because we are "bad" or unacceptable in some way and so we deserve to be rejected, abandoned, ostracized, and/or attacked.

It might be more accurate to call shame a state of being, or a mental/emotional complex, rather than a simple single feeling. This state or complex includes feelings, but it also includes beliefs, needs, physiological reactions, instinctual behaviors, and perceptions. But starting with the "feel" of it, what does this "terrifying feeling" feel like?

In its *most raw*, "in the moment," and acute form, it includes a frightened cringing, constricting, and "creepy" sensation that grips your chest and your belly, a feeling like the bottom has fallen out from under your sense of self, or like you have just been punched in the emotional heart and belly. The experience includes flushing and a hyperawareness of the appearance of your face. Psychologically the experience includes a feeling of being unwillingly exposed as "bad," "faulty," "lesser," disgusting, ridiculous, contemptible, and/or foolish; a powerful impulse arises to hide or disappear; terror, hurt, intense aloneness, and isolation storm your insides; a desperate need arises to "correct" your image and restore your good standing—this in spite of a co-existing feeling of being helpless to do so. This helplessness is caused by the terrifying emotional conviction that you deserve the shame, that you are indeed shameful. Other words used to describe this same experience are "humiliation," and "embarrassment" (which generally is a much milder form of this experience).

Shame is a horrible feeling. Everyone wants to avoid ever feeling it, if possible. We will go to great lengths to avoid feeling it, all the way to killing ourselves or somebody else...or both. Our conversations are managed automatically and carefully by our egos to keep us safe from even the slightest experience of shame, or of its relatives—embarrassment and humiliation. We keep the content of our conversations limited to safety zones, staying away from the exposure of any thoughts or feelings that might risk evoking a shaming judgment from someone else.

## The Ego and Shame

We create our egos in our formative years precisely because of our need to avoid being shamed, humiliated, or embarrassed by the rejection, abandonment, and ostracism of others. As we move through thousands upon thousands of interactions with our parents, siblings, teachers, peers, and larger social circles, we learn which are the ways of being and expressing ourselves that result in our being shamed by those important to us. By the time we reach adulthood, our egos' conditioned, compulsive, reactive, rigid, desperate, and unconsciously-driven efforts to *avoid* any consciously felt experience of being shamed and of feeling shameful are totally automatic. And so we compulsively "seek" to be, do, and have what our ego tells us is safe and acceptable. And we compulsively avoid being, doing, or having what the ego has learned is shameful.

But we don't escape internalizing the feeling memory of shame, produced by earlier externally-delivered shaming experiences. We may suppress the memory, but it stays within us. It is that feeling memory of shame that the Critic uses to either whip us for failing to do our ego's bidding, and push us to try harder to be "good," or to shut down the process of waking up from the ego's gripping trance and realizing who and what we really are.

So it is clear that talking about the Critic, and its controlling use of shame, brings us right into "the belly of the beast (ego)." Outside of abject terror, there is no worse emotional feeling for us humans than that of shame. No wonder we avoid awareness of it like we would avoid the Black Plague.

But our egos' Draconian measures to "protect" us from unacceptability do not end with the work of the inner Critic; next comes the inner Terrorist.

## The Terrorist

As implied by the name, the Terrorist uses every form of fear to keep our thinking, our feelings, and our behavior in line with that which the ego has learned is acceptable and ensures our good standing in our dependency group. It uses two sources of fear to control us. One source is our ever-present (mostly unconscious) terror of being rejected, attacked, abandoned, or ostracized. This terror is instinctual and stays within us throughout our lives. As noted earlier, it is survival based.

The second source of fear it uses are our earlier memories of frightening interpersonal experiences. All our memories of being rejected and exposed to hostile judgments leave a reservoir of fear within us. The Terrorist takes control of our thinking and our imagination and produces vivid memories of the past or fantasies about the future that are filled with threatening and painful images. The terrorist uses feelings of nervousness, anxiety, jitters, fear, or terror to keep us away from any personal expression that might jeopardize our acceptability to ourselves and to others. Its goal is to scare us off any action that risks rejection, negative judgment, disapproval, abandonment, or ostracism; any action that risks the anger, disappointment, or criticism of those who matter to us. It fills us with enough fear to stop us from making choices it has decided are unacceptable or interpersonally too risky.

Again, what choices or experiences your terrorist must scare you away from depends on your ego type. For the bully ego, any expression of vulnerability would be dosed with anxiety. For the people-pleaser ego, speaking up to a boss is terrifying. For the saint ego, being caught in a moment of pride is frightening. For the hermit ego, a surprise birthday party is horrifying. For the star ego, being a has-been or boring is a terrifying prospect.

Again, there are two circumstances in which the Terrorist moves into action. The first is when the host is failing to live up to the demands of the ego for acceptable behavior and the host still believes the ego's rules and regulations are right. The second is when the host "wakes up" to the fact that his/her ego is setting limits on behavior through the use of fear which are damaging to the host's wellbeing and personal evolution. When the host begins to challenge the validity of those fear-driven limits, the Terrorist doubles down.

Examples of the first circumstance could include the following: the terror/anxiety experienced by the perfectionist around getting less than an "A" on an exam; the terror of aging under the rule of an ego that demands youthful good looks; a demotion at work for a power-driven ego; the disappointment of a significant other for the people-pleasing ego. The Terrorist will scare the host into trying harder to do and be the way the ego demands with fear-filled scenarios of what will happen if the host fails.

Examples of the second circumstance occur when there is an action you know you want, even need, to take on behalf of your wellbeing that goes against the approved guidelines of the ego, then an "irrational" fear stops you in your tracks. That is the Terrorist at work. You know you are capable of doing the action, you know rationally there is really nothing to fear, that nothing really dangerous will happen, and you know the action would be beneficial for you. And yet something akin to terror causes you to flee or freeze at the very moment you could take the action. Examples include the guy with the hermit ego wanting to approach a girl; the girl with a people-pleasing ego needing to say "no" to an overly-insistent male; the man with a macho ego worried about his health and avoiding seeing a doctor; the woman with a saint ego who knows she needs to stop feeding her son's dependency with financial support but can't—all stopped in their tracks by the Terrorist dosing them with fearful feelings and filling their imaginations with portrayals of frightening outcomes.

Often when we are challenging the ego's rules, we become really confused about why we can't move into action or make a change. We hate ourselves for our "weakness" or irrationality. We can't understand why reason and rationality don't prevail, why we don't stop feeling so afraid. The Terrorist, like all the members of the ego's management teams, doesn't give a rap about reason and rationality. It's operating in a completely non-rational zone into which reason and reality will not penetrate. It is frozen in the lessons learned about safety as a child. Reasoning with the Terrorist is like trying to reason with a fundamentalist or a psychotic. The Terrorist is not available for rational, reality-based dialogue, and is not available for considering a change in its fundamental beliefs. It is convinced of the accuracy of its beliefs and predictions.

## The Doubter

The last of this threesome, but very, very far from least, is the Doubter. I acknowledged the particular power of the Doubter earlier when speaking about what was happening to me internally as I took on writing this particular piece. Being forced as young, evolving persons to doubt the truth and validity of our felt inner experiences when relating to others, and then being forced to believe that the experience of others is more valid and more important than our own—this is the ground on which the whole operating system of the ego rests. If this core feeling of doubt about the validity, meaningfulness, and truth of our own inner experience was not planted within us before we had the wherewithal to fight it, there would be no ego—there would be no need for it—there would just be our native, natural, intelligent, tuned in, knowing, learning, and evolving self.

The active and aggressive invalidation of our inner knowing, and the forced suppression of the awareness of that knowing, leave us vulnerable to being convinced that what is not true about ourselves is true, and vulnerable to doubting what is actually true. This invalidation and suppression is begun by early important figures in our lives, and then maintained individually and collectively through the activity of our egos.

As I described earlier, and as we will see even more clearly later when I discuss what I call our inner "Truth Place," we are all born with an inner compass for reading relationships, for reading when someone else is in tune with who we really are and what we really need. This compass is in place from infancy. It tells us whether or not someone close to us is empathetically and compassionately attuned with what we are experiencing in a given moment, or not—if they are, we feel safe, seen, valued, and cared for, but if not, we feel unsafe, unseen, devalued, and not cared for. These are feelings, felt senses, *not thoughts*. This equipment is all in place before we even have language and thought. The creation of the initial doubt in this compass, the eventual establishment of a fixed disbelief in this compass, and finally the burial of this compass in unawareness, is what the ego depends on (and enforces) to do its job effectively.

Like the Critic and the Terrorist, the Doubter arises under two circumstances: whenever the host is failing to meet the ego's demands and whenever the host starts questioning the validity of the ego's world view. In both of these circumstances, the Doubter is the one that lays the groundwork for the effectiveness of the Critic and the Terrorist. After all, if the Doubter did not successfully make us doubt our own experience, doubt our own intuition and instincts, our own sense of the truth, then the Critic and the Terrorist would be fatally weakened. If shame and fear is thrown at you but you are solid in the trust of your own knowing, your own intuition and instincts, the shame and the fear would not have as much purchase.

Here's an example I use to illustrate this fact. If some stranger came up to you and said, "Hey, you have orange eyes!" you would either take it as a joke or wonder what was wrong with the person making the statement. You would not for a second believe the feedback because you have no doubt in *your direct experience and knowing* that your eyes are not orange. However, if that same stranger came up to you and said, "Hey, you're an asshole!" there would be a jolt of fear and possibly defensive anger because somewhere inside of you there is a doubt that you are not an asshole. There is what I refer to as "the shameful, fearful maybe..." "Maybe I am an asshole." There is a deeply pervasive "fearful maybe" in most of us, i.e. "maybe I'm not all right." There is not the same *direct experience of knowing* the truth, the truth that we really are all right. It is not a *given* that we are fundamentally acceptable. The doubt is in. This doubt makes us vulnerable to the shame attack of our inner Critic, and so also vulnerable to shaming even from a stranger who knows nothing about us.

So in the first circumstance, when the host still believes that his/her self is the same as the ego, and still believes that the ego's approach to life is the "right" approach, *but* is failing to meet the demands of the ego, the Doubter goes into action to make sure the host has no ground to stand on internally to question or challenge the rules and regulations of the ego. The Doubter makes all other points of view about what is acceptable doubtful, except that of the ego, makes them all not believable. In this regard it serves as back up for the Convincer; it guarantees the host's continued solid belief in what the ego has decided is true and right. This is the basis for our prejudices and fundamentalist inclinations. We *must be right* in order to avoid awareness of the "shameful, fearful maybe" that we might be wrong.

The second circumstance that activates the Doubter is when we begin to question the validity and accuracy of the ego's definition of who and what we are. So, for example, you may have a clear and compelling insight that gives you certainty and clarity about your true nature and which releases you from the limiting grip of your ego. It could be, "Wow, I really am creative," or "I can speak up for myself....I just did," or "You know it actually feels all right to need people," or "I finally really see my confusion between wanting to help others and taking care of myself." These are rich and vital moments. In order to "protect" you from your insight, the Doubter will begin to insinuate feelings of doubt around the edges of the clarity of your insight. That doubt will move, quickly or slowly, to the center of your certainty, and erase it by replacing it with a fearful maybe—"Maybe my insight was not true"; "Maybe I'm wrong."

The ego views your revolutionary insights as dangerous and forbidden. It believes trusting your insights spells interpersonal danger—judgment, rejection, loss of standing, ostracism. The ego uses the Doubter to make sure any liberating insight that may break through into the host's awareness is cut off at the knees before it can find any solid inner ground to stand on.

The Doubter accomplishes this not just by using doubting thoughts about differing points of view, but even more powerfully by pumping the *feeling* of doubtfulness into our chests and bellies. Doubt is not caused just by ideas; it is also created through a unique feeling. We all know this feeling. It's hard to find words for this feeling. I have called it "the fearful shameful maybe." It is a *fearful uncertainty,* the fear that *maybe* you are bad, maybe you are unacceptable, maybe you are an asshole. Once that "fearful maybe" arises, the doubt is in, and in fact so is the belief that indeed you *are* bad and unacceptable. There may remain a desperate hope that you will be able to compensate for or cover up your unacceptability, and perhaps even recover your acceptability, but in the moment you're guilty as charged.

## The Un-Holy Trinity

So whether you are failing to meet your ego's demands or you are now consciously challenging them, the fundamental doubt you yourself have about your acceptability, and that you *feel in your heart and your belly,* forces you to buy into the "truth" of your badness and insufficiency. This doubt, combined with the shaming and terrorizing you feel at the hands of the Critic and the Terrorist, *compel* you to re-double your efforts to be and behave the way your ego says is acceptable, or give up your challenge to its rule.

These three enforcers always work in concert. One may be in the forefront more than another in a given moment. You may be more in touch with the fear and the terror than you are with the shame or the doubt in a certain moment of unacceptability, for example. Or, in another situation, either the feeling of shame or the feeling of doubt may dominate your conscious experience. But all three are always at play. They need each other to do a really effective job on us, to whip us back into acceptable shape and preserve our ego's version of good interpersonal standing and safety.

## Getting Free of the Ego's Grip

When the S/I/C and the C/T/D are functioning adequately, they create inside us a closed circle of awareness. Who and what the ego says we are or should strive to be is all we know, all we are aware of. Any aspects of ourselves, except those included in that circle, do not exist in our awareness. They exist within us, but if the ego is doing its job well, we don't "see" them. And if we can't "see" them, they are not real.

Just as an example, take the person who was raised in a family where free and spontaneous self-expression was met with disapproval. Only conformity to the family rules of controlled behavior was rewarded. In that type of family system, creativity would be suppressed since it requires spontaneity and playfulness if it is to be accessed. Later in that person's life she finds herself in a job in which she has "inadvertently" come up with the solutions to a couple of work-based problems, and her boss remarks on how creative her thinking is. She immediately protests, and believes that she is not creative at all—in spite of the evidence to the contrary. That aspect of herself is not allowed within the closed circle of awareness that the ego compulsively maintains.

So if the ego creates such an effective closed system, how do we ever break free of its grip? If the rewards and punishments the ego uses to control us are so compelling, what could or would bring about a breakdown and/or dismantling of its system? What will make it possible for us to move outside the ego's closed circle of awareness into a broader, more conscious, deeper, and freer embrace of who we really are?

The ego never lets go of control of its own accord. As we have talked about and so many of us know, it is either some failure on the part of the ego's host to meet its demands, or some fortuitous expansion of awareness beyond the ego's closed definition of who we are, or both, that results in the ego "losing its grip." We all need some kind of "wake up call" to start with. From that starting point, the work of staying awake begins, the work of expanding and deepening the awareness of the "more" that exists within us. I will talk more in another document about some conscious, deliberate ways of releasing ourselves from the grip of the ego's relentless host-management teams and about strengthening our access to our true inner moment-to-moment experience.

# chapter seven

# Seeing the Fearsome Threesome At Work Within

## Dialogues Continued

**Lou:** Now that you've read about the machinations of this "fearsome three-some," what are your thoughts and reactions?

**Frank:** I'm clearly in trouble with the ego's enforcers. My whole deal these days is about moving away from my bully/narcissist self. I've been calling that side of me Frank One. I've been working hard on developing Frank Two. He is definitely a work in progress. Frank One is very ingrained and still wants to rule. The experience I had after helping that old lady cross the street is what I want more of. I've come to realize how empty my life has been, how much I have missed in the way of connection to other humans, especially to my two grown sons and their kids, my grandkids.

I've been learning about Buddhism for about three years now—mostly Tibetan. There is this great teacher, Pema Chodren, who I really like. She's very real. She talks about how hard it is to change. She's an American who was married, had kids, and suffered a painful divorce before becoming a monk. She's been around the block. Reading her books and doing her work-shops has really encouraged me. There is this practice called "loving-kind-ness" in Tibetan Buddhism. It's perfect for me. In one sense, it's perfectly aw-ful; it goes completely against what Frank One thinks is good. I guess Frank One would be both sides of my ego—the S/I/C (I love how that sounds like "sick") and the C/T/D. Bullies and narcissists are not loving or kind. So now

I am doing the opposite. Every chance I get to be kind, I take it, even though I don't feel like it in the moment—even though I'm getting attacked on the inside by Frank One. He gets me coming and going. He says I'm being weak and asking for trouble by being kind. And then he also says it's "too late" for me to change. I'm seventy-seven years old and already somewhat disabled from my stroke, so Frank One says, "Why bother?" "It's going to take too long to change." "You're going to die soon anyway." And he says I'm being a phony to boot, that I don't really feel loving or kind so therefore it's all a big fake and I'm a failure.

**Lou:** The "getting you coming and going" is typical of how the ego operates. It really doesn't care if it seems to contradict itself. All it cares about is stopping you from doing what it considers bad for your acceptability, and from what puts you in danger of being rejected or ostracized by whoever matters to you currently. So on the one hand it tries to shame and scare you off practicing "loving-kindness" (following your old bully tribe's rule), and on the other it shames you for "failing" at it (according to your new tribe's rule), as if it wanted you to succeed! It also makes you doubt the value of the change you're making. That is a very common tactic of the Ego and its Doubter henchman. Or, as you said, it makes you doubt your capacity to make the change.

The ego is a shapeshifter, and unscrupulous also. It's a complete opportunist. If you pick a new group to be a member of, like let's say a Tibetan Buddhist spiritual community, and acceptance and approval in that group takes on real meaning for you, the ego will now adopt as "good" what that group considers "good" and will make it compulsive for you to be that way, even if it is the opposite of what it thought was good before you switched your group allegiance.

The ego is always operating on the assumption that you are not already "all right" and that you are not "safe and sound inside your own skin." It has bought into the belief there is something wrong with you that needs to be hidden and compensated for, no matter what group you belong to or seek membership or want the approval of. So now, unless you do your loving-kindness practice *perfectly*, you are a failure and your new group will reject you. And if you do keep practicing it, you'll also take some whacks for failing the membership requirements for bullies!

**Frank:** Christ. What a tangle.

**Lou:** I know. This tangle the ego creates is often what discourages people from keeping on track with their change process. The initial breakthrough or the glimpses of more fulfilling ways of being seem so promising, and then we end up in what feels like the same old, same old—lots of effort and little sense of real freedom and fulfillment.

**Frank:** What do you do to stay on track?

**Lou:** Well, we do have to recognize what gets us off our track. But we also have to have ways of remembering what "the track" is for ourselves. Each of you here has had some experience, uniquely your own, and directly felt by you, that opened up your personal awareness. That experience or set of experiences made you aware that you needed/wanted to change. Most of you here have also had experiences that have given you a taste of a way of being inside yourself that feels "better" in some way—feels more authentic, fuller, freer, more empowered, more natural, more at ease, safer, more connected, full of potential, alive, flowing—some way of being you liked and didn't know was available to you before those "tastes." Some of you are short on these tastes; you just know your way of operating, inside yourself and with others, is not working, and you're trying to find some way of being with yourself, or being yourself, that works better, feels better.

For you, Frank, your experience of helping the old lady cross the street sounds like it captures a bunch of experiences, a bunch of "tastes," that you have had that are for you what being "on track" feels like, right?

**Frank:** Yes. And believe it or not laughing is another one, another taste. I never really had what I guess you'd call a belly laugh before. Now I'm having them at the most surprising moments, with lots of different people. And a lot of them are some good laughs at my own craziness, at the absurdity of my own mind!

**Lou:** That kind of laughter is one of the joys of getting loose of the grip of our egos. It's a sign we've stepped out of the reach of the Critic/Terrorist/Doubter's hammers, at least for the moment.

**Frank:** It's so easy to forget those moments and then discount them. They can seem so "gone," like they never happened, like empty, meaningless memories that really have nothing to do with who I am or my day-to-day living. You know what I mean?

**Lou:** Yes I do, absolutely. They can recede like a dream does. You know that experience when you wake up in the morning from a dream and as you're trying to recall it it is literally slipping back into the vast forgotten? Maybe you remember a snippet, but the vividness, richness, and "realness" is gone—the same with these tastes or breakthroughs we experience. They are then replaced by the experience of ourselves that our ego maintains. That experience can vary from individual to individual, but we all have a kind of "default" setting of our inside experience of ourselves that is maintained by the ego. It is the felt internal experience we always return to when we are not distracted by outside stimuli or activity, when we are quiet, when we are simply by ourselves inside ourselves.

For me, until very recently, when I was quiet in that way my internal default setting was a low grade combination of fear, shame, and doubt—like a lump of oppressive feelings just kind of squeezing and squirming inside my chest and belly behind my diaphragm. Through meditation and some specific self-inquiry, I now have a way to challenge that default setting that I have been putting into practice.

But this forgetfulness is one of the reasons we need to find "fellow travelers." We need the help of each other to remember. I believe we need to create collectives to both help us do the work of disengaging from our egos and to also help us remember and expand our experiences of our true essence, of our authentic selves.

**Frank:** Where do you find the fellow travelers?

**Lou:** That's a really important question. Certainly we could find them in workshops like this one, but where else?

**Mack:** Yeah, I don't know what I would do without my AA meetings. We call it the "fellowship." Having folks I can talk to honestly about where I am in my own skin and in my day-to-day really helps me reconnect with the best parts of me. It's almost like if I can say where I may be stuck or jammed up or fucking up, that alone helps me get back in tune, helps me see what I need to do or stop doing, helps me find my inner compass again, as you call it. I can get really disconnected from my insides, and when I walk into a meeting something just opens inside. It's like my chest relaxes and I can take full breaths again, like somebody said earlier.

**Lou:** There are a lot of people who, while they don't wish they had the suffering of alcoholism, they do wish they had access to meetings like the Twelve-Step ones. The format of the meetings and the Twelve-Step process are brilliant models for collectively working on the kind of stuff we are talking about, not just on substance dependencies. At the end of our workshop we will talk further about resources and groups that can provide connections to other people who are waking up in the way we're sharing here. I'm sure some of you have already found ways and places to connect with fellow travelers. But for now let's continue to explore your experiences of the C/T/D.

**Liz:** Now that you've given them names, I see all three of those guys at work in me. As I was sitting here listening to Mack and Frank talk so rationally, those voices took over my brain. They were telling me that my "fuck you" explosion during the last session is a huge embarrassment and never should have happened, that I've blown my cover and now I've given everybody lots of material to call me crazy with. The Critic is slamming me with feelings that make me want to leave the workshop. The Terrorist is telling me about all the shitty thoughts everybody is having about me, including that you now feel superior to me by getting me to breakdown in front of everybody. And the Doubter is making me question my sanity. If this is what I get for

losing control, it's no wonder I'm a perfectionist. No wonder being in control is such a thing for me. This really feels like an emergency. Frankly I'm
amazed I'm still in this room and talking about this; it goes against everything I've used to protect myself.

**Lou:** In a certain sense it feels crazy to stay here, crazy to talk about this,
even dangerous, doesn't it?

**Liz:** Yes, it does. I hate to admit that I feel frightened right now.

**Lou:** You've gone against your ego's survival system, it's strategies for creating safety for you...interpersonal safety. It's going to feel frightening and
crazy to do that, maybe even suicidal to do that. The ego is operating in a
time warp. The ego has never gotten past what you learned between birth
and seventeen years old about how to be safe in groups of people, how to
protect your acceptability and membership. The dangerous interpersonal
tribal minefields you had to find a safe way through back then were real.
And your ego did a good job of "protecting" you in the best ways available
to you at that time. That's all any of us can do. We truly couldn't know then
that safe ways could exist to both be ourselves and also stay connected to
those who matter to us.

So this is really new territory for you, and you don't know how to take
care of yourself and at the same time feel and express your needs to others.
You're like the crab that has outgrown its old shell and has to leave it in order
for the new larger shell to grow. For a while it can feel like you're completely
exposed and you have no protection. That's why environments and people
that make it safe to do this kind of exploring and growing are so necessary.
You need to be with people who are doing the same thing, taking the same
kind of risks, for it to feel safe enough. You can't be the only one, at least not
in the beginning.

**Liz:** Everything you just said fits like a glove and I still feel incredibly uncomfortable. *Needing* protection feels dangerous to me. You know what I
mean?

**Lou:** It wasn't safe to express or show your *need* for the protection and safety of your personhood or selfhood when your ego was formed.

**Liz:** That is so true. When I let that in it feels so sad to me right now. I don't know what to do with that but I know I don't feel like being hard on myself right now. And that's really different right there.

**Lou:** That's actually a seismic shift. I don't mean to be dramatic, but it really is. The only way you will discover different ways to take care of the safety of your "self," without having to deny your vulnerability, is by not hating and fearing the vulnerability of your "self" the way your ego automatically does. It means letting go of the shell, at least in safe environments, and discovering protections that are not as rigid and fixed as the old ones were—the ones managed by the ego's teams of enforcers and reinforcers. And when you find these different ways, you will see how much more access you have to the full complement of your personal powers, one of which is a deep sense of inner strength, strength that isn't musclebound and limited in its movements, a strength that is naturally subtle, knowing, and skillful. That strength in turn creates a deep sense of being "safe inside your own skin," even in intensely meaningful and conflictual social encounters.

**Liz:** Sounds good, but right now not real for me.

**Lou:** I know. You'll have to feel your way along to discover the truth or fiction of that for yourself.

**Gabe:** I haven't spoken for a while. I have been thinking about getting out of here too. For most of these sessions I have been sitting here feeling pissed off and distant from anyone in the room, and a lot at you. But what Liz went through earlier on and then today has made me stop and think twice about leaving. She and I seem alike—a couple of tough guys—Frank and Mack, too.

But now I find myself questioning the cost/benefit ratio of my ego's operating system. I feel a little ashamed to be admitting I have an ego, not because it's wrong to have one, but because it feels like I am capitulating to you by using that word. I get that's a bit crazy, but that's how it feels. What I am starting to notice is how much I get off on being adversarial. That's when I'm most comfortable. That's when I feel the strongest, and I guess the safest. Although I hate admitting feelings of safety are involved. It feels weak to need safety. I should be impervious. And I try to be. And I feel pretty successful.

**Lou:** Sounds like some curiosity about yourself has been aroused.

**Gabe:** I didn't think of it that way. It feels like a bad kind of curiosity, like the kind that killed the cat. Or at least it seems like a bad idea to be curious about what I'm getting curious about, what I'm questioning.

**Lou:** I know. But if there is nothing to question about your approach to living your life then there's really nothing to get curious about.

**Gabe:** Objectively true. Still it doesn't feel right or smart to do it right now.

**Lou:** Does it make some sense to explore *that* assessment or assumption right now?

**Gabe:** I'm going to stay and I'm going to keep listening. But right now I'm going to stop talking.

**Lou:** Cool.

**Gina:** Recently I have been trying out dating. I've had no real social life since even before my husband and daughter died. I was divorced from my husband for several years before he died. I just focused on my kids, but now I want to learn how to focus on me. But you know what? I can't seem to get beyond my daughter's death.

**Lou:** I'm not sure what you mean.

**Gina:** I miss her terribly. We were close, although now I wonder how close. She died about a year and a half ago. She was twenty-four, beautiful, smart, and an incredible artist and musician. She got hooked on pain meds after a bad fall rollerblading about a year before she died. I've heard so many of these stories since she overdosed.

She was doing some graduate work in fine art and music at a really good school in California. She was doing well. She'd been home for a holiday and she looked bad but when I asked her she said she was just stressed from the pressure of her classes. I asked her about the pain meds but she said she'd gone off them a long time ago. She stayed in her room a lot while she was home, slept a lot.

She went back to school and two weeks later she was dead. Apparently she went online and got some OxyContin and took too much and died. She'd been drinking, too. Her roommate couldn't wake her in the morning. A couple of nights before when we were talking on the phone she said to me, "What if I fail?" She sounded really down. I told her I didn't realize she was struggling and asked her what the problem was. She just blew me off and said, "Oh, don't worry, I'll be okay. I've just got my period and I'm stressing." I pressed her about maybe taking a break or talking to someone, but she changed her tone and just kept saying don't worry.

But now I'm haunted with questions: Should I have flown out there? Should I have called the school counselor? Should I have called one of her friends? She was getting great grades and feedback from her professors. I hate myself for failing her then and all the ways I must have failed her before she got hooked. I had a sense she had a drinking problem for a long time, long before the drugs entered the picture. There were signs of that, too, that I failed to do something about.

**Lou:** So not only are you going through all the sad and painful feelings that come up around missing her as badly as you do, but you are also hating yourself for what you see as ways you failed her. And you said earlier you couldn't "get beyond your daughter's death." I hear what a blow her death has been for you, but I don't understand what "getting beyond her death" means yet. Can you say some more about that?

**Gina:** I'm sorry. I get really mixed up these days. There are a lot of different feelings. One thing is I am scared about my life. I'm scared that I've become so disconnected from people, so alone and isolated. I don't want to be with people. I don't want to answer the questions about how I'm doing. I feel really bad about myself, and like people know I failed. At least once a day or at night I go over in my mind what I didn't do for her, or what I could have done differently. I get so depressed and anxious I can barely stand it. My only escape from myself is reading self-help books and watching TV. But I still end up being preoccupied with blame for her death, or occasionally with a rage at the doctors who didn't see the problem or who prescribed her meds, or the dealers that sold her street stuff.

**Lou:** A death like your daughter's is so complicated to deal with. It's so different from a death due to an illness or the consequences of aging. Death of a loved one from an overdose, from an accident caused by drugs or alcohol, or some other kind of "preventable" accident is a lot like death by suicide. These kinds of deaths leave behind a terrible legacy of doubt, guilt, shame, self-recriminations, and unanswered questions in those left behind. Self-blame is an automatic reaction to these kinds of deaths.

**Gina:** Certainly seems true for me.

**Lou:** The self-blame actually makes it impossible to simply grieve and move along through the difficult process of grieving.

**Gina:** What do you mean? I haven't been grieving? It certainly feels like I've been grieving.

**Lou:** No, I'm not saying that. Let me describe what I think might be your experience of grieving so far: I would suspect that every time you miss your daughter, and every time you feel some real sadness over the loss of her, very quickly a guilty or self-blaming thought jumps into your mind and replaces or smothers the sadness with feelings of shame and fear that there was something you could have done to prevent her death, to have saved her life.

**Gina:** That's right.

**Lou:** So you never have the fullness of your sadness. The depth and breadth of your sadness is actually a measure of your love for her, of how much you meant to each other, of the richness of your relationship. You never can have a deep, full-on experience of crying over how much you miss her, how much you want her back, how much you loved her and enjoyed her, and how much it hurts not to have her around, ever again. You never get to cry until you're done, for that moment, and then again when the next round of missing her comes up. Your *experience* of your sadness keeps getting interrupted or contaminated or sidetracked by the shame and the fear. That's what I mean by not being able to go all the way through the process of grieving.

**Gina:** Just the other day I was doing some straightening up at home and I came across this picture of her rollerblading as a ten-year-old. She was so happy on her skates, and I loved skating with her. I started to weep with missing her, but then I thought about how she died and it was like I locked up inside with the fear that I had caused her death, that I am responsible, that "indulging" in my sadness is somehow copping out from the responsibility. I should have prevented her death, like if I had caused her death I don't have the right to be sad about it. That feels a little wacky as I say it but it also feels really true.

**Lou:** That is such a good example. I want to spend a little extra time on this because it is such a powerful example of the ego at work on the experience of parenting and of the powerful social conditioning of our egos. For the vast majority of us who are parents, we operate with a standard of perfection as the governing measure of how we're doing, or how we did, as parents. Now every parent will be quick to say, "I know I haven't been perfect as a parent." But let's look a little more closely. If you make what looks like a serious mistake with one of your kids, one that hurts the child in some way, that costs the child, and somebody points it out to you, the first reaction is shame and embarrassment, not simple regret. You feel like you are "bad," especially if the mistake becomes public.

Or let's say your kid is screwing up in school or socially. Again the re-action is shame at being exposed as "bad" parents. Your good standing, your acceptability, as a parent among parents, is now in jeopardy. Rejection, shunning, and ostracism loom as possibilities, or are already happening. The S/I/C ego team makes it compulsive that you be a "good" parent and never look "bad." If your kids are meeting all the markers that reflect back on you in a way that say "what good parents they are," then you are rewarded with all the good feelings the S/I/C pumps you with—pride, goodness, superiority, righteousness, etc. If not, then the ego calls in the C/T/D crew and you will be assaulted with shame, fear, and doubt about yourself.

The C/T/D will find every flaw in your parenting skills and assail you with them like bludgeons. And God forbid your kid dies of an overdose or suicide. The social agreement on this is still that this is the ultimate sign of failed parenting. And if you are the parent, then you deserve to be blamed and shamed. Just like alcoholism and addiction are still blamed on the al-coholic or addict. This zone of behavior where human choices, and not strictly physical causes, are involved leaves us caught between a hard-nosed condemning moral viewpoint that makes people feel bad but doesn't seem to lead to much learning or change, or a "soft," compassionate point of view that seems to leave people unaccountable for the consequences of their be-havior—sort of the "liberal" vs. "conservative" dilemma. This is fertile terri-tory for the ego.

Coming back to Gina's experience of her daughter's death may help us think this through, or feel it through. What I see you experiencing, Gina, is very familiar to me with parents who have gone through a similar kind of loss. There are two things going on simultaneously that are really different but get all mixed up together.

One is the experience and ongoing process of grieving—that is simply *feeling* every bout of pain and sadness and missing that arise from the loss of your loved one. The second thing that is going on is the ego jumping on the experience of this loss with all its compulsive need to manage and protect your acceptability and your safety within your tribe or dependency group, as well as within your own inner sense of acceptable selfhood. Does my de-scription of what I believe is going on inside of you fit your experience at all?

**Gina:** Yes it does. I can just barely see the difference between the two inside me; they are so tangled up. But yes, I can kind of *feel* the difference between the two. They really are different. Your description of mourning or grieving actual made me yearn for that experience. It feels like it would be such a relief to be simply sad, to just feel *that* and not all the shame and fearfulness about being a failed parent. But I don't know if that's possible for me. It still feels like a cop out.

**Lou:** Yes. Yes. This is really tricky, especially when we *have* made mistakes as parents, have actually hurt our kids in unintended ways, diminished them, disempowered them, abandoned them in ways we may not have even re-alized at the time. Because of our blindness to our own vulnerability, we are not as attuned to the vulnerability of our kids, to their desperate need for our approval operating right along side their powerful need to be them-selves, to express who they are, to become more and more autonomous.

We react out of our conditioning, out of our own blindness, automat-ically. I have often used the analogy of the blind woman in the bus, who, having arrived at her stop, opens up her folding cane and inadvertently pokes another passenger's eye out. She didn't even *see* the other passenger. But she put his eye out. She did it. Nobody else did. What does "blame" mean in that situation? And is "accountability" different from "blame?" Is "I am a bad person" a more useful conclusion than is the ownership that "I did that, and I will deal with consequences of my blindness as best I can?"

**Gina:** I'm sort of stunned into silence right now. I feel like you threw a monkey wrench in my machinery. I don't mean that in a bad way. I think I feel right on the edge of that grief and regret—a terrible sadness, a terrible recognition of powerlessness, something terribly humbling, like a recogni-tion of my failures, of my blindness about me, about my daughter, about so many things, about how much of my own life I've missed that I wasn't really present for, that I never claimed, never enjoyed, because I was trying to be all right all the time, trying to be acceptable; so afraid of not being accepted, of being bad in some way, never being at ease, never really feeling safe with anybody. I don't know. I just feel so sad right now.

**Lou:** Can I ask you to take a look around the room right now and check out the faces of the folks who are here with you?

**Gina:** I'm scared to.

**Lou:** What do you expect?

**Gina:** Something like emptiness, nobody really there.

**Lou:** You don't have to look.

**Gina:** (Looking around, quickly, then slowly, then staring, then smiling, crying a little, laughing.) I see what looks very unfamiliar to me. I don't know how to name it. But your eyes are letting me in. I see your eyes are with me. It feels a little scary, but in a good way. It feels okay right in this moment, but I don't trust the next moment.

**Lou:** So from the looks of their eyes, it seems they have not moved away from you, are not closing themselves up over what you have talked about. Would you be up for hearing some of their experience while you spoke?

**Gina:** I don't think so.

**Lou:** So you want to let that go for now?

**Gina:** Yes. If they're going to respond, I don't want to have to respond back. I'm done for now.

**Lou:** Okay. Again, being able to make the choice you just made, to say "no," is vital to protecting ourselves as we enter these territories of deep vulnerability. To be able to say "enough for now" is critical.

**Gabe:** I had an older brother who committed suicide when he was sixteen. I was ten at the time. I hated him. He was nothing but mean to me. So I was as mean as a younger brother could be back to him. I found him. I had to help my mother take him down from where he had hung himself. She was screaming the whole time. I don't remember much of what happened after that. An ambulance came and took him away. Listening to you and Gina talk took me back there. I realized that my biggest reaction when I found him and had to tell my mother was that she was going to be mad at me because he killed himself, because I didn't stop him, because I hated him. I was horrified by what I saw, by what he did, but I was more afraid of being blamed—terrified, really. I still don't know what to make of it.

**Lou:** Jesus. That would be horrifying to anybody, much more so to a young boy. Does this relate to what we've been looking at here?

**Gabe:** Well it's clearly an experience of when what someone thought about me really mattered to me—meaning my Mom. Maybe that was the last time, come to think of it. She never talked to me about it. After that she just shut down, went on like nothing had happened. She never spoke about him again, unless somebody asked, and even then she cut it short. So I don't know what she really thought about me.

**Lou:** Where was your Dad in all of this?

**Gabe:** They had divorced a couple of years before. I don't remember him being around much.

**Lou:** So there was no one to help you sort through this traumatizing experience.

**Gabe:** No.

**Lou:** Well it would make a kind of sense, wouldn't it, to do your best not to care what people thought about you after that, in a certain sense, not to need people.

**Gabe:** Yeah.

**Lou:** You know your ego, in the only way it knows how, is trying to prevent you from being traumatized again...ever again. Your ego is actually terrified of your vulnerability, and terrified of ever being powerless to prevent you from ever feeling that kind of horror and that terror of retribution again. It both hates and fears that powerlessness.

**Gabe:** Let's say that's true. What am I supposed to do about that?

**Lou:** Actually, if it's true, then your ego has made its mind up and it is not going to change its mind just because you or I or anyone else thinks it could or should. It's convinced and won't be unconvinced. So there is nothing you can do about that.

**Gabe:** So where does that leave me?

**Lou:** Well it brings us back to the exploration of whether or not there is a "you" in there that is really different from your ego. If there isn't, then we're just playing around with words and ideas that are useless regarding helping us find more satisfying and safer ways through the hurts and wounds our lives brings us. Right?

**Gabe:** I'm beginning to see what you've been driving at. I should say I am beginning to *feel* what you mean. I just had a flash inside that for me to be different from my ego means I could feel some sympathy for myself, and that means I *am* going to feel vulnerable. That already feels really risky to me, really dangerous, even foolhardy.

**Lou:** It is risky, even dangerous. But it doesn't have to be risky in a foolhardy or completely powerless way. It's what I've been saying all along; we are afraid for good reason. We really do need each other's approval, from some more than others. This is no joke. This is serious. We can and do hurt each other...badly. And so it does feel really risky and scary to lose the approval and acceptance of others, just like its scary to lose your oxygen supply. You can be really hurt as a person, as well as a body. You could even be wiped out as a person, or a body. People are wiping other people out, as persons and as bodies, every minute of every day somewhere in or not too far from where we're sitting right now.

The problem is not that we need other people's approval and acceptance—just like needing oxygen is not a "problem." The problem is we have to pretend we do not need acceptance. The problem is we think the best way we can protect ourselves are in the ways we learned when the only way we could protect ourselves included doing harm to ourselves, chewing off the proverbial leg. We did not have the "weapons" to fight with, and we had nowhere to run. The best we could do was some kind of perpetual freeze, to hold our breath and get through. And we're still holding our breath to this moment.

So if you come to your own conclusion, based on your own inside experience, that there is a "you," a "self," inside that is not your ego, and you choose to move toward supporting the emergence of that "self," you will be going against what the S/I/C believes is safe and acceptable for you, and as a result the C/T/D is going to come after you, call you a "fool," terrorize you with some worst case scenarios about people's reactions, and make you doubt your own experience. That's its job.

**Gabe:** So not only will I be vulnerable to getting hurt by those I let in, the ones who matter to me, I am also going to be attacked on the inside by the C/T/D for doing so! Wow! What an inviting proposition! Why would I want to do that!?

**Lou:** You might not choose to.

**Gabe:** I know that. I've already made that choice. I'm asking why I would want to make a different one.

**Lou:** Listen, Gabe, I hear your question. And I believe I hear what's inside it—the past hurt and abandonment, the aloneness, the fear, the anticipation of more of the same. I could not possibly answer your question in any way that will make personal sense to you, that would answer it *for* you.

Right now it sounds like it doesn't make enough sense to you to change what you see as your relationship game plan, and what I see as your ego's.

Given your current expectations, I can see where that makes the most sense to you right now. I will say this: The pain of the experience you described to us is terribly real and lives in some unfinished ways inside you. I believe the way you had to deal with that horror around the time it happened and afterwards is costing you *now* in diminished personal freedom and satisfaction in your relationships. You're like a wounded warrior. You've survived a nasty battle, in a certain sense you were even victorious, but you're bleeding internally. I hope that doesn't feel like a judgment or a put-down.

**Gabe:** I get where you're coming from. It might have felt that way before all this talking. Listening to Gina got to me. I felt really bad for her. So I suppose it should be all right for you to feel bad for me. I know one thing I don't want from anybody is pity. I didn't feel pity for Gina, just sad and like I could feel a pain in me like hers. That felt okay. What you said didn't sound like pity.

**Lou:** It wasn't. It was something like what you felt about Gina.

**Gabe:** Yeah.

**Lou:** Shall we leave it there for the moment?

**Gabe:** Yeah.

**Mack:** Thanks, Gabe. Talking about that piece of history and hearing how you've dealt with it got me a little clearer about me. I'm in a different place than you but we're a lot alike, too. One difference though—and in a way you helped me see this more clearly than ever before—is that I *do* have an ego. Boy, do I have an ego—a big one. I'm the man. I'm the go-to guy. I'm the guy you want fighting next to you because I'll kill someone if necessary. I can do that. I know I can. I've come too close for comfort a couple of times.

I like my ego. I'd say I love my ego. I see now so clear I could never have survived what I survived without it. I like that guy. He's actually not a bad guy, just a really tough guy, somebody you don't mess with, and you don't mess with anybody he cares about either. But, you know, as much as I like him, he nearly killed *me*! For one thing he wouldn't let me see I was alcoholic. Me?

Out of control? Forget about it! Fuck you! You know what I mean? I was the guy that kept order. It took a near death experience for me to wake up. That's a lot of years ago now. And now I know there is another me that is not my ego. I can be a tough guy when I need to but not all fucking the time. I needed help; I needed somebody to care about me, to set me straight in a loving way, a respectful way—no pity for sure, just straight honest stuff. My guys in AA have been that for me. But you know what? I am right up against my ego again!

**Lou:** How so?

**Mack:** In my marriage. It was the tough guy who won my wife. She loved that guy, loved how he loved her, loved how he made love to her. Our sex life has always been intense, a big part of our staying together. She's tough, too. We're two tough guys. We've had some pretty spectacular fights, but up until now never physical. But I'm afraid. I can feel it coming. She's having a meltdown of some sort. She doesn't like it when I get caught up in work. She's paranoid I'm seeing someone else. She's going into my phone and my computer looking for evidence. Any communication with a female is suspect. I cheated on her when I was drinking years ago, so it's not like there is no precedent, but I'm not now. She's really looking to hurt me now—telling me she's gong to get with someone else, telling me she doesn't want to make love with me, telling me I'm not a man, I'm just a big show with no substance. My tough guy just wants to whack her! I don't know if the other guy I've become can hold up, can deal with this.

**Lou:** So the way she's dealing with her fear of being rejected by you is to blame you, shame you, and be aggressive, go right to where your ego feels most ashamed and vulnerable. That is a "tough guy" strategy. For sure she is not showing you her fear, her hurt, or her vulnerability.

**Mack:** She's busting my balls.

**Lou:** So naturally your tough guy ego wants to strike back and not show your fear and hurt and vulnerability either. You're in the combat zone, and when you're in there it's kill or be killed, right?

**Mack:** Jesus, this is so fucking familiar. I feel like I am eighteen years old again.

**Lou:** So what about the other guy? The one you feel is not your ego? What's he up to?

**Mack:** He's hurting, and scared. He feels desperate. He keeps going back for more, begging her without really begging her. He just wants her to love him, to think he's great. When I leave the house when it gets really bad, I can't stay away. I can't really get free, or separate, or something. It's like I have an emotional umbilical cord attached to her. I can't stand how I feel when I'm away from her and I know she's angry with me. I have to text her or call her or something to make contact—even if it's to fight with her some more and just be yelled at. I feel crazy. And I hate myself for being such a weakling.

**Stew:** Man, do I know how you're feeling.

**Liz:** Me too.

**Lou:** I'll bet a bunch of you do. It's like you're caught between being the tough guy who needs to believe he doesn't need anybody and some little boy inside who is desperately dependent on the one he needs and loves, a little boy who feels like he is going to die if she doesn't let him back into her embrace.

**Mack:** Well I didn't think of it as a little boy, just some weak version of me.

**Lou:** Yes, I know. Let's look at your situation closely, because I think it really is an example of the battleground we enter when we come to the conclusion we are not our egos and we want to include more of ourselves in how we live. If you were still in the place where you completely identified with your ego, "my ego is me," then you would just have to be a better tough guy and do whatever your ego compels you to do to be that, or suffer all the shaming that the C/T/D would dose you with for being a failed male. Right so far?

**Mack:** Yeah, but I know different now.

**Lou:** Yes, and that's what complicates a complicated situation even more. It's no longer black or white for you like it is for your ego. It's no longer having to chose *between* feeling only your "love" or only your "power" for you. You have some sense, some personal experience, that says you want to have both. You just don't seem to know how to experience both with safety and integrity in this situation with your wife, how to keep your integrity, how to be authentic in your own self-expression, how to protect your dignity, how to maintain a genuine autonomy, and at the same time feel your love for her, as well as feeling your need for her love and approval in return.

Now you know you are afraid of losing her love and approval because you are *feeling* that fear. You've lost your capacity to deny that fear, or to deny the hurt you experience when she rejects you. Your ego's defenses against feeling the intense hurt from her shoving you away have been crashed. And, on top of that, you have decided to no longer buy your ego's belief that it is "good" to deny your need for approval and acceptance. You want to respect your need for human connection and support, especially to and from those who really matter to you. *Now* it feels really risky and dangerous to lose that connection and support. But if you can only preserve a particular connection to someone who really matters to you at the cost of your dignity, your self-expression, your freedom to be your essential self, what then? How do you keep both your "power" and your "love" in a relationship that's currently demanding the kind of compliance and accommodation that cuts into your wholeness and respect as a person?

**Mack:** I hadn't put it that way to myself, but, yes, that seems to be my dilemma.

**Lou:** Your ego's response to someone treating you this way is to insist that any choice you make be jammed into an either/or framework, either tough guy choices (acceptable) or wimpy choices (unacceptable). In that system, if you feel your love and need for her, and then choose to stay in the relationship in an effort to make it work by struggling to talk and listen to each other, you are automatically judged as weak by your Critic and terrorized by your Terrorist with the threat of ostracism from the male community for being a failed male. The only acceptable feeling you can feel in this situation according to the ego is anger or rage, and the only acceptable behavioral responses are aggressive ones, like criticizing, yelling, put-downs, etc., all the way to hitting and or killing her.

**Mack:** I'm feeling too close to those last two options. But look, the problem seems pretty clear. What about a solution? There really is no "talking and listening," only arguing. And she is being really nasty with my friends, too. If I really look at what's going on, the only really safe option for me right now, and for her too, is for me to get out of the house and go stay somewhere else for a while, maybe a good long while. At least that way we're not in each other's faces escalating shit. But it's my house. It feels like I'm accommodating in a bad way. And besides, though I hate to say this, as soon as I'm away from her for a little while I feel like I have to see her, or at least talk to her. I really feel crazy.

**Lou:** No wonder it sometimes feels necessary to shut our feelings down.

**Mack:** Sometimes?!

**Lou:** You said something a moment ago. You said, "If I really look at what's going on…." and then described the best action for "right now." "Really looking," as you described it, may be the answer—or rather the way to get to an answer, to get to some choices that make enough sense to you to make them for "right now." When we've stepped away from the ego's narrow-minded set of response options, and open up to all of what we may feel and think about a difficult life moment, we can sometimes be flooded with feelings and thoughts about what to do, and with some contradictory ones as well. We can end up in a spin in our heads, especially when the ego is still at work frightening us and making us doubt our own feelings and thoughts, our intuitions about the right choices—especially our intuitions.

So if my head is spinning, and I'm trying not to listen to my ego for answers, where else can I look for clarity? Where can I "really look," as you put it? Maybe "look for real," or look for what feels real and right to me in the moment, for a response that feels trustable in the moment. There really is no right or wrong response to your situation, no formula. There are responses that are going to work better than others regarding taking care of yourself, taking *yourself* seriously. Whatever they are, they will have to make enough sense to you or you won't make them. The choices you have in a situation like yours are all going to be uncomfortable, to put it mildly, so they have to *feel* right *enough* to you, in spite of the discomfort. Even then you may feel too afraid to make them. But if any response is going to move you along a path that takes your own wellbeing into consideration, that response at the very least has to feel right enough to you. Does this make sense to you?

**Mack:** Sure, intellectually. But I don't think that's where you're headed.

**Lou:** You're right. Where I am headed is not into an intellectual territory. We may need to begin there and create a map. But I don't want us to stay in the map, just like we did when exploring the "ego," not as a concept, but as a direct personal experience. We're now going to head into a whole differ- ent territory of our personal experience, one that is very different from the territory the ego creates and manages, an inner territory of experiences that the ego does not want us to know about or explore or pay attention to. I am going to have to be "intellectual" about what this territory looks like to be- gin with, in the sense of mapping it out a little with words, ideas, and images. But we will then be going into the territory that the map points us toward in order to discover whether or not what the map *says* is there is *actually there*, in your own felt experience.

When I put the call out to you and others who might be interested in this workshop I summarized three objectives for us. We have fairly thor- oughly accomplished the first objective regarding coming to more clarity about what an ego is and how it operates within us. We are now moving toward the second and third objectives. To remind you, I will quote them again:

- Second, we will explore how to bypass those ego-driven limits and how to access a different, deeper source of internal knowing. We will discover how that source can give us a direct experience of what we need to know to sustain our interpersonal safety and our personal wellbeing, as well as genuine self-respect, in any given moment. This internal "compass" provides us with a trustworthy basis for operating moment to moment, on our own personal authority, while we evolve within ourselves and engage in our important relationships.

- Third, we will share methods that release us from the limits of the ego, as well as methods that help us access this source of evolving self-knowledge, authenticity, and wise personal power and authority.

So the territory we will be heading into now is the inner territory of experiences where that "different, deeper source of internal knowing" actually exists.

But before we head there, some of the words we use to name the internally felt experiences within this different territory could use some clarifying, especially those words or phrases that we use to name the *felt* qualities in this "non-ego" territory that are different when we are probing inside ourselves for what we "really" think and feel about something, about each other, or about ourselves.

Some of these words and phrases have already become clichés, and some are in danger of soon becoming so. Clichés are words or phrases that once pointed to true experiences, but have now been stripped of any connection to a "felt" truth, and as result have become superficial and meaningless concepts. This stripping of meaning is what the ego does in order to maintain its control over how we use our own awareness. The word "trauma" is right at that point of becoming meaningless, of actually hiding the reality it is supposed to be pointing our attention towards. The word "trauma" most often now keeps us safely in our heads and far away from any personally *felt sense* of the complexity and intensity of the painful *experience* we are trying to explore and help each other with.

Some of the words and phrases that we need to get clear about include: "real," "authentic," "being in the moment," "being present," "presence," "true," "truth," "deep and deeper," "looking in," "felt," and "feeling." There may be others that need some discussion on our part in order to be clear about what kinds of experiences we are talking about, but we'll work with some of these for now. And I say "experiences" because these words and phrases are not meant to exist as abstract concepts; they are meant to point to actual felt internal experiences.

We will be "looking into" our "real" experiences within this inner non-ego territory, otherwise we would just be floating around in a word-filled mental space completely separated from the actual "felt" experiences of what we are trying to explore with each other. It would be like pulling out a map of Alaska, looking at all the names of cities, mountains, and bodies of water, and talking about it all as if we had actually been there, as if we actually "knew" Alaska from direct experience.

I picked up earlier on Mack's phrase of "really looking" at what he thought. Mack, you said it in a flow of other thoughts about actions you could take and of thoughts about what you were experiencing with your wife. You passed over it quickly, almost like that was just a throwaway thought. But let me ask you to go back to the thought that emerged from what you called "really looking." Can you look a little more closely at whether that was different somehow from other thoughts, and if it was, how so?

**Mack:** That's the one thought I really *don't* want to look more closely at.

**Lou:** How come?

**Mack:** Because I know it's true and it's frightening. I'm scared to leave her. I'm afraid I'll lose her for good if I do, and I'm afraid of her wrath at me for abandoning her.

**Lou:** So you *know* it's both a "true" and a frightening thought. What I would like to do right now is put the looking into the fear part aside for the moment and look into what you mean by "true." But for your sense of safety's sake, let's agree for the moment that knowing the truth of this thought does not bind you to act on it, that for now, in this space, you're allowed to know something is true for you but are not obliged to translate that into a decision. Okay?

**Mack:** You bet! That let's me off the hook.

**Lou:** For me it's not so much letting you off the hook as it is this: a choice may be just too frightening for you to make, for now. To me the choice to not choose is a legitimate one, even a necessary one, if you are going to take your own experience seriously and use it to figure out your best course of action. Very often the fear of or doubt about a choice comes into our heads and bodies so fast that you really don't get "time" to think about what makes sense and what feels doable.

It's as if there is a rule that says: "If you think it's the right choice then you have to make it, and right away." But if you can give yourself the permission to not have to take any action right away, it can make it possible to look more closely and fully into all the ramifications of the choice. It gives you "time" to see the sense, the meaning, and the consequences of the choice with more clarity.

But let me ask you: What are you indicating when you say that the thought is "true" and when you say "really look" at something?

**Mack:** I was not so conscious of this before, but there is a part of me that seems to be involved when I am "really looking" at something that is not there when I'm just thinking normally or spinning around in circles. It's a little hard to describe, but there's a feeling there when I'm looking that way and when I *know* something is true. It's a feeling in my body, somewhere in between my chest and my belly. It feels good, sort of chunky, solid, like some kind of felt "yes." Weird.

**Lou:** So "really looking" and "true" include more than just the thought; there is a feeling that goes with the thought that let's you know that you know the thought is true for you, a felt "yes," as you so wonderfully just put it. Is this experience of "true" or "truth" ringing bells for anyone else?

**Stew:** I have the same experience when I'm writing a song. At least it sounds the same. So it's not about thinking, or following a line of thinking, but it's about following a line of sounds. And it's really following, like the song is coming up sound-by-sound, or clump-of-sounds-by-clump-of-sounds. Most times I have to sort of fool around with sounds until that something we're talking about gives me the "yes" feeling. Some sounds fit, and some don't, but I know it when a sound or clump of sounds works. Sometimes I'm lucky and a song comes up in one whole clump, totally perfect. That's like magic.

But it is a feeling in my chest and belly like Mack's. It's like something just clicks in there; I can feel it. But "feel" isn't quite right either, close but not quite.

**Lou:** I like that name for it—the "yes feeling."

**Lucas:** I felt like I was living in that "yes feeling" continuously after that workshop. Everything was so clear, felt so real. I've had moments of that feeling since—mostly unhappy ones, like knowing I'm really missing something, feeling that in my gut; knowing I'm angry; knowing I'm sad. That's actually different for me. I was not so in touch with my feelings before. Even though the feelings lately have been unpleasant or painful, I'm glad I'm feeling them. They really let me know where I am inside my own skin.

**Lou:** So there is that word "real." What is that pointing at? Can you describe what you're getting at by putting that word on your experience?

**Lucas:** Jesus, man, you are really pushing on this experiential thing, aren't you?!

**Lou:** Yes.

**Lucas:** All right, let me see if I can find some words for the feeling. It is a feeling. Well I said two things: that everything was so clear and felt so real. The "clear" part was visual in a way. like somebody had turned the three-way lamp up from dim to bright. Everything I looked at seemed brighter, sharper, richer, visually. It was the same with sounds and smells and things I touched. It was like I was living in some kind of haze before that and the haze had lifted. Nothing had changed except how I experienced it. I guess that's what I mean by more "real" also. It was kind of like, "Oh, whadaya know! This is all really here. Damn. Will you look at that! I had no idea being alive was like this!" Maybe *I* felt more real, like I came out of some kind of trance or dream state. It seems like it has precious little to do with thinking, with thoughts. It's more like being than thinking, more like present, here now. Maybe that phrase "being in the moment" fits here.

**Stew:** Sounds psychedelic, man.

**Lou:** Would "being in the moment" also fit for when you were knowing that you were angry or sad?

**Lucas:** Those are not necessarily moments I want to inhabit, but, yes, I guess it would.

**Lou:** Let's pause a moment and look into this notion of "being in the moment," into what that phrase means. That phrase is actually a good example of something becoming a cliché or a fad. Certainly everyone in the self-help world and on a spiritual path would agree that "being in the moment" is a good thing. It's the way to be, sort of the "holy grail." right? People will often describe what they consider a "good" moment with a statement like, "I was really in the moment." Or they will criticize someone else for "not being in the moment." It's become this "better" way to be, right? It's actually a terrific example of the ego taking an experience, capturing it in a set of words, a concept, and then turning it into a new demand, a new way of being "good" or "bad," of passing or failing the test of acceptability, now in your spiritual or self-help tribe. It's even gone mainstream as a "good" way to be, a new quality to compulsively strive for: "I'm really trying to be more in the moment." Advertisers now sell their products as taking you "into the moment."

Let me pose a question to you: Is it possible to be in any other moment but this one?

**Gabe:** Logically, no.

**Lou:** Any other way?

**Gabe:** Physically, no.

**Lou:** Any other way?

**Gabe:** I suppose mentally you could be in another moment, like when you're thinking about something that happened yesterday or that may happen tomorrow.

**Lou:** But you're doing that thinking right here in this moment, right? Same if you're upset about something that happened already or that might happen in the future. You're still upset right here, right now, right? In fact we're totally stuck in the moment we're in right now. We may not want to be, but we are. Just because we can think and feel and imagine about the past and the future doesn't ever mean we are not right here, right now having that particular experience. We may "forget" that truth, or choose not to pay any attention to the reality that we are right here, right now in this moment, and get lost in our thoughts, feelings, and fantasies about the past and the future, but we cannot escape this moment.

So maybe "being in the moment" doesn't have anything to do with the reality that we actually *are* in this moment, but with what our awareness *includes* within it in any given moment. If our awareness is lost in thought in a given moment, that is only one particular way of being in or experiencing a given moment—same if we are lost in feelings or fantasies.

**Gabe:** So what?

**Lou:** Good question. What's the big deal about being in the moment when we really can never be anywhere else?

**Lucas:** For me, being in the moment *is* no big deal. Being more and more aware in the moment is the big deal. Letting whatever is happening in the moment *in* is the big deal—not just what is happening outside of me but what's happening on the inside of me too. More and more, I'm discovering that there always seems to be more going on inside me and around me than I am aware of in the beginning moments of *any* experience. The experience sort of unfolds if I let it. If I let myself open, open my senses to both inside and outside, I discover more and more of what I am experiencing. I've realized I was kind of pretending to be open before, pretending to be "real," pretending to be myself. I was really always editing out stuff I was feeling and thinking, like that was normal, mostly like I didn't even notice a lot of stuff that was there. I must be sounding confused.

**Lou:** You sound like you're getting clearer about your own experience of experiencing. So this may sound like a dumb question, but what's the big deal about being more and more aware in the moment?

**Lucas:** It's not just the "more and more" part. It's a lot about what I am letting into my awareness that matters. When I let in what I'm feeling or sensing in a moment with someone, then I know what the experience of that moment with that person means to me. When I know what that moment means to me, then I know what my response in the next moment needs to be. I'm not guessing at how to respond or trying to respond in some "right" way, or responding just in some automatic, unconscious way. I know what I want or need to do. I feel like I have an inner guide I can count on, I can trust.

**Lou:** So maybe "being in the moment" doesn't fit so well as a name for what we are talking about. Maybe something like "dropping into the moment" would capture it better. Being in the moment sort of feels like an event, and like something constant. And what is "the moment" anyway? Aren't we really talking about *this* moment, and then *this* moment, and so on? What we're describing is more like a process, more like, as you put it, an experience of the "unfolding" of an experience, moment to moment to moment.

**Liz:** I'm losing you, guys. Can we get out of the words here? I need a sample of what you're talking about. I've always felt I've been very real. I'm a sort of a "what you see is what you get" kind of girl. I don't believe in beating around the bush. So I guess that would mean I'm "in the moment," too. So this is all starting to sound like it doesn't take me anywhere I'm not already.

**Lou:** Actually, if you remember the other day when we did that exploration of your "pissed off" feeling, the experience you had of dropping into that experience and following it as it unfolded from pissed off to empty and sad to feeling a wider space inside, and so on, was exactly what we were talking about.

**Liz:** But that sort of feels like an unusual moment, a special moment, not a normal moment. Like right now nothing is going on inside me. I'm not feeling anything, except maybe a little disconnected from your conversation with Lucas and Gabe.

**Lou:** So good. Let's put into practice what we've been talking about. What we're looking into is the possibility that there is always more going on in any given moment than what we are initially aware of, and that if we deliberately use our own awareness in certain ways we can allow into our awareness more and more of what is happening in this given moment. So let's do it instead of talking about it. Here we are in this moment, Liz. Let's first let our awareness expand outwards, not be so focused solely on each other, but look around and let in the others in the room with us, the room itself, any sounds that may be going on, okay?

**Liz:** Sure.

(A couple of moments of silence as we both look around the room.)

**Lou:** Now let's take a moment to look at each other without speaking and use our awareness to notice both what we see about each other and also what we're feeling and thinking inside ourselves.

(A couple of moments of silence while we do this.)

**Liz:** You first.

**Lou:** Sure, but keep using your awareness to notice what you were feeling inside when you said "you first," and also what you may think and feel while I tell you my experience.

So when I looked around the room I was aware of some shyness and embarrassment inside me. And at the same time, as I looked at the different faces, a big smile came up in me. I noticed how I blocked out everybody so I was only slightly aware of their presence until I started looking around.

Then I noticed that I didn't like the room we're in, that I thought it was ugly and kind of dead. And I felt grateful for all the aliveness I felt from everybody being here.

When I looked back at you I was again aware of feeling shyness, embarrassment, and some nervousness, like I didn't know what to do with my body. Then I caught your eyes looking at mine and there was a moment or two of intimacy, just letting you in and looking into you. Then there was a kind of shut down and a feeling of isolation. Then I noticed a feeling of liking you, and I felt connected again in me and to you. Then you said, "You first."

**Liz:** I didn't like that much. I think that's why I said, "You first." I felt uncomfortable most of the time. Just the silence was uncomfortable. And then seeing people looking at me made me feel really awkward. Like you said, I didn't know what to do with my body. There was like a rushing sound in my ears so I didn't hear much and I don't think I saw much either. I was kind of enclosed in my own body and head.

When I looked at you I felt pretty much the same way except for that moment we looked into each other's eyes. It even makes me uncomfortable to say that phrase—"look into each other's eyes." But I felt the intimacy, as you called it, of that moment. I liked that when it was happening, but afterwards I felt awkward again. That pleasant moment seems like a small reward for all that discomfort. Who wants to feel all that uncomfortable stuff?!

**Lou:** Nobody "wants" to feel uncomfortable.

**Liz:** So why feel it if you can avoid feeling it!?

**Lou:** Would you avoid feeling the pain in your butt if you happened to sit on a tack?

**Liz:** I'd jump up and remove the tack!

**Lou:** But you wouldn't be looking to be unaware of the pain, right? You'd respond to the pain, of course, but you wouldn't avoid feeling it. You'd seek to end it. You would naturally use the pain as information that something was hurting you, that your butt was experiencing something that was not good for its health and wellbeing. Right?

**Liz:** What are you getting at?

**Lou:** Maybe "all that uncomfortable stuff" is trying to tell you something about your relationship to the people in this room and to me. Maybe, just maybe, there is some information in that "uncomfortable stuff" that could be useful to you if you "dropped into" that.

**Liz:** What possible usefulness is there in feeling all that awkwardness?!

**Lou:** You probably would not be up for trying out dropping into the experience of awkwardness in order to see what valuable information it has to tell you about your relationship to yourself and your relationship to us, would you?

**Liz:** Don't assume. You do piss me off. But hey, I'm here. Let's see what happens.

**Lou:** Do you want to drop into "pissed off" or "awkwardness?"

**Liz:** I prefer feeling pissed off, but let's do awkwardness...just for the fun of it all!

**Lou:** Let me guide this a little. What we've been doing, and what you're about to do, is no different than if I asked you to bring your awareness down to your right foot and feel the sensations in that foot. You can feel the sensations there when you do that, right? The pressure of the floor, the warmth in your shoe, your skin in your sock—all going on before you moved your awareness down there, just not noticed. In the same way, what I will be asking you to do is deliberately place your awareness on the internal experience you are calling "awkwardness"—the actual sensations of it, the feel of it in your body. Like you didn't think about "what might my foot feel like?" you just directly felt what your foot felt. So here, too, you are not going to think about what awkwardness is, you are going to directly feel what "awkwardness" feels like inside you, inside your own skin, so to speak. Understood so far?

**Liz:** Think so.

**Lou:** What you will have to keep in mind is that your ego probably has some negative judgments about feeling awkward, so your ego will be working hard to keep you from dropping into that experience. It will want you to turn away from it. Okay? So close your eyes for a moment and recall your earlier experience of either looking at the folks here or at me and see if the feeling of awkwardness arises again?

**Liz:** (After a moment or two) I feel humiliated by my awkwardness, embarrassed about it being there. It feels weak. I feel like people will look down on me, maybe make fun of me. That has happened to me. Shit. There's that need for approval. That feels weak, too—and scary.

**Lou:** So keep your eyes closed for a little and stay with what you're feeling, but see if you can put the feeling of humiliation and embarrassment a little to the side and put your awareness back again on the feeling of awkwardness, right directly into that experience, and see what emerges.

**Liz:** I need to be liked. (Weeping) And I just need to be loved. Just as simple and frightening as that. (Crying)

**Lou:** I'm going to suggest you do something that is going to feel risky, so if you don't want to do it that is really fine. Respecting your fear is as important and as valuable as choosing to challenge it. I'm going to suggest you open your eyes and look around the room again at the people here and be aware of what you see outside of you and what you feel inside of you. Does it feel safe enough to take that risk or not?

**Liz:** (Turning to group without speaking; looking around; crying softly; looking away; looking again; several folks crying with her; looking some more; laughing and folks laughing and crying with her.) (Turns, looks at me, right in my eyes, we both have tears streaming down our faces, crying and laughing.) Who wants to look at all that uncomfortable shit, right?! (Laughing)

**Lou:** I'm really happy you had the experience you had as a result of dropping into it. I feel such gratitude that the experience unfolded the way it did for you. I figure you can see that you never would have gotten to this if you didn't take the risk of dropping in, the risk of deliberately being with your awkwardness and all the shame you felt about it. It takes a form of real courage to do what you did. It's courage that doesn't feel muscular and all geared up in an armored suit of denial and invincibility. It feels "weak," vulnerable, like you really are in danger, like you're shaking in your shoes, and you do it anyway.

**Liz:** Yes, not that I like the process of getting here all that much.

**Lou:** Understood. One way to name what you just did could be to call it being "more real," or "more authentic," or "being present to what was true for you moment to moment," or "going deeper into your experience." All of those phrases could fit. But the important thing is they now are pointing to an actual experience that we have all shared, thanks to you, an experience that was meaningful, powerful, enriching, and freeing, amongst other things. Let me ask the others in the room a couple of questions. Does anybody have any feeling of doubt that what Liz shared with us was exactly what was true and real for her, moment to moment? Raise your hand if you have any doubt at all.

(No show of hands; lots of shaking heads)

**Willa:** I felt so connected to you, so much care for you, and admiration.

**Frank:** You opened my heart.

**Gabe:** I have to admit I was really touched by what you told us, but I was also scared imagining myself in your shoes, being honest like that.

**Stew:** Me too. It's scary being that vulnerable.

**Gina:** You made me feel safe in this room. I got real quiet inside, which I don't feel a lot.

**Mack:** I just wanted to hug you.

**Liz:** Well come over here! (They embrace and cry a bit together.)

**Mack:** Thanks.

**Liz:** Thank *you*! Thank you all. This is very, very different for me. According to Lou, I'll probably lose this good feeling, but, hey, it's in the memory bank. I'll keep it there.

**Lou:** The path of being more real, more authentic, more present, and going deeper is a very challenging path. It is the path of stepping away from the incredible grip of our egos and stepping into the power of our inner place of personal in this moment's truth. Its rewards can be astonishing and its costs extraordinarily scary and painful. Not always—sometimes the rewards are subtler. And it can get less and less scary and painful.

We need to be aware that the ego has a huge investment in our not dropping into our truth place. The ego believes intensely that it is dangerous to go there, that nothing good will come of it. and that lots of bad, humiliating things will happen to us regarding our standing in our tribes if we do. It will do its best to scare and shame us off course and make us doubt our own experience of personal, experiential truth, and doubt and demean its value to us. It will make us feel like being our authentic, real, true self in the moment is not worth it, not worth the risk. And there is risk.

So, Liz, I want to ask you to do one more thing that helps build access to your "truth place" as I call it. What seems to help build connection to this part of us is, after we have had an opening like you just did, to look back on it a little with our objective mind and make a mental note of what we learned, discovered, uncovered, or saw about ourselves.

Like you said, the good feeling will pass, as all feelings do. But you want to make sure the fruits of what you learned *do* get into the memory bank. Consciously noting your discoveries, even writing them down, helps to make a solid deposit in the bank. The ego wants you to forget what you experienced and will do its best to erase it from your consciousness. So this is a helpful counter step to the ego's shenanigans. Looking back on what you moved through, what were the discoveries, the surprises, Liz?

Liz: Well, I guess the big one is that there does always seem to be more going on inside of me than I am aware of to begin with. And if I want to discover what "more" there is all I have to do is stop, look, and listen, you might say.

Lou: That's a great way to capture the learning, naming it like that. What else?

Liz: That what I call awkwardness is really embarrassment and shame. And those feelings stop me from looking inside. They're the first blocks I meet if I turn inside. What I found underneath or just past the embarrassment was my need for love. I still feel some fear and embarrassment about that need, but I saw, or I felt, how good it felt to feel the need and have it met. I haven't felt that open and connected to people in a long time. But I guess I'm still scared of feeling it and not having it met.

Lou: Of course. That fear is natural. You can be hurt if you open your heart and show your need. You can be. Chances are you will be from time to time. Is the hurt feeling shameful too?

Liz: (Closes her eyes) Wow. I'll say. A lot. Like that's the big shame. That's the really dangerous admission. Then I'm at the mercy of someone else. I feel powerless then. And I hate that.

Lou: I admire how you just went inside yourself and saw what you saw. And what you saw is so, so important for all of us. This shame of feeling hurt is at the root of a lot of our difficulties with each other and with ourselves. What we need to discover is that we were powerless as kids to protect ourselves from the chronic hurtfulness of those we depended on or who mattered to us. But we are not powerless as adults. If someone hurts us now, we have the choice to confront them and seek their willingness to address the hurt. Or we have the choice to step away from that relationship, for the moment or for good. We did not have these choices as children; certainly we didn't have the choice to leave.

**Mack:** Sometimes it feels impossible to leave.

**Lou:** True. But the possibility exists. I want to mention something else before we move on. What you all experienced with Liz is something to really pay attention to. When one person in a group of people drops in to a deeper level, something happens within the whole group that is unexplainable but true; that person's openness causes each of you to either be more open or be more closed yourselves. If your ego is not too freaked out by the person's openness, you will find yourself spontaneously opening to a deeper place within yourself, and you will feel something of what that person is feeling in your own heart space. Many people here were clearly feeling what we typically call "moved" by Liz's experience. Her risk-taking made it safe for you to open. This is the power of a group that is deliberately looking to become more open, more authentic, and more conscious as a collective. One person's willingness to step into what the ego considers a "radioactive zone" inspires courage and willingness and a sense of safety in the rest of the group.

And the group can offer a special gift back to the individual. By being connected to the person's experience and in a sense feeling it along with that person, the group gives back a "yes, we see you and feel you." This response penetrates that person's experience with an energy that gives his/her experience "flesh and bones" it didn't have before. I have heard this experience described as "feeling felt." It "substantiates" that person's experience, literally gives it substance and makes it more real for the individual.

Or the opposite can happen for some folks. Some members of the group will find their egos assaulting them either with judgments about the person who took the risk (he/she is stupid, weak, crazy, etc.), or with shame, fear, and doubt about their own participation in such a group (you are a fool for being here and taking this seriously). These negative and destructive eruptions can be very powerful.

In a group of people who are truly seeking to be more open, authentic, and conscious, everyone's experience would be accepted and not judged. The understanding would be in place within the collective that everyone's conditioning (ego reactions) is automatic and not a choice, so there would be compassion for all responses, whether open or closed, negative or positive. It would be safe enough to do what we've been doing in this room—getting to know our egos, spotting them at work, and then "telling on" them to each other. And it would be safe enough to use personal awareness to connect with what was happening within us that lies outside of the ego's controlling and limiting reach.

This is actually the description of a group that has created a safe space within itself. It is a group committed to both more and more openness, authenticity, and awareness, and to the acceptance that our conditioned reactions to our movement in this direction are not in our control. These conditioned reactions of closing must be accepted as a part of the process of opening. Opening, deepening, and expanding are never going to be "once and for all," "all or nothing," "all at once," or a straight line.

Any questions?

**Gina:** You know what? All of a sudden I feel safe not feeling safe. I can hear my ego saying, "Don't buy this." But I got that in here I am allowed to be wherever I am in the moment, including feeling not safe. Weird. But that makes me feel safe. I am actually allowed to feel not safe if that is where I am. I don't have to pretend. Pretending makes me feel really unsafe.

**Lou:** Precisely. Despite how contradictory that may seem to our logical minds and how threatening it is to our egos, the only condition for deepening the experience of safety in a conversation is that you remain willing to share where you are as *your own* reaction and not impose it as "truth" on anybody else. This is critical for the maintenance of a "safe space" within the collective. So if you have a prejudiced or defensive reaction to a group member's experience, you need to share that reaction with the awareness that those reactions are your ego's and not your native self's. We need to adopt the perspective that our first reactions are most often far from the whole story and be willing to look under and beyond them, to open to our deeper feelings, intuitions, and insights.

This is a good place to fine-tune our understanding and exploration of your personal awareness—first of all, what it is, and then how to use it to separate yourself, your "me," from the conditioned reactions, beliefs, and behaviors of your ego. When that happens it becomes much more possible to contact the *source* of your unconditioned responses to whatever is happening in a given moment, to contact the "more of you" that is going on within you just below the level of awareness allowed by the ego. Liz let us witness an experience of doing just that.

This "source" is actually located within our bodies. It is there that the unedited version of our *experience* abides and emerges. We very much want to foster our ability to separate from the ego, and then foster our ability to touch into the *felt* experiences emanating from our unconditioned source of knowing. To do this we must become more and more proficient in the deliberate, conscious use of our personal awareness. If we practice using our personal awareness, it will help us both to find this source and not get diverted by the ego on the way to dropping into it. So I'm going to give you another document to read and then we will reconvene and continue our discussion from there.

# Section Two

My Truthplace and My Self

# chapter eight

# Using Personal Awareness to Expand Beyond the Grip of the Ego

"In the inner landscape of the soul is a nourishing and melodious voice of freedom always calling you. It encourages you to enlarge your frames of belonging—not to settle for a false shelter that does not serve your potential. There is no cage for the soul. Each of us should travel inwards from the surface constraints and visit the wild places within us. There are no small rooms there. Each of us needs the nourishment and healing of these inner clearances. One of the most crippling prisons is the prison of reduced identity.... Each one of us is inevitably involved in deciphering who we actually are. No other can answer that question for you. 'Who are you?' is a surface question that has vast, intricate rootage. Who are you behind your mask, your role? Who are you behind your words? Who are you when you are alone with yourself? In the middle of the night, when you awake, who are you then? When dawn rescues you from the rainforest of the night, who are you before you slip back safely beneath the mask and the name by which you are known during the day? It is one of the unnoticed achievements of daily life to keep the wild complexity of your real identity so well hidden that most people never suspect the worlds that collide in your heart. Friendship and love should be the safe regions where your unknown selves can come out and play. Instead of holding your friend or beloved limited within the neat cage of frightened identity, love should liberate both of you to celebrate the festival of complexity within you. We remain so frightened to enjoy the beauty of our own divinity.

"There are no manuals for the construction of the individual you would like to become. You are the only one who can decide this and take up the lifetime of work it demands. This is such a wonderful privilege and such an exciting an adventure. To grow into the person that your deepest longing desires is a great blessing. If you can find a creative harmony between your soul and your life, you will have found something infinitely precious. You may not be able to do much about the great problems of the world or to change the situation you are in, but if you can awaken the eternal beauty and light of your soul, you will bring light wherever you go. The gift of life is given to us for ourselves and also to bring peace, courage, and compassion to others."

—*The Cage of Frightened Identity* by John O'Donohue,
from "Eternal Echoes"

By using our personal awareness we can become more and more skilled "spotters" of our egos as they operate within us. But before we can even begin to develop this skill, we first needed to see for ourselves that there was more to us than meets the "I" as defined by our egos. We needed to experience some form of an un-mendable crack in the rigid, limited ego-identity we believed was "me." We needed to be dis-illusioned. *"I believed I already knew everything there was to know about myself. Now I know I don't know everything there is to know about myself. Now I know there is a lot more to me than I realized—more about me that I really like, and more about me that I really don't like. I also know that some things I believed about myself are not accurate. I now know that I most likely still hold false beliefs within me, and that there are discoveries about more of who I am that have yet to be made."*

We then needed to understand where this inaccurate self-perception, what we've called the "ego," came from, and to uncover the purpose it served and still serves. All three prior documents and all the dialogues in the workshop to this point have been dedicated primarily to uncovering and describing the ego, as well as dedicated to discovering that "I am not my ego; my ego is not "me"; it is not my native self. It is an altered version of my native self.

These documents constitute a kind of "ego owner's manual." We needed an "owner's manual" that describes the mechanics of the ego so we could see its machinery, cranking away inside of us from moment to moment, trying to control and limit our perception of ourselves. We needed a manual to help us bring our egos out of the shadows of our own unawareness and ignorance.

We needed this manual to aid us in becoming better at what I describe as "spotting and then telling on our egos." First we need to "see" our egos ourselves. But then we need to find others who are doing the same inner exploration. We need a community of "fellow travelers" to help each other fend off the ego's relentless and insidious methods of keeping us from seeing it. The ego wants to remain a "ghost in the machinery," unseen as it goes about its single-minded agenda. We need to tell each other about our egos, share with each other what we've spotted our egos doing. Remember, your ego hijacks your own thinking, creativity, and imagination for its own purposes; this makes it hard to see it as something that is not you. A group of conscious, compassionate "ego busters" can be a powerful aid to seeing what you may be blinded to about your own ego.

## "Seeing" and "Spotting" The Ego: Personal Awareness

Throughout these documents I have been talking about "seeing" the ego, and now in this one, I will talk about "spotting" the ego. What is it within us that has this capacity to "see" and "spot" the ego? It is what I have been calling our "personal awareness." The discovery and use of this personal awareness is as crucial to our personal and collective evolution as is the uncovering of the ego. So I want to make sure you are clear about what inner capacity I am pointing you towards by using the words "personal awareness."

First a bit about "awareness" in general. Let me see if I can describe some common experiences that might help you differentiate your personal awareness from your general or functional awareness.

People who have become comfortable driving a car will often experience, especially on long trips on a highway, that they can go on automatic pilot as far as driving goes. Their minds can range around and think of other things and indulge in a variety of fantasies but not necessarily be actually thinking about driving. When something happens on the road that's out of the ordinary, for example an animal crossing the road or a car veering out of its lane, your attention is instinctively and automatically pulled out of your thinking and fantasy world. Your attention becomes singularly focused on driving and managing your car and avoiding whatever needs to be avoided on the road. The placement of awareness in both parts of this example is not deliberately chosen. In one part it sort of "drifts along," following the trains of thought and fantasy. In the second part, it is "captured" by a sudden threat to physical safety.

In a similar way, we go through our day doing our work, having our conversations, eating our meals, partying, and not paying much if any attention to anything but whatever grabs our attention in the moment. Or, if nothing has grabbed our attention, then we sort of drift along in our mind's flow of thoughts and imaginings. It doesn't occur to us to deliberately expand our attention to include more of what we may be experiencing inside ourselves but which lies outside of our momentary surface awareness, to look, for example, for what feelings or intuitive senses might be arising just underneath our surface awareness. The great bulk of our attention and our awareness is captured by whatever is most compelling in the moment. There's no sense of directing our attention, deliberately or intentionally from one source of knowing to another, for example from thinking to feeling or from thinking to sensation, etc. Our attention is moved around for us.

Again, what shifts our attention is when something unusual, threatening, or extra pleasurable happens. Then our attention level shifts out of that automatic, drifting mode of awareness into something more alert, maybe more alarmed, or more interested. That shift is an internal experience, not just an external one. You are aware of that shift in a sharp, heightened way. But that shift to heightened awareness is also automatic, conditioned. It is not a deliberate choice. We might describe it as a more focused and alert awareness. But, even here, the focus is mostly on the *object* of our awareness, not the experience of the change in awareness itself. You might say our conscious awareness is always in the background of the object of our awareness. Typically we don't notice awareness; we notice a "something" within our awareness.

So these kinds of shifts in awareness do not involve deliberately *choosing* where you place your awareness. You are more aware of *something* that has grabbed your attention. Your awareness is more alert, but it happened automatically, instinctively, not by choice. These are passive, stimulus driven shifts in attention or focus.

Most of us don't realize we don't have to wait for some stimulus to heighten or direct our awareness. We don't realize that we do have *some* conscious control over the use of our own awareness. And if we do have some awareness of this control, we don't practice using it to explore our *internal* world. The heightened attention is kept for the external world and for our thoughts.

Most of us are not taught to become skillful in utilizing our awareness for a wider, deeper *exploration* of our *inner world*. Our childhoods were a long and intensive training period regarding the use of our awareness. Our native selves were trained where to place our awareness and from where to withdraw it. We were taught to shrink what is included in our awareness to fit the confines of tribal safety and acceptability. The natural curiosity and openness of our native selves to all of our experiences, both inner and outer, was significantly curbed. Typically we were taught to direct our awareness away from our interior experience. We were never taught to consciously and deliberately choose to place our personal awareness on our internal experiences. Thankfully, there is growing understanding that this ignorance about and avoidance of the deliberate use of our awareness to explore our internal world does not have to remain our fate. Witness the growing popularity of mindfulness training, including training for children at young ages.

The "piece" of awareness that is in our control is our "personal awareness." When we do consciously and deliberately choose to expand our awareness to include more of what's happening in a given moment, our experience of our own awareness changes. Now we experience that our awareness is not strictly stimulus-driven. Now the experience is of my "self" choosing how to use my awareness, where to place it, and what to include within it. My awareness now becomes a tool that I can actively apply for my own self-exploration, rather than something I simply passively experience. As many of you have probably discovered, the regular use of this tool leads to many valuable self-discoveries. It allows us to have more informed and fuller experiences of ourselves and of others, *in this moment* and on into the next. And as these more conscious moments accrue over time, our embodied sense of self becomes richer, deeper, and more substantial.

It turns out that by shifting our personal awareness to an internal focus, we discover our access to internal sources of guidance, such as our intuition and insight, our emotional intelligence, and our creativity, as well as other inner capacities. Access to our sources of internal guidance allows us to know and to follow the true course of our emerging authentic inner experience from moment to moment. This guidance is accessed by using our personal awareness to follow the flow of our own inner experiences *more deeply and more inclusively* from one moment to the next. This inner guidance allows us to know if we are relating to ourselves and to others in ways that are either on or off this true course. It is our guide on the path to consistent personal authenticity, authority, and compassion. Our personal awareness allows access to both the "unknown you" and the "suppressed you."

I will speak at length about this inner resource, which I call the Truth-Place, later. Right now I want to keep the focus on the use of our personal awareness. If you don't know what your personal awareness is and how to use it, then your awareness will always be at the mercy of the conditioned, compulsive, and limiting rules and regulations of your ego.

## Using Personal Awareness to Separate from the Ego

As we proceed, we need to remember that our egos do not want us to use our awareness to include *any* experiences that our egos believe endanger our acceptability or our standing in our tribes. The ego's job is to "protect" us from having or revealing any experience that it believes might jeopardize our being personally and interpersonally acceptable and safe. So if and when you do decide to deliberately place your awareness on any such "unacceptable and dangerous" internal experience, and if you actually make an effort to feel into it intimately with your awareness, your ego will try both to seduce your awareness away with rewards of good feelings as long as you obey its directive, or, failing that, to block your awareness by dosing you with feelings of shame, fear, and doubt, should you persist in disobeying its directive. The ego is not curious about anything outside of its safety zone.

I call the self that remains curious about finding out more about *whatever* we may be experiencing below the surface in a given moment the "native self." I do this to help distinguish this native, unconditioned self from our egos. It is this "self" that has the ability to use our personal awareness to widen and deepen our conscious experience from moment to moment, in spite of the efforts of the ego to stifle this expansion.

I want to describe as clearly as possible how what I'm suggesting we do with our awareness is different from what our awareness may already be doing automatically. I want to answer the question, "What specifically *is* this different way of using our own awareness that I am encouraging?"

In short, it is a way of deliberately and continuously expanding, in "this moment," *what we are including* in our awareness of our *internal* experience. The source of this internal experience is located within the trunk of our bodies, primarily inside the chest and belly areas of the body.

So it is an *extended*, deliberate use of our personal awareness, not just a "hit and run" use of awareness. It is a conscious practice. It begins by pausing and interrupting the automatic flow of experience, by waking up from the unnoticed, trance-like functional awareness that gets us around our day to day. It is in that pause that our personal awareness "pops back up" into our consciousness again. In that moment we realize, "Wow, I was running on automatic there for a while." "I" becomes more conscious. One way it might be experienced is, "Oh, I'm in here. I forgot." We have regained our personal awareness.

The next step in this practice is to deliberately place our awareness within the trunk of our bodies to include what we are experiencing in there, for a more extended period of time. The practice includes doing this on a regular, daily basis. "Looking" at your inner experience, inside your body, with this awareness has a more intimately personal quality than everyday functional awareness. You might call it a kind of "I-sight."

Many of you are familiar with a deliberate, conscious use of personal awareness from your meditation practices. The familiar meditation practice of placing your awareness on your breathing, and holding it there, rather than letting it stay in your thinking mind, is one way to deliberately use your own personal awareness. It's a way to free our awareness from the captivity of our constantly-thinking minds.

In the exercise I will invite you to do, we will place our personal awareness deliberately and for extended time periods on our experience inside our bodies. What do the words "inside our bodies" point to? As mentioned above, they point to experiences within an area of our bodies located primarily *in the chest and belly region*, although they are not limited exclusively to that location. This area of our bodies is the location of our emotions, feelings, intuitions, insights, sense of meaning, etc. It is where our own life-guidance system resides, and from where it speaks to us. There are many other ways you could direct your personal awareness, for example, to listen intimately to someone else. But for this exercise it will be directed inward within the body.

Several participants in the workshop have already done this deliberate "placing of awareness" within their bodies as we dialogued together, and they followed my suggestions to look into what they were feeling in a given moment. Feeling happens within the body, not within the head.

The use of our awareness in this deliberate and intimate way can only happen in "this moment." We can only expand our personal awareness to include more of our experience in *this moment*. We cannot expand our awareness to include "more" of our internal experience in a moment that is already over, or in one that isn't happening yet. We're not there now. We are here now. It is true that through our memory and imaginative functions we can take a past moment, bring it into our awareness in this moment, and re-visit it more consciously than we did in the original moment. And we can also create an imagined future moment. But in both cases we are doing so in this moment.

So we are speaking of a "moment to moment" method of personal discovery and "pathfinding." We are not talking about this method of inner exploration being used to answer such questions as, "What is the meaning of life?"; "What does the future hold for me?"; "How do I find enlightenment?"; or "Who am I?" These questions are for a philosophical inquiry or a deep meditation practice.

No. We are only exploring a way of discovering and knowing *more* about what we think, feel, believe, need, or want *in a given moment*; *more* about what really matters to us; more about the meaning of this moment to us; more about what satisfies and what frustrates us in this moment; more about what makes us feel safe and what makes us feel endangered inside our own skin and in our relationships, in *this moment...and on into the next.*

This is a way of discovering *more* than what we *already know* at first glance; more than what we are already conscious of *initially* in any given moment. We are exploring how *not* to be limited by our egos to running and skipping over the surface of one moment to the next. Instead, we are learning how to pause the flow of functional awareness in "this moment," and then use our personal awareness to "drop into" this moment more deeply, more inclusively, and more intimately. It takes practice using this method to experience its profound benefits.

## The "Dropping In" Exercise

Here is a simple instruction in how to "pause" and "drop in" to this moment:

- Until this moment your awareness has been focused through your eyes on reading this document and on the thinking mind in your head as you take in the words you are reading.

- First sit straight in your chair in a comfortable but erect way. Then take five nice full breaths in and full breaths out. Try to really feel the breath come in and go out of your belly and your chest.

- In the next moment, close your eyes and deliberately move your awareness away from your eyes and your head and down into your body. Take a few moments to make some felt contact with your body. You're not looking for anything in particular right now. You're just feeling the different sensations going on in your body as your awareness scans around all the different areas of your body.

- Now bring your awareness to your spine. Feel its presence in your body from the base up to the back of your head. Just move along the whole length of it with your awareness. Focus your awareness specifically on the back of your spine; feel along the length of it.

- Now bring your awareness around to the front of your spine and feel along the length of the front of your spine.

- Now move your awareness to the inside of your chest and belly, and with your awareness just notice whatever physical sensations may be happening there. Keep noticing physical sensations for a couple of minutes and then come back to reading the rest of the instruction.

- (Pause)
- Okay. What you experienced may end up being similar or very different from what anybody else may have experienced. There are a great variety of experiences possible inside our bodies, including an absence or numbness.
- Now I will ask you to do the same thing—that is move your awareness down into the trunk of your body, your chest and belly area—but this time use your awareness to notice what you may be feeling about doing this exercise. Close your eyes while doing this. Keep your awareness there in your body longer this time. If you find your thinking mind captures your awareness and takes it away from the trunk of your body and up into your head, just take your awareness back, and place it again inside the trunk of your body, and keep noticing what you may be *feeling* about doing this exercise. Notice what that feeling really feels like; feel the sensations that make it up. Get intimate with it. Keep placing your awareness into the feel of the feeling, the nuances of the feeling itself. After about five minutes come back to reading the instructions.
- (Pause)
- Okay. Again, there will be many different internal experiences discovered or uncovered as a result of using your awareness this way. Right now I am most interested in being as clear as possible about this "way," this method or practice, of using your awareness. This is the *method we will be using to separate from the internal grip of our egos and finding our way to a fuller contact with our inner experience.* This is the method for moving beyond the limiting grip of your ego in a given moment and dropping into contact with your own authentic experience, not just the experience that is edited for acceptability and safety by your ego.
- What you feel about using awareness this way can and will vary enormously. Maybe this time it felt stupid and useless or boring. Maybe you felt confused about using it. Maybe you had an insight as a result of using it. Maybe you fell asleep. Maybe your thinking

mind kept your awareness captive in your head and you never entered the trunk of your body. Maybe you touched feelings that felt too powerful and frightening to feel. Maybe it felt very familiar and comfortable as a method of using your awareness. Maybe you felt empty. Maybe you felt angry and frustrated. Maybe you felt like you failed some test. Maybe you felt peacefulness. Maybe you felt you became one with everything. Whatever you might have experienced, I just want to be clear that this is it. This *is* the method of expanding your awareness to include *more* of what you are experiencing internally in a given moment, and from one given moment to the next. This is the method I have been using in the Workshop and will be using going forward. There may be other methods you have used to "expand your awareness," but this is the one we are using here and we will be exploring in the dialogues in the workshop.

In a nutshell, this method of using your personal awareness has two steps: one, "pause" the narrowly focused automatic flow of your functional, surface awareness attending to your outside environment or the thoughts in your head; and two, "place" your regained personal awareness on the inside of the trunk of your body. There may be three steps. The third one being: keep taking charge of placing your awareness on the inside of your body for an extended period of time. Allow whatever is happening in the trunk of your body to keep arising into your awareness. This is an invitation to the deeper parts of you to speak to you—and they will. If you "visit" their neighborhood often enough and sit with patient, curious presence, the "residents" there will speak to you.

A caution: When using this method, at times, you will likely touch into feelings that can feel like they are too much to bear in a given moment. Kindness and gentleness toward yourself are absolutely necessary attitudes to hold in place as you do this kind of inner work. Permission to step away must always be present, otherwise the ego can take over this inner exploration and turn it into a torturous, shaming, terrorizing, and self-destructive process under the guise of doing "good," i.e. "perfect" self-exploration and self-discovery.

## More on "Spotting" Our Egos
## and "Telling on Them"

Our egos will never be gone, and they will never give up doing their job. As we discovered earlier, they never listen to reason and they don't give a damn about evidence to the contrary of what they believe is necessary for our interpersonal acceptability and safety.

However, we do need to absolutely "decriminalize" possessing an ego. Everyone has one. They come with the territory of being a dependent and vulnerable human being. They served a necessary protective function for our vulnerable, dependent selves in our early development. They were created to protect us from fully being and expressing ourselves at a time when fully being and expressing ourselves endangered our connection to those we depended upon for our continued existence. They were a necessary evil, if you will. We need to let go of any shame or judgment we may be carrying within us for having an ego, and for how it can rule us.

The "trick" with our egos is not to argue with them. What works best is to see them and "tell on them." To know my ego as "not me," but rather as something I possess, is the beginning of loosening its grip. It is the beginning of "possessing" an ego rather than "being possessed" by one. We need to become skilled in spotting them in action, to see what specific rules and regulations my own Seeker/Inflator/Convincer has decided are compulsory for me to follow, and to see exactly what my Critic/Terrorist/Doubter throws at me when I choose to challenge those rules and regulations. To name what our egos are doing and trying to accomplish is to continue to disempower them. Egos don't want to be seen, because if you "see" them you are already a bit separate from them. Our egos want us to stay merged with them. "Egos are us" would be their sales pitch. They want the "I" or "me" to be buried inside the experiences the ego creates or allows. They want us to be "m'egos."

Telling on your ego, both to yourself and to others, is a powerful consciousness-expanding practice. It is a practice of waking up from the ego-induced m'ego trance of no awareness of unawareness, of moving into a state of awake-ness to the existence of *both* awareness and unawareness, to the existence of *both* the known you and the unknown you, of *both* the "allowed" you and the "suppressed" you. In acknowledging, "I have an ego," and telling on it, i.e. "this is what my ego looks like, and this is how it is trying to control my awareness right in this moment," we paradoxically move out of the powerless position of our personal awareness being possessed and ruled by our egos and we move into the empowered position of consciously using our awareness both to see our egos and to step away from them. Consciously seeing and owning our egos and their efforts, and then sidestepping them, leaves us with way more options in living our lives than being unconscious of them and simply suffering the consequences of their relentless and compulsive directives.

We must become disillusioned from the delusional belief that we are totally free agents, making free choices based solely on reason and present circumstances, disillusioned from the belief that "what you see is what you get." We must be humble enough and courageous enough to admit when in a given moment our egos are in control of us. The ego will shame and terrorize you for doing this, but the more you do it, the less power that shame and fear has over you. In fact, down the road a bit, the ego's efforts can become something of a joke.

So as you may have already experienced, whenever you have used personal awareness in the method I described as "dropping in," you automatically bump into some activity of your ego. We all do. The ego doesn't even want you to *remember* that you have something called your "personal awareness," and that you can make choices about using it. To successfully move your personal awareness "down" into the home of your unknown or suppressed you, and then stay there for any length of time, you will need sharp inner eyes (I-sight) to spot the ego's diversionary and disruptive efforts to keep you away from that source of knowing. And we all will need the help of conscious "fellow travelers" to keep getting better at spotting and telling on our egos, and in finding ways of successfully tapping into and navigating our rich inner world.

# chapter nine

# What Do I See Inside Me With My Personal Awareness?

## Dialogues Continued

**Lou:** Okay. Welcome back. We will talk about your experiences of using your personal awareness to "drop in," and to "spot" and tell on your egos, both in the little exercise you just did and going forward, as we continue our conversation together. The experiences you share here will give us some practice in being clear about using our personal awareness. Your experiences will also give us some practice in distinguishing which inner experiences would fall under the heading of the "native self" and which would fall under the heading of the "ego."

I think a useful way to start would be just to go around the room and have each person describe what they experienced when they did the awareness exercise in the document.

**Gina:** I had a really hard time getting out of my head. I kept thinking about whether I understood the instruction or not and questioning if I was doing it right. I got confused about whether the trunk of my body meant the outside of the trunk or only the inside, and what was inside and what was outside. All I could feel in the trunk of my body was tension.

**Gabe:** Me too. I felt this kind of thick sensation in my head, like it was stuffed with something dense. It was sort of repellant. I didn't want to feel it. Thinking was more interesting. I don't think I got my awareness down to my trunk at all—maybe just to feel some tension, like Gina.

**Willa:** After a bit of back and forth between my thinking and my body, in the second dropping in it felt like just for a moment something settled, a deep breath came, and I felt very relaxed and at ease. I felt a warmth and connection toward everybody in the room. I realized I *felt* safe. And then in the next moment I got a jolt of anxiety right beneath my breastbone, and that brought me back to the outside.

**Frank:** I've never understood what "going inside" meant, except to see what I thought. It was helpful to have a location for "inside." But I had a lot of trouble finding my awareness to put it anywhere. You know what I mean? I got caught up in trying to figure out what my awareness is!

**Stew:** My awareness kept getting pulled into other parts of my body. My legs and my arms and my hands got all jumpy with energy and wanted to move or shake or do something. I don't know how to describe it other than jumpy. I was thinking, too. Mostly I was thinking, "When is this going to be over?"

**Liz:** The first "dropping in" was too quick for me to have much of a reaction. In the second one I felt really uncomfortable, a jumble of feelings, kind of swirling around, all mixed up together. I couldn't sort anything out. And then this thought popped up—"you miss him" the "him" being an ex-boyfriend. And I started crying again. But it wasn't bad. It was kind of peaceful—sad and peaceful.

**Lucas:** Both times were very quiet for me, like a big stillness. My head kind of worried about it, but mostly I just felt the quietness.

**Mack:** I couldn't much get out of my head. I kept thinking about my wife, or fantasizing about her, imagining her with another guy. When I tried to put my awareness in my chest or belly I could only keep it there for a couple of seconds. But I know I mostly felt fear and anger, and I wanted to quit the exercise.

**Matt:** The first "drop in" was just being present to my breathing. I didn't want to stop the second one. In my meditation practice I try to just let everything go—feelings, thoughts, insights, whatever. When I meditate, I really practice coming back to the breath and staying there. So this was different for me. I used my breath as a focus to begin with, which of course is in my chest where you asked us to put our awareness, but I let my awareness move out from just my lungs to the rest of my chest and my belly and just let it stay there in that bigger inner space.

Well what happened next was quite amazing. I had a series of insights about my relationship with my oldest kid. He's twelve. The first one was that I was afraid of him! And I saw how embarrassed I was about that; like I'm the adult and I'm not supposed to be threatened by my twelve-year-old kid. But I just let it be so and the next realization was that he can hurt me, hurt my heart, and that was what I was afraid of. But again, like I wasn't supposed to be vulnerable to a twelve-year-old. And then I saw that he really matters to me. In my heart he matters to me, but he acts towards me like I don't matter to him, that what goes on in my heart, the feelings in my heart, do not matter to him in his heart. It felt like he was deliberately making a point of not letting my feelings matter.

I know there is more about this, but then I stopped. And, you know, those were really upsetting discoveries, but I felt relieved to know, to really know what I feel about him and let it be. It's like now I can actually look at what I want to do about what the truth of my relationship to him is instead of trying *not* to be in the actual relationship I have with him. That was a lot to get in a few minutes.


**Mary:** I was really surprised by what happened to me. In both "drop ins," almost immediately an image of the sacred heart of Jesus appeared in my mind's eye. I don't know if it was in my body but it was really quite vivid. Some of you may not be familiar with image. It is a picture of a heart with a crown of thorns around it, and flames coming out of the top of it and a small cross sitting just above the flames. Often there is a light all around the heart. That was what I "saw." As I looked at it in the second "drop in" I felt a bunch of different feelings, besides surprise—fear, hope, a little awe, confusion, wanting it not to be a Catholic thing, shame. A bunch. I have no idea what it means.

**Willa:** During the second, after a little while of being distracted by my thinking, at first I felt into a place in my chest, around the breastbone, where a lot of what felt like squeezing and squirming was going on. I stayed with that sensation and I felt it translate into a feeling of urgency, a pushing out, almost like a physical seeking or "trying" of some sort. It felt really, really familiar, like that feeling is almost always there. And then that feeling of warmth and connection came. Like Matt said, initially squeezing and squirming was not a pleasant feeling at all but I liked knowing it, if that makes sense. I felt stronger or safer or something. I still feel that.

**Lou:** Okay. So there were a lot of different experiences. I want to be really clear that what you *experience* as a result of using this simple method is different from the method itself. Some of you were not even sure you were "doing" the method, either at all or properly. Others used the method and had experiences that were more or less compelling. These were a mix of native self experiences and interfering experiences generated by the ego. Any of these experiences of using the method could set you up with expectations about what the method can or cannot do the next time you use it, or discourage you completely from using it again.

In either case, your attention will be taken away from simply applying the method and seeing what happens, without either negative or positive expectations. Expectations are natural, but they are in your head, in your imagination, and paying attention to *them* the next time you "drop in" is not placing your awareness in your body, which is the method. Running with the thoughts or fantasies in your head is not being more present in *this* moment, being more inclusively present to what is happening *now*. It is being in an imagined past or future experience. The next time you use it, you could end up surprised again or disappointed, bored or engaged with something emerging from within, numb or amazed. The key is in letting go of what was so a moment ago and letting your awareness receive whatever comes, whatever emerges, from within your body right now—and then in the next "right now."

For those of you that felt you didn't do it right, or didn't experience anything meaningful, or experienced something unpleasant, you would naturally be less motivated to use the method again. Who wants to sit and fool around with something called awareness and just experience tension, confusion, or inadequacy, right? So if you are going to decide to use it again, it will have to be more on blind faith than it will be for those who found the method opened them up to something meaningful. So Tina, Gabe, Frank, and Stew your experiences are common, and it is important to understand they are not failures but part of a learning and discovery process, or a skill building process, and they are also the effects of the ego at work blocking access to your TruthPlace.

Most people are confused initially about what "my awareness" is. Like when Frank said he felt he couldn't "find" it, most people don't think there is anything about awareness to find. We experience it as a condition. When we are sleeping we are not aware and when we are awake we are. Awareness is not a "something" we have a say about. It is there or it is not. You're in a coma or you're not. There is no choice involved. Even in the notion of "paying attention or not," we don't think of choice. If we were not paying attention it is "because" our attention (awareness) was distracted by something else, or we were sleepy, or bored, or something else outside of our choosing. Awareness is seen as kind of passive and reactive. It goes wherever the strongest call is coming from. And this is very accurate, just not the whole story.

This is what I earlier called "functional or surface or general awareness." It might also be called "simple" or "ever-present," and we experience it as "just there." The experience is more like it follows us around or accompanies us. So wherever I direct my eyes, ears, or touch, awareness is there, so I see or hear or feel whatever I'm "pointing" my senses at. We don't think about these movements of attention as choices about where we are placing our "awareness" but as choices about what we are doing with our senses.

If you think of awareness as the light in a room, we don't look at the light; we look at what is lit up. So most often what we call our "awareness" is very bound up in, or merged with, experiencing experiences but not in noticing the awareness that allows us to experience the experience. We just go from experience to experience not noticing the "light," and we take that as the end of the story about awareness. And our egos want to make sure that this ending of the story remains unchanged.

It turns out this is very far from the end of the story. Becoming aware that awareness is a very real "something" that has very particular qualities is an unfolding story once you discover its accuracy. The discovery that we can have a direct say about where we place it in our outside and in our inside worlds is a turning point in how we can experience and live our lives. And it is a direct challenge to our ego's exclusive control of where our awareness can go within us and what it can include.

Our egos are like herders and hoarders of our access to awareness. They create pens and prisons, hydraulic and plumbing systems, architectural structures, and policing and rewarding systems that hold awareness and direct its flow. The S/I/C and C/T/D are examples. The ego also wants to be sure you are not using your awareness to be aware of the ego *itself*. Once you are aware of the ego, you have the potential of escaping its grip, its control—you've pulled the curtain on the Wizard Ego and it is seen for what it is: a bunch of conditioned survival strategies posing as a "self" and not our true "I."

So in my book, "finding" access to your *personal* awareness and discovering you can move it around inside of you is a very big deal. It opens a lot of doors. So, Frank, I want to spend a moment with you if you're willing to see if we can clarify together what we're pointing to with the word "awareness," okay?

**Frank:** Sure.

**Lou:** And Gina, Gabe, and Stew, this may help clear things up for you, too. So, Frank, my take is that your experience is a good example of your Doubter deep at work within you. I think your ego decided a long time ago that it was dangerous for you to allow into your awareness many painful, scary feelings you felt as a child. And it found ways to keep your awareness out of your body. This is where these feelings are felt. And it wants to continue to do so. So enter the Doubter. It made you doubt you could find your own awareness so you couldn't take it down into your body. Let's see if we can bust the Doubter's grip and get clear what we are calling "your awareness"—not by talking about it, but by helping you find it, experience it. So the instruction was simply to place your awareness inside your chest/belly area, right? Without looking, if you close your eyes, can you point to where your chest and belly are in your body? Just point with your finger.

**Frank:** (Points)

**Lou:** Now were you able to point correctly because you remembered in your mind that was where your chest and belly are or because you could feel their location?

**Frank:** Maybe a bit of both.

**Lou:** So at least in part you could locate your chest and belly by feeling them?

**Frank:** Yes.

**Lou:** That experience of feeling your chest and belly is following the instruction to place your awareness inside your chest and belly area.

**Frank:** That's it!?

**Lou:** Yes.

**Frank:** But that's nothing!

**Lou:** Yes. It feels like nothing, purposeless, even stupid. But it is actually not "nothing." You did deliberately move your own personal awareness to somewhere other than your thinking, did you not?

**Frank:** Hmmm. I think I'm seeing what you mean.

**Lou:** The trouble with "awareness" as a "something" is it feels like a "nothing." And it *is* a "no thing." It is not a physical thing that you can touch or see. So it is an easy target for the Doubter. But it is a something. And we can deliberately re-locate it, so to speak, to and from different places internally.

**Frank:** Yes.

**Lou:** Let me share an experience with you that is like the one you just had. It was one of many early experiences I had of discovering my own personal awareness and taking control of it back from my ego, and specifically my Doubter. For a bunch of reasons in my history, my ego decided that minimizing the amount of awareness I had of my body and its senses was a good idea for my interpersonal safety. I'm not going to go into all the details of that history right now. I'll just give one example of my ego at work suppressing awareness of my senses.

In my late twenties I worked in a hospital in New York City. One day as I was walking from one location in the hospital to another, the thought struck me, "I can't feel my feet," I was shocked and puzzled. To my rational, logical mind, the thought didn't make sense. I deduced, and I mean logically *deduced*, that I must be able to feel my feet since I am successfully walking from one place to another. I'm not tripping and falling down. But I doubted I could feel them. And I believed that doubt. I did not know at that moment that I could move my awareness down into my feet and feel them. I could only deduce or "think" that my feet must be feeling the floor or I would have tripped and fallen. All this was happening up in my head.

It then struck me: "This is crazy. 'I' *can't feel* 'my' feet??!! They're mine! They're attached to my body. I must be able to feel them." And so without any instruction, I started to explore around in my body to see if I could "get down" to my feet and feel them. It helped to move them a bit. And I discovered I *could* feel my feet. It was kind of like "duh," but also like a minor revelation. The consciousness of it, the deliberateness, and, in some sense, the intimacy or personal-ness of it was a revelation. It was a bit like consciously owning my feet for the first time. Does that make any sense?

**Frank:** That's crazy! For sure it makes *me* feel not so strange. And it helps me get what we're after here, I mean with this method. I mean, in a way it's not even a method; it's just realizing you have some choice over where you put your awareness and then choosing to do it.

**Lou:** Exactly. And it is crazy. Believe it our not I had to do the same thing with my eyes, with my voice, and with thinking for myself. But that's another story.

**Stew:** Wow! You mentioned the intimacy of it. I like that. Sounds sexy.

**Lou:** Sometimes it is. You can consciously place your awareness on your sexual experience and as a result feel your sexuality more fully. You can place your awareness anywhere. The spreading of the practice called "mindfulness" has popularized this knowing. But here we are talking about placing it in a particular area of the body. You had trouble keeping your awareness in your chest and belly area because of the pull of sensations in other parts of your body. Having difficulty keeping our awareness deliberately in one place is par for the course. So can you locate your awareness in your chest and belly area?

**Stew:** Sure. It was just difficult keeping it there for more than a few seconds.

**Lou:** For some people, body sensations have more of a pull on their awareness than thoughts do, or at least have as much pull. You strike me as a guy whose ego has always thought bodily sensations are a really good thing—at least the pleasurable ones, and maybe especially the sexual ones.

**Stew:** Being a highly sexual guy has always been an ego trip for me. I love it. I love playing with it and blowing people's minds with it. I love turning women on. It turns me on, and it does make me feel powerful and really cool.

**Lou:** Your pleasure and ease with your sexuality is a strength for you. You could say it has a lot of positive meaning for you. It gives you lots of good feelings about yourself as a man, as well as a lot of physical pleasure. That's simple native self stuff, not ego stuff.

**Stew:** You said it right. But what do you mean not ego stuff?

**Lou:** The ego's involvement in your experience could be your Seeker at work. Let's say your ego, and specifically your Seeker, believes that being sexual is a safe and acceptable way of sustaining and enhancing your membership in your tribe. Then your ego will certainly use that experience to bolster your membership. But perhaps more importantly, it will also use sexual experience to keep you away from experiences that endanger your standing in your tribe. This is an example of the ego using simple natural, native self, pleasures for its own agenda.

So what is relevant here is that if you place your awareness in your chest/belly area, and there are feelings or knowings that emerge there that your ego has a problem with, your ego will probably use your sexual feelings to distract you from keeping your awareness on those unacceptable feelings, just like the ego uses people's thinking, attachment to power, admiration, wealth, goodness, or whatever to pull their awareness away from unacceptable or frightening internal experiences. Your ego will compulsively use whatever it can to stop you from including in your awareness whatever it considers unacceptable and dangerous. Your experience could be an example of the Seeker/Inflator/Convincer doing its job of keeping you away from contact with the Truthplace. It automatically and rigidly keeps you seeking the sensual pleasure and convincing you this is the place to keep your awareness.

So like I said to Frank, it is not unusual to have difficulty keeping your awareness anywhere or on anything except what your ego has already deemed "good" or acceptable, and what makes you feel interpersonally valued and, therefore, safe.

**Stew:** So any stuff that might hurt my image of myself is a "no-no" to my ego.

**Lou:** Right. And your ego is going to try to beat you to the punch, too. It wants to stop you from looking inside yourself before anything unacceptable even has a chance to pop up in your awareness. Don't even go inside. Don't look in there. Just keep your attention on what your ego has already decided is acceptable. That's why turning our awareness inside of ourselves is such an uncommon and foreign thing for most of us to do. It never occurs to most people, and if it does it seems like a pointless and/or simply uncomfortable thing to do. Why bother? "Don't dwell on your feelings." How often have you heard that comment? Many people even see pausing to look inside ourselves as an invitation to the devil or to evil thoughts. Keep busy, keep doing stuff, don't look inside. "Idle hands are the devil's workshop." Culturally we are largely opposed to what we might call "emotional introspection," what some would disparagingly call "navel-gazing." We will introspect intellectually (maybe) but not emotionally. Even the word "emotion" is degraded. It is a lessor realm of experience than the rational realm. Feeling is childish, primitive, or "feminine," in the negative sense of that adjective. Thinking is adult, evolved.

By moving your awareness inside yourself you are actually opening yourself to so much more than what the culture would call "emotions." You are accessing a form of knowing, a source of knowledge, that is just as important for our survival and wellbeing as our rational knowledge or our intellectual memory are. As just one example of the importance of this internal 'non-rational' (not irrational) knowledge, it is the source of knowing the truth, without the shadow of a doubt, that, in regard to this adventure of living, we are all in this together. Until we know this in our own hearts and guts, we will continue to do harm to each other and our environment. The intellectual knowledge of this is not enough to produce a sufficient change in our behavior. We have to feel the truth of it in our chest and bellies.

But this is a glimpse of the larger meaning of what we are doing here. There's no need at the moment to get into the bigger implications. Let's stay with the meaning of this use of your personal awareness to "drop in," and for spotting and telling on your egos, for each of you.

So, Gabe and Gina, you both expressed some difficulty or confusion with using your awareness this way. But if I remember right, you both said you felt tension in your chest. So it sounds like you were able to locate your awareness in the chest area. Is that right?

**Gina:** I think so. I mean I did feel the tension there. But I felt so confused. My mind was spinning around and I felt really nervous about doing it right. I also felt nervous about what I might see if I looked inside.

**Lou:** So confusion, judgments, and fear. You know, it figures given the nature of your ego. Your ego, like everyone else's, does not want you to find your own unedited experience. So it will use its standard ways of disrupting any attempt to place your awareness where that experience lives, like inside your chest and belly area. Your particular ego believes it's safest to never feel safe and to never trust your own authority, safest to stay in doubt and to always be wary. So your Terrorist and your Doubter were really pushing you around inside.

Remember, the ego never learns, never changes its "mind." It is unable to process current reality. So it doesn't care that you may reap great benefits to your survival and wellbeing from becoming more intimate with your own inner experience of yourself. So it is going to keep you confused, scared, and doubtful as much as it can. It will pull your awareness into those thoughts, beliefs, and feelings and away from inside your body.

It will also make you feel confused and doubtful about what I am saying right now. So I am going to suggest that, as much as possible, we don't rely so much on concepts and thinking and ideas and stick as close to concrete experience as we can. I would like to go back to the actual practice of you using your awareness by placing it in or on your chest/belly area. If you don't want to right now, that's okay. We can always come back to you later if you change your mind. And as a good ego-challenging practice for you, answer with a simple "yes" or "no." Can and will you do that?

**Gina:** Yes. (Squirming around in her chair)

**Lou:** So do you want to try it now?

**Gina:** No. (Clearly restraining herself from saying more)

**Lou:** Okay. Shall we come back to you later to see if you want to then?

**Gina:** Yes.

**Lou:** Beautiful. So, Gabe, you felt a thick sensation in your head that you didn't like, and if you felt anything in your chest it was some tension, like Gina. Right?

**Gabe:** Lots of fun. I must say I am finding this whole conversation incredibly aggravating and boring. This whole deal feels to me like much ado about nothing. I'm not saying I won't play, although at this point I am really not sure why. I guess I have to admit I am finding stuff about me that I didn't know was there, like the feeling in my head and the tension in my chest, but it's like "so what?" Other folks seem to have found something meaningful or pleasant for them, so I'm holding the possibility that I might too. But, Jesus, this really seems pointless to me right now.

**Lou:** I am glad to hear that "right now" you just said. If you or anybody is going to discover whatever there is to discover using your awareness this way, we have to be willing to accept that what we discover in any given moment is just for "right now" and is not the end of the story. There is going to be resistance to using this method. Your particular ego, your Seeker, believes that being rational, logical, an independent thinker/decider, in control of your feelings, is the only acceptable way to be. It is not surprising that it would seek to keep you up in your head, keep your awareness up there, and keep you being logical and rational. Our unconditioned, unedited experience is not in our control, or the ego's. It is a spontaneous discovery of fresh insight and intuition. It can and will challenge old knowledge, old conclusions, and old convictions. It can produce surprises in regard to self-discovery. The ego will have none of this. Your old egoic way of operating has had some benefits, but it has cost you substantially. That's really why you are here.

So to test this method out for yourself you're going to have to be patient and diligent in behalf of giving yourself a chance to discover its power and value—again, somewhat on blind faith. Reclaiming ownership of your personal awareness is a kind of an internal battle for most of us. And your Critic will give you a hard time for being willing to stay and explore. It's likely to give me a hard time also.

**Gabe:** You said it! But that's also why I'm sticking. Using your Normandy Beach analogy, I guess you could say I've been a Nazi sympathizer without really knowing it. I don't want to do that. But it's hard to give up that allegiance to rationality.

**Lou:** It's giving up a *compulsive, rigid, and monolithic* allegiance to rationality, an allegiance that demands the *exclusion and degradation* of any other sources of knowing. Rationality and logic are always available when useful. It's just that we are disempowered and diminished as persons if we are not allowed to access *all* our ways of knowing our truth moment to moment.

**Gabe:** Thinking of internal feelings as "other sources of knowing" helps me find some value in them.

**Lou:** Good. They truly are. Do you want to try the practice again just to make sure you know you can move your own awareness around in your body?

**Gabe:** No. I know I can do it. There's just a lot of noise from my ego to contend with.

**Lou:** Great. Gina, do you want to revisit your experience of the practice?

**Gina:** I've just had an amazing few minutes while you were talking with Gabe. First of all it was *incredibly* difficult for me to just say "yes" or "no" to your questions without giving a whole explanation...justification really. I just want to say that. Incredibly difficult! It left me reverberating so much inside I wasn't paying attention to your conversation with Gabe. And then I remembered you saying to yourself that it was crazy that you couldn't feel your feet and I just said to myself, "of course I can feel my chest," and I put my awareness right there without any trouble and I felt this little surge of joy right in my heart, like a "yes, yes you can." I felt happy about this little recovery. That's what it felt like—a little recovery of myself, of my will, of my own permission to decide about my own powers, you know? To decide what I do with my own abilities. Seems silly in a way to make such a big deal out of such a little thing, but it felt really important...period!

**Lou:** (laughing) I love that "period!" It just *felt* important, period. No need to explain or justify! *You* know it. That's good enough. That's what accessing your true inner experience feels like. You simply know whatever arises from there is true...period. It's not so important whether the discovery is "big" or "small." What matters most is that *you know* it's true...*period*. And that it had meaning for you! And that you know you have a place inside you that you can choose to turn to that is a trustworthy source of knowing exactly what is so for you in this given moment. That's not an ego experience. That's a native self experience. And your joy in what you called "a recovery of self" is a feeling that arises when our need to be true to ourselves is met. You are recovering your true autonomy from the ego's oppression of it, from the ego's scaring it to death. Allowing the emergence from within of some true self knowing, and claiming it, brings feelings of joy and pride and freedom and dignity...in the moment.

This reminds me of a conversation I had with a client the other day. We were talking about his desire to be more authentic when he spoke about himself in his AA meetings. He found himself rehearsing what he wanted to say before he said it and he felt that was not being spontaneous, or real. It was not being true to himself. His sharing was too prepared and focused on his need to be seen in a good light by the group.

I suggested that he could simply share *that.* Just reveal that what is true for him in the moment is that ego-need to rehearse. He could feel that doing that felt risky, like he might be judged for that as being an inauthentic person, a fake. I said that he might be; that's the risk of being yourself in certain moments, the risk of "telling on your ego" when it has a grip on you. And then I said something that I think struck me even more deeply than it struck him.

I said: "The only 'self' we ever have is the one that is happening in this moment." I found myself laughing at the obviousness and accuracy of that statement. For me, it was like, at least in that moment, I had let go of seeking for my "real" self, or for any version of a "better" self. I realized that seeking was unreal, that the only "self" that is ever real is whatever version of self I am experiencing in this very moment. *Period.*

I also realized that the *only* thing about my experience of myself that I had *any* real say about was just how much I *opened* my own awareness to include all the nuances of the experience of the "self" that I was having in a given moment. That's it. Period. Whether I like it or not. Opened, closed, enlightened, endarkened, loving, hateful, peaceful, fearful, whatever. End of story. I could then choose to share that with someone else or not. Moving in the direction of hiding or denying what was so in the moment was the ego at work. If I "spotted" that my ego was controlling my experience of myself in a given moment, okay. Then that was the "self" I got to be in that moment, a "self" whose ego is in charge of my experience in this moment. I can see it and I can name it, and then I can "tell on it" to someone else if I choose to. Being truly authentic is about letting whatever is so about myself in a given moment be exactly the way it is. Period.

Like you, Gina, those were experiences with a "period" on the end of them for me. You actually did exactly what I was just now describing realizing. Without putting my words on it. You just *did* it. You didn't have to think about what you were doing. You sat in your chair being with the "self" you were experiencing in that moment. a self that was "reverberating," in your words. It was probably not very comfortable, but you kept your own personal awareness open to that very experience, to exactly what was so for you in the moment. That is the only power we have in regard to "being ourselves" in any given moment.

And there is no predicting what will happen next when we exercise that power. What happened to you? A "knowing" popped up from your inner truth place. A direct experience of knowing, "Yes, I can. I can choose to place my awareness somewhere in particular." No doubt. And you did. And then you experienced what emerged within you next: a "surge of joy," a happy feeling, a sense of a small bit of "self" recovery, of personal empowerment, an experience of *self-possession and autonomy*. It is true that the experience that followed your choice to place your awareness in your chest could have been very different. But you got what you got, in that moment of using your awareness. Like I said, there is no predicting. We can predict that in any given moment you will always get something, even if it feels like "nothing," and then, in the next moment, something more or something different. So it goes.

**Gina:** Well great. I don't know if I get all that. But it doesn't matter. Like you say, "I got what I got" and that's fine with me.

**Lou:** Perfect. Or maybe "period." Do any of the others want to explore their experience of using their awareness?

**Willa:** Yes. I feel pleased with my experience but doubtful at the same time. I'm a little perplexed with experiencing something that felt so safe in one moment and then so anxious in the next. I sort of don't know what to make of it.

**Lou:** Why make anything of it?

**Willa:** Well, I don't know. Maybe I'm just saying I liked feeling safe and didn't like feeling afraid.

**Lou:** Can you check with yourself and see if that's true and not a "maybe?"

**Willa:** That's true. But it feels like there's something more. I think I want to know where I'm going with this "dropping in" business. Where is it taking me? What's going to happen? And, maybe, why do it if it's not going somewhere good?

**Lou:** Valid questions. Really, like what's its usefulness to you? Especially if it may at times be uncomfortable to do, right? Like Gabe is exploring. Like everyone is really.

**Willa:** Yeah.

**Lou:** Obviously those of you who are somewhat new to a body-based method like this are going to have to experience that using your awareness this way produces enough value for you or you won't continue to do it; nobody will. The difficulty with this is that not only is there a learning curve involved, like with any new practice, but there is also a conditioned aversion to the practice itself that arises regularly. The C/T/D can fill you with doubt and fear and shame about doing the practice and demotivate you. So the willingness, the courage, and the patience to do the practice may be hard to come by in the beginning, and maybe even more so at different, particular times as you practice over a lifetime.

As you all know, an interest in doing this practice at all, let alone a sustained one, does not arise to begin with unless some experience or set of experiences has in some way pushed your ego's management system beyond its capacity to control your image of yourself and your sense of acceptability and safety. And as a result you've now got things going on inside of you that you were not aware of before, positive or negative. And you're trying to manage and make sense of this change, and maybe having trouble doing so. Some of the experiences that emerge from within our hearts and bellies can feel frightening and shameful; some can feel like blessings and healings. The method is the method regardless of what you discover or what arises. Part of the learning curve is discovering how to use the method with courage, compassion, and care, and asking for help when you need it, particularly when really difficult encounters occur with internal traumas and emotional wounds.

Or maybe you've been on this path of self-discovery and "uncovering" for a while already, and you keep bumping into your ego over and over again. It can be discouraging. The ego is as clever and creative and intelligent as we are. It uses our native capacities for its own agenda. In the psychotherapeutic world there is a saying: "Intelligence complicates psychopathology." The saying is a nod to how our interpersonal survival strategies can be rationalized and defended in elaborately creative and "reasonable" ways even when they have ceased to be acting in our best interests—in fact even when they are destroying us.

**Lucas:** It's been interesting listening. The peacefulness, or quiet, I felt during the exercise hasn't left me. I was able to empathize with everybody's experiences, really kind of feel them, and yet not lose that stillness. I found it really valuable, like everyone was doing some exploring for me, letting me know some of the stuff that might come up. And I felt no doubt or fear about my stillness. It feels real, a kind of presence. Speaking about it right now some fear comes up about losing it, but I know it's in me. I feel more trusting that I can find it again if I lose it. And if the practice of dropping in is helpful in that way, I'm grateful for knowing it.

**Lou:** I'm glad for you. You have dropped into a relatively ego-free space inside your native self. And in that space the qualities of peacefulness, stillness, and empathy spontaneously effortlessly arise.

**Liz:** I'd like to talk about my experience a little. I said I felt sad and peaceful about missing my boyfriend. I realized as you were talking with the others that I felt safe inside, too. It was not an emergency to miss him, you know? I felt really sad but not scared. I didn't think that was possible, like I was all right without him, just not happy. And, you know, as I'm talking right now I have this sense of liking myself, of caring about myself, like a friend might, you know? That's a surprise too. Jesus, what a nice feeling that is. And like Lucas, talking about it also brings the fear of losing it. I would be really unhappy about that. I can feel right now how much I don't want that to happen and that it's happening a bit as I speak. Shit.

**Lou:** Try taking a breath...and consider the possibility that it is not an emergency if you lose it, if your ego shuts it down. Let it go if it goes.

**Liz:** Hmmm. Interesting. Hmmm....I'm feeling some of that spaciousness I talked about before.

**Lou:** Again I made a suggestion and with your personal awareness you took it inside and let it touch you there. You might not have been able to do that and then you would have had a different experience—*what* we don't know, but different. You used your awareness to be inside and be with my suggestion. And then you had the experience you had—spaciousness. The practice is being willing to keep your awareness placed in your body, in the knowing of your body, not your head, and not your ego. It is in the ego's nature to hold onto any experience that makes you feel safe, to try to control that experience and prevent it from ending.

Your ego is going to create the feeling of emergency every time there is an experience that it cannot control, that it can't either hold onto or push away, depending. Being out of control of your internal experience is always an emergency, as well as shameful, for the ego. Your native self and your personal awareness know it's not an emergency and know that the ego will create the feeling that it is. Your native self and personal awareness allow both knowings to co-exist, are present to both, are "still" with both realities, when both are there.

**Liz:** I'm confused about this "native self" dude.

**Lou:** It's just a name I use for whatever it is in you and me that remembers it can use its own awareness in the way we are practicing. There is more to it than just that, but that's a sufficient description for our purposes right now. Right now I want to come back to the discovery of inside safety you made and tie it into Matt's experience of internal relief in knowing the "awful truth" about his relationship with his son.

It seems that when we manage to sidestep the ego and drop in, to settle into this place in our bodies, no matter what we discover or what is revealed, there is a sense of "no emergency," a sense of a kind of safety and all-rightness that abides there. This is a lovely surprise every time it is rediscovered freshly in a given moment. What we discover within may have urgency to it, even real destructive potential, but somehow the knowing of it from within the source of our true feelings, the source I call our "TruthPlace," and not from the ego's perspective, embodies a trust in our capacity to know what to do and how to respond in real time, again, a sense that I'm all right even though I've got some serious shit to deal with.

This is the opposite of Mack's experience of being tortured by thoughts and images and fantasies of his wife's abandoning and betraying him—definitely an emergency. According to his ego, Mack is definitely not all right unless his wife loves him and is faithful to him. And also according to his ego, Mack is weak and worthy of shame for needing his wife the way he does. This is the ego creating the experience of an emergency and shaming its host both coming and going, the C/T/D at work, convincing Mack that if she abandons him he is worthless, and his acceptability to himself and his tribe is seriously endangered, and if he needs her approval, the same.

This difference in response, between the ego and the Truthplace, regarding a challenge both to our interpersonal dependency needs and to our need to be true to our separate, authentic selves can be quite striking. Since your experiences capture this difference, if it's all right with you Mack, and with Liz and Matt, I would like to explore in real time the difference this difference makes in our capacity to respond when we feel threatened in a relationship.

**Liz, Matt, Mack:** (All agree)

**Lou:** Good. So Matt, when you described your experience it sounded to me like you were able to keep sidestepping the Critic and just be with the truth of what you felt. The Critic kept saying you "shouldn't" feel what you felt, but you were able to slip past the grip of any embarrassment or shame it threw at you.

**Matt:** It's funny. You're right, but I would not have focused on that as important. What I found out, what stuck with me, was not so much *how* I got there but *what* I found there. But now that you mention it, I can see that on another occasion my need to avoid the feeling of shame would have diverted my attention or just stopped me from keeping on "dropping into" what I was discovering I felt. I see it's helped me to grasp that shame is a disrupter of my relationship to myself and is an enemy, that it does not protect me, it actually harms me when the Critic uses it. So now when it comes up I don't seem to be so afraid of it and I can act against it inside—sort of like disobey it.

**Lou:** Yes! That's a great way to put it. You are in fact disobeying your ego's rules and regulations, both by not doing or being the way your Seeker/Inflator/Convincer says you have to be, and then by not letting the Critic, the Terrorist, or the Doubter bully you around inside by using feelings of shame, fear, and doubt. Of course, sometimes the feelings the ego creates inside us will be so powerful that it is impossible to sidestep it and drop in to the Truthplace. When that happens, it's somewhat like having an emotional flu...you just have to ride it out. Your Truthplace can be the equivalent of bedridden, temporarily, by the ego's vomiting and diarrhea. But when you *can* locate your awareness in your Truthplace, that feeling of safety and all-rightness is right there.

This battle between you and your ego, and perhaps most intensely between you and your Critic/Terrorist/Doubter, will be ongoing. There is a lot written about different ways to be effective in this combat. In Appendix A of the book that underpins this workshop, you'll find a list of books that are particularly useful in this regard.

Like Liz felt about feeling her sadness, the expression "the truth shall set you free" takes on meaning here. I would change it up a bit to "knowing your truth of the moment shall set you free in the moment." It's not some "big truth" we are discovering. It's not some truth that sets us free forever. It's more like discovering and rediscovering what's true continuously. It is knowing our own moment-to-moment felt truth as it unfolds. It liberates us to continually discover and become ourselves. And this is so, and only so, when *both* our dependent need for the embrace by our tribe *and* our need for own autonomous experience are respected and included. We need both our "power" and our "love," as Dr. King put it. Matt, you also said you knew there was more to discover about what you discovered, more unfolding to occur.

Matt: Yes. And I can see that means using the awareness practice some more.

Lou: Exactly.

Mack: I'm feeling more and more foolish about being stuck in this shit about my wife—more and more like a real wimp.

Lou: So your ego really has a grip on you right now. When that's true it's like there is no place inside where it is all right to be; nothing about you seems acceptable. You've got the ego-flu. And now because you're here and what we're doing here is becoming meaningful to you, and maybe the people in this group are starting to matter to you, your ego is also comparing your "performance" to theirs and beating you up for not measuring up and endangering your acceptance.

Mack: You read my mind. Problem for me is that I don't see the difference between me and my ego right now. I believe all the crap in my head right now.

Lou: We could call what you're stuck in right now your "m'ego". Your "me" and your ego are merged. Instead of the Swine flu you have the M'ego flu.

**Mack:** Great. That doesn't fucking help me feel any better.

**Lou:** I know. And it does feel like an emergency doesn't it?

**Mack:** I hate to admit it but yes. I hate that feeling. I'm not even sure what it means. I just know when you say it, it fits what I'm feeling.

**Lou:** Afraid?

**Mack:** I hate to admit that too.

**Lou:** In a sense, that's the difficulty for you right now. Your ego won't let you simply be afraid. Your ego, your Seeker, and Convincer, have you convinced that feeling that feeling is wrong, shameful, and dangerous, that you must be strong, fearless, and not need anybody. Matt was able to dodge that bullet from his ego and simply feel afraid because he saw the shame was coming from his ego not from him...and then he could look to see what the fear was about. His ego for one reason or another didn't have such a powerful grip on him as yours does right now. Maybe we can help you get a little separation from your ego. Let me ask you this: Do you feel you are creating everything that is going inside you right now?

**Mack:** Yes.

**Lou:** So you are making yourself afraid?

**Mack:** Yes. (Angry)

**Lou:** How do you do that inside? How do you deliberately make fear come up in your body? And if you are, why would you want to?

**Mack:** You ask the most fucked up questions. How do I know how all this shit happens? It happens. I should be able to control it, that's all.

**Lou:** So it happens. You don't make it happen. You just should be able to control it, to stop fear from happening?

**Mack:** Look. I'm getting pretty pissed off right now and you don't want that to "happen" believe me. Things can get pretty ugly pretty quickly.

**Lou:** You're right. I don't want that to happen. Then *I* would be feeling fear for sure. Listen a minute. What I was doing was trying to corner your ego a bit so it would reveal some of its own crazy rules and beliefs so you could see them as the ego's and maybe not necessarily yours. The trouble is you don't see your ego as something different from who you are so it feels to you like I'm trying to corner *you*. I'm really not. I was just trying to put a little wedge between you and your ego. I'm sorry if that's making things worse for you, really.

**Mack:** I know, I know. Sorry. This shit really can fuck me up. I *can* see I'm just hating on myself all over the place right now.

**Lou:** It may not seem so to you right now, but it's a big deal that you can see that and say that right now. That's the beginning of the wedge. Some part of you is watching you hating on yourself, not just joining it. That "watcher" is not your ego, it's something different. It is a moment of your besieged personal awareness spotting and telling on your ego. To some degree you can see "you" are not doing it. Self-hate is just going off inside you. It's like vomiting. It happens to you. Self-hate is really out of your control, like a rogue tape recording just repeating and repeating inside your head and your body. What's "happening" inside you right now makes it completely unsafe to be yourself. It's what I have called a "Normandy Beach" moment. The ego has you pinned down, like the Nazis had the Allied forces pinned down upon first landing on the beach.

**Mack:** That helps a bit. I feel a little calmer inside.

**Lou:** The map helps identify where the enemy is located and helps you find a little mental cover from the ego's sniper fire. See if you can stay out of your head for a bit. Treat it like a tape recording that maybe you can't turn off, but you can direct your listening, your personal awareness, to something else—maybe just the sound of your own breathing. Don't join your ego's noisy, shouting party.

Just so you know you're not alone, how many of the others in the room have had a bout with self hate like Mack is having? (Six raise hands; several "oh yeah"s)

Let me tell you this too, Mack. I've been where you are right now countless times. I've had to weather the storm of self-hate you're experiencing. When you fail to obey, or you go against, your ego's commands, you can get caught in a real shitstorm internally. These days I am rarely caught in a self-hate storm. But it is not gone. I wake up every morning more in touch with feelings of shame, fear, and doubt than I am in touch with the joy of being alive for another day. Where I've arrived on the inside is kind of paradoxical. I can feel contentment and quiet and "all-rightness" inside me, right alongside those negative feelings. That's kind of my resting state. There are times when the fear, shame, and doubt are all but gone and I'm immersed in other different, easy, pleasurable, empowering feelings. And there are times when the fear, shame, and doubt dominate. The difference now is I have more of a steady experience of being separate from all the feelings, of being "something" more than my feeling experience of the moment, whether painful or pleasurable. I hope this all makes you feel a little less isolated. We'll come back to you later if you want, okay?

**Mack:** Yeah. Good. Thanks everyone.

**Lou:** Mary, do you want to talk a bit about your experience?

**Mary:** Sure. That image of the sacred heart has been coming up over and over again. I "see" it in my chest. Every time it comes up I feel better. It's like each time it gives me a little shot of peacefulness and pleasure. I've never had an experience like this before. I've taken a lot of comfort from Catholic rituals, but I've never felt like this before. I'm saying to myself, "Could this be a spiritual experience? Could this be God giving me something, a blessing of some sort? Do I dare think this? Am I worthy of this? And, of course, will I screw it up, make it go away?"

**Lou:** Well, those are all interesting questions. Some of them sound like your ego jumping in the act and some don't. Maybe the best action you can try in your behalf right now is just to stay with your experience as it unfolds. Maybe don't try to figure it out; just have it. You know what I mean? See what happens next, and next, and next.

**Mary:** Yes. I can see I want to hold onto it and think about it. But I think you're right. My thinking about it doesn't get me anywhere—probably mostly my Doubter at work. I'll practice just being with it best I can, just placing my awareness on the experience, not the thoughts about it. Thanks.

**Lou:** You're welcome. Your experience is a good example of the different ways the Truthplace communicates with us. Sometimes it's through images like yours, sometimes through memories, sometimes through feelings. As an example, I sat down to meditate the other day and what arose immediately was a memory of being teased by my older and younger brothers when I was about six or seven years old. I couldn't remember what they were teasing me about. But they were both teamed up making fun of me and rejecting me. I began to cry and I went to my mother for help. That was the worst thing I could do according to my male sibling tribe. I was being a "momma's boy," a "big baby." She intervened in some way I don't recall but then left me with my brothers. They looked at me with scorn. I felt compelled to tell them, to lie to them, that I had made myself cry, that I could make myself cry whenever I wanted to. The shame I felt about needing their approval and needing my mother's protection was fierce. Showing my hurt was already totally unacceptable. In my meditation, this led me on an inner exploration of my vulnerability and sense of self. I ended up rediscovering how safe I feel in my own skin now compared to then, how much I have come to accept and respect my need for acceptance. You never know ahead of time where you're going to travel to in this kind of inner self-exploration.

What I would like to do now is give you a document describing more fully what I have been calling the Truthplace. Hopefully it will flesh out the territory of internal experiences and capacities this name is a verbal label for. Then we can talk further next time we meet to see if my description resonates with your own experiences.

# chapter ten

# The Truthplace

I am using the word "Truthplace" for two reasons. For one, the word captures the essence of what it refers to: a *place* where we can go to gain fuller access to our *true* inner experience in a given moment. And the other reason is simply that it works well as a heading, under which can be gathered for our exploration, certain inner capacities for discovering deeper self-knowledge. These inner capacities empower us to skillfully fulfill both our deep need for the acceptance and embrace of our tribe(s), as well as our deep need to be true to the development of our unique selves.

Our Truthplace is not a "thing," even though it does have a physical location within the trunk of our body—just like our "Rational Mind" is not a "thing" but has a physical location within the head. We would say the source of our Rational Mind is located within our brain. And we would say the source of our Truthplace is located within our hearts and our guts.

The numerous capacities of our Rational Mind are wonderful resources for certain ways of knowing and interacting with reality. Through analysis, logic, deduction, abstract thinking, mental problem solving, creative theorizing, and conceptual learning and memory, we have a set of powerful tools with which to understand reality, and hopefully to bend it to the purposes of our collective safety and beneficial evolution.

The numerous capacities of our Truthplace are also wonderful resources for certain ways of knowing and interacting with reality. They are fundamentally different from, and complementary to, the capacities of the Rational Mind.

Let me give you a couple of examples of the nature of the Truthplace through the experiences of two clients re-discovering theirs. The first is a young woman, we'll call her Jane, in her mid-thirties, who had been in psychotherapy for a number of years prior to beginning work with me. She also had been practicing meditation for a number of years and had had a few powerful spiritual experiences. So she was not new to the exploration of her inner life. She had an abiding curiosity and openness about looking within.

She sought my help because she was feeling stuck in some inner pain. Her previous therapy did not help alleviate this pain, and the spiritual experiences she'd had, while wonderfully liberating, did not last. One thing that became clear pretty quickly was that she was living with a very harsh and active inner Critic. She was very identified with her Critic and believed the nasty judgments it continuously made about her. Her Critic was subverting any value she could gain from her strong capacity for self-reflection. Her Critic kept her up in her head "thinking" about herself in very hurtful, shaming ways. After a few sessions and some mapping of her ego, she was beginning to be able to spot her Critic *as her Critic* talking to her and not as herself thinking those thoughts. She began to see the automatic nature of this thinking and how the conclusion was always the same: "You're bad; you're weak; you're doing it wrong," etc.

She always began our sessions smiling very shyly, glancing at me, and trying to be polite and present. But she was clearly uncomfortable. We had frequently identified her Critic being at work in these beginning moments. In the session I want to share with you, she was again looking uncomfortable as she came in and sat down. After just a couple of minutes she noted her discomfort. I said to her to just take a few moments inside herself (dropping in) and just let whatever was going on to just be there and not try to change anything.

She closed her eyes and went inside. I watched her silently and could see her body gradually relax. She took her time, which was beneficial. When she opened her eyes, she looked at me directly and began describing what had happened. The first thing she saw was her Critic telling her that she had nothing of value to say and that I did not want to listen to whatever she did have to say. It was telling her I was bored with her problems. That she just keeps repeating the same complaints. The next thing that happened surprised and pleased her. She spontaneously dropped down out of the thoughts in her head and down into her body. She said it felt like she left the Critic somewhere behind and dropped into a safe space in her heart. She stopped worrying about what I was thinking. She said it felt really good, that it felt like "coming home, "like she was okay, like she could just be herself. It felt very natural and amazing at the same time.

And she knew this place inside of her. It was familiar. She had been in it before, for example while participating in a couple of different awareness workshops. She knew from past experience that she could trust what she would discover there, that what came from there was not about thinking and judging. It was just "about knowing," and "knowing for sure," was how she put it. She loved when that kind of felt clarity happened, even if what came up for her was painful or troubling. She still felt safe and able to deal.

The trouble for her was she couldn't hold onto what she discovered and couldn't stay down in this "heart-knowing." She would lose contact with this "home base." As she talked about this she noticed her Critic starting up again, shaming her for not being able to hold onto her truth, telling her she should be able to by now. It made her feel despairing and sad about her future.

Without being fully aware of it, Jane had used her Personal Awareness to first spot her ego, the Critic/Terrorist/Doubter, at work, and then move that awareness down into her body, into her trunk, and drop into her Truth-place, "coming home," as she called it. She named some of the qualities that are characteristic of the self-knowledge that can be found there: knowing what you know for sure, knowing that the knowledge is trustable, and that it has a felt clarity. She also described some of the qualities that are inherent characteristics of this inner space I'm calling the Truthplace: a feeling of inner safety, a naturalness, i.e. like "coming home," and a permission to just be yourself, to be exactly where you are in the moment.

Her experience is also a good example of how the ego tries to keep us away from this source of self-knowing, both by keeping us out of contact with it from the start, and then by finding a way to disqualify and degrade the experience afterwards with shame, fear, and self-doubt.

Another client of mine, we'll call him John, had been working with me for a year or more. A man in his sixties, he had lost his wife to a ravaging illness a year and a half before we started working together. He loved his wife very deeply. In the large circle of friends he and his wife shared, John was considered the "go-to guy." If you were having problems, whether they were personal, family, work, or spiritual, he was the man to talk to. He never said "no" to a request for help. And his wife supported him in this role. You could say he was the ultimate "good guy." He was also a very successful business owner, and amongst his friends this was an important piece of his credibility. John treated his employees like family, and indeed some of them actually were. You could say, until his wife's illness and death, he had lived a charmed life.

A year after the death of his wife he fell in love with a young woman half his age. When they found out, his three grown children and his friends were terribly upset with him, and he was upset with himself. He knew the young woman was not someone he could spend the rest of his life with. He could see the signs of her immaturity, her overwhelming dependence on him, and her frightening lack of respect for the social boundaries he was trying to keep on the relationship.

And yet he was powerfully drawn to her. He loved her in some sense of that word. Their sexual connection had an intensity he had never experienced before. When he was with her, particularly when making love, there was a kind of timeless quality to their connection. He discovered a passionate side of himself that he was unfamiliar with until their meeting. And yet, when not in the spell of that intensely felt connection, he could sense the unbridgeable mismatches inherent in their relationship, not just in terms of age but in many other meaningful ways.

After months of "shoulds" and "shouldn'ts," numerous times of leaving her and going back to her, we had a conversation about his Truthplace, without naming it as such. We talked about the quality of "knowing" that comes from the internal connection to a felt sense of what is true in the moment. He kept putting his hand on his heart as he talked. He said he had always trusted his intuition before he lost his wife. It was clear he knew where his Truthplace was located, and that the kind of knowing produced there was not new to him.

His wife, being a deeply intuitive person herself, was someone who had always helped him connect with his own intuitive knowing. She was a true soulmate whom he loved dearly, and whom he counted on for validation of his intuitions. Up until the death of his wife he said he had very much lived from his Truthplace. He realized he had lost contact with it during her long sickness and her death. Her long and painful illness had rendered her less available as someone he could check in with around his intuitions. This unavailability, and her ultimate death, were overwhelming emotionally, just too much for him to consciously bear. So he emotionally disconnected. He lost his feeling-self, and with that loss he lost his "intuitive self," as well as losing his wife. Beyond re-visiting the pain of the loss of his wife, the pain and consequences due to the loss of access to *his intuitive self-knowledge* hit him hard in our session. Without putting it in these words, he realized he had lost his own personal internal compass.

In the past sessions, he would describe his confusion and his inner conflict, but always in terms of conflicted and confused *thoughts*. He felt bad that he could not get clear and resolve the inner conflict. He felt weak and ashamed of himself. The Critic was definitely working on him. His ego demanded that he be the guy with the answers for everyone's problems. His ego had no tolerance for confusion. Confusion, especially persistent confusion, was a failure, was unacceptable.

In the session I want to share with you, I told him, "You are only going to find your way through the confusion and conflict if you can allow yourself to really have your confusion and stop trying not to have it. Stop 'should-ing' on yourself and let yourself be where you are." I asked him, "Do you know you are confused and conflicted right now, right in this moment?" He said, "Yes." I asked him again, "for sure?" in order to bring him into his experience in this moment, to make him check in with his current *felt* experience. He paused before answering. I could see him looking inside his body for the answer. And he said, "Yes." I said, "Then that is your truth of this moment, and that is re-connecting with your own intuition, with your Truthplace. You are confused and conflicted...period. There is nothing you can 'do' about the truth but accept it. If you can let it be true, and not try to get rid of it, then you will move on from there. And you will move on *only* from there. Not from where you think you should be or want to be, but from where you are. Guilt won't change you; truth will. Only your truth will move you, unfold you, moment to moment."

He got it. I should say his native self got it. The self that is not controlled by his ego got it. He dropped into his felt truth of the moment and just let it be so inside of him. "God, I really am confused and conflicted," he said with rueful acceptance. And do you know what he then said, after a self-reflective pause? He said, "You know, now I know I will be all right. Do you know what I mean?" Kind of a surprising statement, yes? But I knew exactly what he meant. He *did not* mean that he had suddenly gotten un-confused and un-conflicted. No, he had instantly and simply remembered from his past experiences just what the bodily feeling of being inside his Truthplace felt like. And he knew he was back *in* there. He could feel it, maybe for the first time without his wife's help. Our Truthplace is trustable and brings a sense of safety even when conflict and confusion reign supreme. You connect, like he did, with a felt sense that "now I can find my own way." But you need the courage and self-permission to own the knowing that emerges in each moment from within your Truthplace. And guess what? The ego will be trying, through fear and shame and doubt, to scare you off taking ownership.

You can't be where you or others think you "should" or "shouldn't" be regarding your own inner experience. If you can't be present to yourself now—here—then you are present nowhere. You don't even have your own two internal feet to walk with because you're not standing in your own shoes. You're trying to run ahead of yourself—or backwards into some imagined preferable inner state. You're up in your head, spinning around in your rational mind, driven crazy by your ego's efforts to keep you in its version of safety and acceptability, like my client was. Once he dropped down out of his head and into the truth of his heart and gut, my client could re-start his journey of unique personal exploration and discovery for himself. He could seek the courage within to be true to where he actually was. And he could trust what would emerge from his own direct inner experience as being true, being accurate. Even if it meant he may remain confused and conflicted for a while, he knew the "intelligence" he was tapping back into could be trusted to ultimately steer him in the right direction.

He knew, or "remembered," that his rational mind could not resolve this kind of confusion and conflict. Only the native authority of his own intuitive knowing could help him find his way to clarity. This moment of insight reconnected him to his access to that intuitive knowing, to that place of felt knowing. Regaining this access had the result of opening an inner door to some felt discoveries about his relationship with his young lover. In that same session, he had two important realizations. First, that if he chose to let her go, of course, that alone was going to be emotionally painful. But even more daunting was the realization that letting his lover go would also mean he was going to feel like the "bad guy" for hurting her. His saint ego demanded that he always be seen as the "good guy," never disappointing another. Doing the right thing but being seen as the bad guy was a criminal offense that his Critic/Terrorist/Doubter would make him pay for with deep shame.

The second realization he had was that letting his lover go would also open the door for the re-emergence into his awareness of his suppressed, unfinished, painful grieving over the loss of his wife. He now knew, from his own direct inner experience, that his avoidance of that grief was part of what was keeping him stuck in indecision about letting his lover go. He felt how much courage and support it was going to require to take the action his intuitive knowing told him was the right one. For the moment the "should-ing" of the Critic was not happening. It was not an emergency requiring immediate action. He just knew he'd make his way to the right decision and he was allowed to be afraid of and guilty about it along the way. Now instead of running from the fear and guilt (from being the "bad guy") by running in circles in his head, he could look right into those feelings and check to see whether or not what they were telling him was accurate and to be believed.

## Your Body Knows Your Truth

Both of these clients' experiences are examples of touching into an experi-ence of insight and intuitive knowing. These kinds of "bodymind knowings" have a very different quality to them than the knowledge that is generated by thinking, deducing, analyzing, or remembering. Insights and intuitions are fresh, alive knowings that are *felt* to be revealing, meaningful, and accurate in the moment. They are more in the nature of discoveries than convictions, beliefs, deductions, memories, or speculations. They are not abstract. You know one in a physical way when you have one. Our egos may make us dis-regard it, forget it, or doubt it later, but you know it when you have it. You recognize your own knowing as true, as accurate.

And if you manage to stay connected to your Truthplace, then you will be guided by what is actually true for you from this moment to the next, and the next, and so on. It operates in this moment, whether responding to something happening right now, or planning for and preparing to respond to some future experience. It knows it can't control outcomes but that it can participate, respond, influence, and open to the flow of experience in this moment and the next. The Truthplace doesn't swim against the flow of inner experience. It follows the current, knowing implicitly that the current knows how to direct itself. It is passionately interested in learning about, exploring, and dealing with all the domains of being alive, including the painful, threatening ones.

The Truthplace wants you to know everything about you, without exception, inside and out—every thought, every feeling, every sensation, every insight, every intuition, every opening and closing of your heart, every meaning, every confusion, every experience of being lost and then found again. It is inherently curious and attentive to all experiences. It is inherently curious about other people's experiences also. It is not interested in controlling or avoiding the flow of our life experiences or in judging or controlling others. It is very interested in learning skillful responses to all aspects of life that it comes in contact with or that come into contact with it, including hostile ones.

The Truthplace has no permanent attachment or aversion to any experience or way of responding. It's only interest is in experiencing and moving through whatever is actually so in a given moment with conscious presence, grace, skill, engagement, responsiveness, wisdom, and compassion. If the Truthplace has an aversion, it is to what is not real, not whole, not genuine. Like the body has an "aversion" to being abused or misused in any way, the Truthplace has an "aversion" to what is false. The body responds to abuse and misuse with physical pain. The Truthplace, when allowed, responds to any demand for falseness with a "twist" of discomfort in the heart or the gut. This twist functions like an "autonomous alert" for inauthenticity or untrustworthiness.

Egos don't produce this kind of knowing or have this kind of curiosity. Egos only affirm and confirm past conclusions and beliefs. They fear insights and intuitions because they do not come from the rational, logical mind. The ego has the power to direct the rational mind to think thoughts that suit the ego's rules and regulations, meet the ego's standards for safety and connection within your tribe, or with an important individual in your tribe. In terms of self-knowledge the Seeker/Inflator/Convincer aspect of the ego keeps you thinking "in the box." And the Convincer will convince the host those thoughts are right and good and accurate.

But the ego cannot direct the internal source that produces insights and intuitions. It cannot force this source to come up with only *certain kinds* of insights and intuitions. So the ego would rather just shut this source of knowing down completely, and most often succeeds. However, our native self can be helped to remember the Truthplace exists, and that it can be found. Our native selves, through the consciously directed use of our personal awareness, can restore access to our Truthplace.

## Other Inner Capacities Found Within The Truthplace

Insight and intuition are just two of the capacities for self-knowledge located within the Truthplace. There are several other valuable capacities "in there" that can also be accessed by consciously placing our personal awareness in the physical neighborhood of the Truthplace (i.e. the trunk of your body), and keeping it there for a while. One of these capacities has come to be known under the heading of "emotional intelligence." Our emotions and feelings are essential sources of information about our interpersonal environment. They let us know "what means what" in our relationships. They let us know when an interaction with another person feels safe or dangerous. They let us connect with another through empathy. They let us know the meaning of each of our relationships, the heart-felt meaning. A meaningful sense of purpose is also a felt experience, not just an abstract, dry idea in our minds. Love, joy, excitement, comfort, solace, peace, ease, contentment, satisfaction, gratitude, warmth, acceptance, and appreciation are all felt experiences emanating from within the Truthplace. And these feelings can keep deepening and expanding when given the regular and sustained attention of our personal awareness.

The emotions and feelings we tend to view as unpleasant and unwanted are also vital sources of information for us. This is true as long as they are not twisted and distorted into self-destructive forms by the rigidity and compulsivity of our egos' rules and regulations. Fear is meant to alert us to dangers, and to move us into protective action. Anger and aggression are expressions of our instinct for survival and self-care. They move us to act against what is harmful to our native wellbeing. Grief and sadness are expressions of the painful loss of someone or something that we cherished and felt connected to. The hurt of betrayal, abandonment, and rejection is an expression of our need for each other's embrace and cooperation. Outrage is an expression of a wounding to our inherent dignity and worth as human beings.

Without full access to our emotions and our feelings we have lost access to our internal compass, the compass we need to make beneficial life choices and navigate interpersonal relationships. The Truthplace is naturally open to the experience of every emotion and every feeling. It has no problem with co-existing feelings that may seem contradictory to the rational mind but make sense in the lived experience and complexity of a human life. Combined with intuition and insight, emotions and feelings are powerful guides and informants for understanding and navigating all the meaningful aspects of our lives. We are flying blind without them.

Besides the sense of inner safety and of "coming home" noted above, the Truthplace, when accessed with our personal awareness, has other qualities that distinguish it from the ego. It is not rigid, compulsive or automatic in its movements. The compass the ego uses is locked onto directional settings that often guarantee collision courses. Responsive movements generated from the Truthplace are naturally mindful, calm, and fluid. It has no turbulence, like a master of martial arts who operates from a stillness in his center as he responds with great clarity and power to an attack. There is no inner emergency while responding to an outer one. Energy is being expended, but there is no strain, no inner conflict while the outer conflict or challenge is being responded to. Our Truthplace responds to reality precisely as it is in this moment. Past and future do not rule, there is just the flow of present moments and the emergence of the responses that the present moment calls for.

Sometimes our personal awareness opens very deeply and continuously to our Truthplace. When this happens an extended state of "flow" can be created. This is the word we use when whatever it takes to participate in an experience seems to happen easily, naturally, and almost without trying. Sometimes a sexual encounter happens this way. Sometimes a dance or the singing of a song happens this way. Sometimes a moment of playfulness with a child happens this way. Sometimes a conversation happens this way. Sometimes sitting in the sun or walking in the mountains happens this way. Sometimes responding to a crisis happens this way. Sometimes creating something happens this way. Sometimes self-discoveries happen this way.

There is energy being spent in these kinds of experiences. But the expenditure of energy feels effortless, without any strain. We know exactly what to do and the actions just flow out of us, usually with more skill and effectiveness than when we are not in a state of flow. It can be kind of a continuous surprise. One's senses are heightened and sharpened. A feeling of joy or deep pleasure accompanies our actions and our discoveries. This heightened capacity can feel quite surprising while at the same time feel very natural. Athletes speak of being "in the zone"; artists speak of having "creative runs"; workers speak of "finding their rhythm"; actors speak of being taken over by their characters. There is a famous quote from the basketball great, Bill Russell:

> "Every so often a Celtic game would heat up so that it became more than a physical or even mental game, and would be magical. The feeling is difficult to describe, and I certainly never talked about it when I was playing. When it happened I could feel my play rise to a new level. At that special level all sorts of odd things happened. It was almost as if we were playing in slow motion. During those spells I could almost sense how the next play would develop and where the next shot would be taken. Even before the other team brought the ball in bounds, I could feel it so keenly that I'd want to shout to my teammates, 'It's coming there!'—except that I knew everything would change if I did."
>
> (Russell, B., 1980)

Flow is a natural state of being. It is not an altered state of being. It is an unaltered state of be-ing. Thinking, judging, fantasizing, worrying, and controlling are not happening; they would alter the natural state of flow. Russell knew intuitively that if he used the state of flow to "control" the game, "everything would change." He would lose contact with flow. He would alter the state. He would move back into the socially-accepted altered state of consciousness called "normal."

We live in an altered state of being that we accept as "normal." And *it is* normal in the sense of most common. It has become our "second nature." It is not our "first nature." It is not natural. It is altered, just in an "acceptable" and extremely common way. This alteration is maintained by our egos. The ego does not allow for "flow." Of course, because it feels so good and "works" so well when it happens, the ego will take credit for it after the fact, and try to "bottle" the experience for its own controlling purposes. But, while it is actually happening, to the ego it feels too much like being out of control. The ego must avoid any possibility of unplanned and uncontrolled surprises.

## The Truthplace And Personal Awareness

The Truthplace can and does operate without the conscious cooperation or participation of our personal awareness. Sometimes it sends a "message from the interior" in spite of a dedication to maintaining unawareness on the part of the person on the receiving end. It can show up as a sinking feeling after making a bad choice, or as that whispering inner voice trying to alert you to a danger or to an opportunity, or as a funny feeling you get around a particular person, or as a surge of joy following an important decision, or a sudden understanding of a situation that puzzled you until then, and so on. These are all blessings, sometimes unwanted, sometimes welcomed, that we experience as "out of the ordinary" of our typical day-to-day experience. If our lives remain limited to these occasional unsought messages from our Truthplace, then we are settling for living on a starvation diet of person-al truth. The limiting and destructive consequences of this truth-deprived diet are myriad, personally, interpersonally, and collectively, consequences stretching from unhappy individuals and families to all out wars, and to all manner of suffering in between.

All our ego-driven seeking is compensatory. If what we are seeking is a substitute for what we really need, then we will never get enough of it. The substitute satisfactions we seek are designed to fill the painful inner hole created by the socially-induced disconnection from our Truthplace, and by the substitution of our ego-distorted selves for our true, native selves. Most of us are living in the chronic pain of that disconnection and distortion while doing our best to compensate for it, or to medicate it, or both, in one way or another. As Thoreau once said, "The mass of men lead lives of quiet desperation and go to the grave with the song still in them." A *"quiet"* desperation—meaning a desperation hidden, unspoken, secret, not shared. We need to stop lying about how we need each other, how we have been hurt, how we hurt each other, and how we continue to do so and deny it. We need to admit we are not relating to each other in ways that make it safe for us to be our authentic selves fully and openly, *both dependent and autonomous.* We need to step away from those ego-driven ways of relating. And we need to step into an honest search for the genuine safety that will allow us to be both fearful and courageous as we put our hearts and minds together for the benefit of both our collective and our individual wellbeing and evolution.

The Truthplace resides, intact and complete, within in all of us...but our ability to access it varies widely. Given the differences in our early conditioning, by the time we move into and then through our adult lives, each of us is left with more or less access to our Truthplace. The question is, "Have I arrived in my adulthood completely possessed and identified with a bully ego, or saint ego, or hermit ego, or rebel ego, etc? Or is my identification with and possession by my ego more partial, more situational?" The degree of accessibility I have to my Truthplace in any given moment of my experience is very much dependent on the degree to which I am possessed by and identified with my ego in any moment. The logo of my consulting company, EgoMechanics, Inc., asks the question, "Do you possess an ego? Or does your ego possess you?"

But beyond whatever level of access we may have been permitted to carry into our adult lives, the quality of our lives going forward very much depends on the deliberate and regular practice of three things: remembering the presence of our personal awareness; using it to spot our egos and separate from their grip; and then allowing our personal awareness to drop into and hang out with our Truthplace.

What I call a "real ideal" is to make living from our Truthplace become ordinary and normal—not some special momentary occurrence, not the result of a surprising instant of open consciousness, but of a "normal" flow of continuous awareness. After all, *it is* our natural source of personal truth. Since we have been conditioned out of contact with our Truthplace, in order to make this shift we must make a practice of using our personal awareness to both keep spotting our egos at work and dropping into contact with our Truthplace. We must stop living on a starvation diet of personal truth. This takes courage, as well as skilled, conscious effort. The regular, deliberate, and conscious joining of our personal awareness with our Truthplace is the key to living and responding with wise inner guidance. Without our deliberate use of personal awareness to continuously spot our egos at work, separate from them, and then drop down into our Truthplace we will never become whole, empowered, autonomous, and compassionately connected human beings. If we don't do this, we certainly will not thrive as human beings, and there is the increasing game-ending probability that we will continue to create the conditions that endanger the very survival of our human species.

# chapter eleven

# Living From
# The Truthplace
## Dialogues Continued

**Gabe:** I'm feeling angry again. Are you serious about me using my heart as some kind of GPS for living!? Give it a rest. That's crazy. I've been hanging in here but this is too much. My mind is my guide, my reality checker. Feelings are fine but they're not rational. They can't analyze a situation objectively. They're going to make me do things that are not good for my health. All these "feel good" workshops seem dangerous to me. "Follow your bliss!" Yeah, sure, right into drug abuse. Right over the waterfalls just downstream on your lovely river of bliss. Bullshit.

**Lou:** So your "reality checker" says what I have described is bullshit and dangerous to boot?

**Gabe:** You heard me.

**Lou:** So this is not your heart talking?

**Gabe:** For sure.

**Lou:** What about your gut? Is it talking to you? Is that a part of what you're listening to besides your mind?

**Gabe:** Don't fuck with me.

**Lou:** Let's take a minute here. This is actually an opportunity for me to practice what I preach about vulnerability. I can feel my reluctance to just openly tell you that I've got some fear about moving our conversation along. I see and feel you're really angry with me, and that right now I may not be your enemy but I'm certainly not your ally. Your disapproval and anger are scaring me, and part of me has some fear that you could get angry enough to hurt me physically. Part of me doesn't think you will, but that fear is there. So we're not in a conversational safe zone at the moment. Something is not safe about the space we're sharing right now. We're a threat to each other in some way. Can we agree on that?

**Gabe:** I don't feel threatened by you, just kind of outraged and ready to walk out of here.

**Lou:** Okay. So the difficulty I'm having is this: What I need from each of you for this workshop to accomplish its purpose is an interest and willingness to look inside and see if some of what I have been describing with words actually fits your inside felt experience. So this is not an intellectual discussion or a debate about different ideas. This is not something we can get clear about by verbally debating the accuracy or inaccuracy of the fit between the words and your experience. If it doesn't fit, and that feels final for the moment, then that's about as far as we can go with any hope for useful conversation.

I understand that what I am asking of you requires that it make enough sense to you to look into your own experience and see whatever you see there. If this exploration feels too much like it is violating your own sense of your personhood, your common sense, or your dignity, then, at least for the moment, you may have to honor that experience and stop. In a real sense that is your Truthplace for this moment.

And it also *has* to feel safe enough to do this exploration in this public forum. To find and open to your inner Truthplace means going into inner territory, into your heart and your gut, where the feelings of hurt, fear, and shame are actually felt. The Truthplace will not continue to speak to you if you're not willing to listen to it when it's telling you that you are feeling afraid, hurt, or shameful. That willingness is the price of admission. The willingness to actually allow ourselves to feel our "hurt-ability," our fearfulness, and our shamefulness is the price we pay for acquiring the freedom to continue to evolve into who we are. For our authenticity, our personal authority, our personal power, our capacity to create and sustain loving and empowered relationships, and so much more, we must allow for our vulnerability. The stakes are high. And we can't fake or force this.

So, Gabe, we may have reached a real impasse for the moment, maybe permanently. You're not experiencing fear but you are feeling this doesn't make sense to you and violates your common sense, maybe even your sense of personhood. Powerfully. Correct?

**Gabe:** Yes. I feel boxed in here.

**Lou:** Boxed in where?

**Gabe:** Between leaving and staying. I hate this feeling. I hate feeling stuck. I hate feeling confused and indecisive. I hate it. I hate this whole fucking process.

**Lou:** Loud and clear. What's up about leaving?

**Gabe:** A moment ago I was angry, and clear enough to do it. Now I feel stuck. I hate to admit this, too, but I'd feel embarrassed to get up and walk out. Shit. This really sucks. And I hate you right now for putting me in this position.

**Lou:** So the way I would talk about your dilemma is that it is not safe enough for you to stay and it's not safe enough for you to leave. You lose something important either way.

**Gabe:** I don't like the word "safe."

**Lou:** I can relate. Here's what might help: I've been trying to figure out when to give you all some of my thinking on the issue of safety. Even though this is close on to just giving you a piece of writing on the Truthplace, it seems like perfect timing to give you what I have written about safety and its relationship to feelings of pain and pleasure. What you're feeling, Gabe, relates to all of us. You may not think of it as having to do with safety, but I believe it does. So I'm going to give all of you what I have written. Read it. We'll take a break for an hour and a half, and then come back and we'll continue talking. And Gabe, this gives you a chance both to see if the document relates to you and some time to decide do you want to stay or not. Okay?

**Gabe:** Good.

**Lou:** If you decide to leave the workshop, just let me know, okay? No questions asked.

**Gabe:** Agreed.

# chapter twelve

# On Pain, Pleasure, Safety and Wellbeing

The experience of pain, the unique feeling of it, is meant to let us know that something is happening that poses a threat to our safety and wellbeing.

The experience of pleasure, again, the unique feeling of it, is meant to let us know that something is happening that is both safe and beneficial for us.

In order to keep ourselves safe and foster our wellbeing, we must *pay attention* to *both* feelings of pain *and* feelings of pleasure, and not avoid the awareness of either.

*Compulsively avoiding* the experience of either pain or pleasure is not natural. Likewise, *compulsively seeking* the experience of either pleasure or pain is not natural.

The words "pain" and "pleasure" cover many different experiences. Pain, for example, can include physical pains of many different kinds, as well as emotional hurt and sadness, fear and anger, feelings of emptiness and worthlessness, depression and despair, simple unhappiness, feelings of insufficiency, and many others. Pleasure can include the many different physical sensations that feel good, as well as emotional experiences such as joy, happiness, excitement, love, contentment, comfort, connection, and feelings of worth, fullness, and acceptance. But whatever the pleasurable or painful feeling, each one gives us specific information about what is happening to us. If we pay attention to each feeling consciously, intimately, and with real curiosity about its message, we will know how to respond to whatever is happening to us in ways that protect our safety, and promote our wellbeing and personal evolution.

*To be safe and to thrive,* all of our sensations and feelings must first be given the respect of our full attention and deliberate curiosity. We must then discover effective ways to respond to the information they provide us, and be allowed to respond in attunement with that information. And finally we must be open to the feedback our responses bring us, and refine our responses based on that feedback. We are all equipped from birth to evolve and learn in this way. But this evolution will unfold only if our early interpersonal relationships were open and responsive to the entire range of sensations and feelings that arose within us in response to how persons on whom we depended related to us. In a genuinely supportive relationship, it would feel safe for us to be dependent and safe for us to be autonomous.

We have already seen that the acknowledgment and responsiveness to the *full* repertoire of our feelings of both pain and pleasure by those who matter to us is not the current norm. Certain expressions of feeling are deemed acceptable and others are not. This in turn creates the need for the ego and its internal actions to block our access to our Truthplace. As a result, inner sources of knowing become "disqualified" and become stunted in all of us, to the extent that we are then stunted in our capacity to relate to each other safely, wisely, and compassionately.

## Safety — The Body

There is no absolute safety for our bodies, only relative, conditional safety. Every single thing we take for granted as being permanent is not. Nothing. No thing is. Every living thing will die. Every living thing, including us, can be physically hurt, damaged, or destroyed. This is a fact of our human lives.

And it is a fact that most of us do our best to keep in the deep shadows of our unawareness. Our awareness of this profound vulnerability arises only when a real threat to our bodily safety and wellbeing presents itself to us. Soldiers in combat zones have this awareness every day and night they are in that kind of zone. People who live in dangerous neighborhoods have this awareness. People who are the subject of prejudice have this chronic awareness. People living in countries with oppressive governments have this awareness. First responders do. We all felt it here in New York City on September 11, 2001. We have all experienced this physical vulnerability to each other at points in our lives. But right now, most, if not all, of you reading this document live in relatively high safety zones regarding physical safety.

Maybe some of you have come from physically dangerous circumstances in your earlier lives. But typically the acute awareness of our vulnerability to one another physically, our *dependence* on each other for our bodily safety, remains in the recesses of our consciousness. It is safe enough for us to assume we are physically safe right now, and for most of us in our day-to-day lives this is true. We are very lucky in that regard.

It is also a fact that our capacity to respond to threats and promote our wellbeing is extraordinarily effective compared to other living creatures. We have survived and thrived as a species as no other species has before us. Our survival equipment is magnificent. *And a major piece of that equipment is our capacity to bond and cooperate with each other.*

We have survived as well as we have not as individuals but as collectives, large and small, from families, to social groups, to larger organizations. Instinctively, we know we are *safer* as a member of a group. And we know also that the possibility of *thriving* is greater within a cohesive group than as a solo individual. Consequently, the security of our membership within the group we depend upon for collective safety is experienced as a paramount *need* in each of us. This felt need to be bonded with and embraced by each other is there to promote our survival, our autonomous functioning, and our wellbeing, not to inhibit them. That need for connection is not neurotic. It is existential. Our need for air is not considered neurotic or weak by anyone; neither should our need to *feel* bonded with and embraced by each other. But it is.

## What Creates Safety?

So what *does* it take for us to feel safe within our dependency group or tribe? What are the collective operating agreements that create safety within such a group?

The agreements that make us feel safe as *physical* beings within our tribe are clear to everyone, although in our "first world" lives we often take them for granted and don't notice they are operating. They include agreeing not to physically harm each other, to make sure we all have sufficient shelter from the elements, food to eat, water to drink, and clothes to wear, and also to agree not to abandon our sick and frail.

## Safety—The Self

The reality of our physical nature is obvious and universally agreed upon. There is no debate about what a human body is. And there is no disagreement that to be a human being you must have a human body, and that that body can be either harmed or protected.

But we also all have a sense that a human being is more than just a human body. We have a sense that there is something inhabiting that body, something we generally refer to as a "person" or as a "self." However, we do *not* agree as to what a person/self *is*. As a species, and as separate tribes, we are still in the process of discovering what actually constitutes our essential personhood or selfhood. There is much disagreement about this, some of it leading to enlightening dialogue and exploration, and some of it descending into brutality, murders, massacres, and wars.

Clearly our sense of personhood or selfhood matters greatly to us, regardless of our confusion about what it is. Whatever personal and group belief we may have about what it is, we feel a powerful need to successfully fit that definition, and our fitting into that definition becomes something we feel a powerful need to maintain and defend fiercely. Notice how often the protection of our *sense* of meeting the acceptable definition of personhood trumps even our basic need for physical safety—our own and that of others. We are willing to risk our lives and kill others for the sake of protecting whatever we consider essential to our sense of having an acceptable, valid personhood. Religious suicide bombers, whose need for a personal sense of value and acceptability is met and bolstered by blowing themselves up in order to murder "infidels" (bad persons) are a current example of a tribally-created, self-destructive belief of how to get this need met.

Our need to create and maintain some current acceptable version of personhood seems even more compelling than our other inherent and powerful need to fully self-express all aspects of our human nature. If it comes down to a choice between exposing something about ourselves that threatens our acceptability versus choosing to protect our acceptability by suppressing that self-expression, we will typically choose to suppress that particular self-expression.

Given our confusion and disagreement about what authentic, full personhood is, it follows that the agreements about what constitutes danger and what might make us feel safe as *persons* (not just bodies) within our tribe, and across tribes, are not clear. We settle for agreements that make us physically safe but leave us blundering through the minefields of inter*person-al* safety and danger.

In a very fundamental way we are all continuously afraid of each other as persons. None of us is completely acceptable—either to ourselves or to our significant others. None of us get through childhood and adolescence being accepted for *all* of who and what we are by those who matter to us. We carry a deep, often hidden, uncertainty about our value and our acceptability. A child's worst emotional nightmare is the experience of his/her power-lessness and helplessness to prevent being rejected, neglected, devalued, or abandoned emotionally by the person or persons the child depends on. The experience of that same powerlessness in adulthood is the ego's worst fear. It is terrifying and shaming.

Animals have only one option when primitive fear arises in them: feel the fear and act to protect themselves. The protective actions available to any given animal are limited by the nature of their bodies and their brains. The protective actions an animal takes may not always work, but that's just how it is. There are no further adaptive actions available to animals. They must either fight, flight, freeze, or collapse. They can only take the actions genetically available to them, *and* they *cannot* avoid experiencing the accom-panying feeling of fear. It is different for humans.

## The Power to Supress Feelings

Humans have two options when this primitive fear arises. One is the same as our fellow animals—feel the fear and act. We of course, given the more evolved development of our bodies and brains, have a much wider range of protective actions we can call on. However, as with our animal friends, our protective actions of fight, flight, freeze, or collapse do not always succeed in removing the threat that is triggering our fear. But for us humans, if those protective actions don't work, and we are stuck in a chronically threatening situation (within families, peer groups, organizations, institutions, etc.), we have an alternate option animals don't have.

As we have seen in earlier documents, self-protective responses to threatening situations can themselves become dangerous. For example, if as a child I get angry (fight) and I am shamed, or shunned, or hit for that response; or if I show fear and try to flee (flight) and that response brings greater danger; or if I don't respond at all (freeze) and I am punished for not responding. All of these instinctive responses are reactions to frightening hurts and threats. But, as humans, if endangered we have the added option of suppressing the responses themselves, as well as the fear that generates them. Animals can't do this.

The development of this human capacity to suppress the *feeling* of fear itself is awesome, although self-destructive. The dangerous or hurtful situation may persist, but we no longer feel the fear of it. And without the awareness of the feeling of fear, then we can more easily suppress the self-protective responses to what is fearful when those responses might in fact endanger, rather than protect, us. We end up treating the feeling of fear as if *it is* the problem. And we "solve" the problem by turning against our fear, fighting it down, shaming ourselves for having it, convincing ourselves we shouldn't be afraid, and doing everything we can not to feel it, including drinking alcohol and taking drugs, and countless other forms of medicating (numbing) our feelings.

So, first and foremost, we will do all the behaviors we have available to us to avoid or defuse the threatening experience of rejection and unacceptability. But because our acceptability to those who matter to us, from birth forward, ends up being profoundly and chronically conditional, we end up living with a chronic (hopefully suppressed) fear of rejection. Acceptability is never a given. It depends on the continued suppression of vital, but unacceptable, aspects of who we are. Those repressed parts of us don't die; they live on in our unconscious and continue to press from within for recognition and expression. We are always in danger of slipping up in meeting the demands for acceptable membership. Somewhere inside we know we are on or near the risky edge of rejection. "We are constantly at risk of being ourselves" (*A Conscious Life,* 1996). Living in the experience of chronic fear/terror is an intolerable inner state. The urgency and sense of emergency inherent in the feeling of fear insists that we act on it in some way. We must discharge it, suppress it, or numb it.

We have learned to be ashamed of this deep chronic uncertainty and fearfulness about our acceptability. The *feeling* of fear itself is a sign that there is, or may be, something "wrong" with us, so we do our best to deny that we feel it. So we all, to one degree or another, join in a socially accepted and required rule. As noted earlier, the rule goes like this: "I should not be hurt, frightened, or shamed by your rejection of me, ever. So I must do my best to hide those feelings from you and from myself." We must *pretend* in order to obey this rule. We must come to believe this pretense is true; that it is not a lie. But it is a lie. Perhaps, given the circumstances, a good and necessary lie; necessary for keeping us from feeling unsafe in our relationships, and necessary for maintaining our sense of personal dignity and self-respect.

If we were truly completely all right with our need for each other's approval, if it was acceptable and safe to express our fear of rejection, and if it was acceptable and safe to seek approval and reassurance there would be no shame or fear in asking for it, or in sharing our need for it. This would allow us to operate in our particular worlds, big and small, in much easier, more vital, and cooperative ways. The compulsive need to hide our vulnerability to and dependency on each other for our emotional safety would be removed. We could recover from mistakes and failures, and inadvertent hurts to one another, because we could talk and listen to each other about them without judgment or rejection. It would not be so dangerous to be with each other in ways that were more open, creative, curious and compassionate. The experience of being hurt could be used as an impetus towards finding what was necessary to heal. Instead, we all hide our vulnerability to rejection, and suffer from a chronic fear of that vulnerability being exposed. We live our lives defensively or offensively, or, more commonly, alternating between these two poles of denied insecurity.

We do our beat to create tribes of safe people, all of whom agree about what, for them, constitutes an acceptable or an unacceptable person. And then we hope that each member of this safe tribe will keep the agreement not to point out or cause the exposure of the unacceptable parts of any of its members. But our defenses against the unacceptable internal parts of ourselves betray us. They are inherently "leaky." These parts, which are aspects of our essential selves, are pressing from within for their own expression, and they will find undercover ways of coming out, ways we might not notice but others may. So we suffer a chronic "social anxiety" and engage in a constant, semi-conscious to very conscious effort to present and maintain our acceptable version of personhood, while, for the sake of our sense of dignity and autonomy, simultaneously pretending we don't need that acceptance.

Even when we are doing all of this well, the frantic, frenetic "high" that can result is a reflection of the fragility of the temporary escape from the chronic underlying anxiety about the insecurity of one's ongoing tribal membership and standing.

The fact that for *all* of us actually *feeling* our fear of each other's disapproval and rejection has become unacceptable and needs to be hidden from each other's view complicates our relationships enormously. In an effort to suppress this fear, we deny our natural and profound human *need* for approval and acceptance. We "pretend" we don't need approval, or, more insidiously, we pretend we don't fear disapproval. We end up fundamentally dishonest with each other. We cannot openly and proudly let each other know how much acceptance means to us. Admitting to that need "proudly" seems a total contradiction in terms. Needing each other's approval is shameful, and anybody who shows that need does so with a sense of shame and inferiority. Strong people don't need other people's approval, right?

Actually, the most unsafe of all interpersonal circumstances are those in which we cannot be honest with ourselves about the real fears and the real risks we experience when considering being open and authentic with each other. Those circumstances in which we have to pretend there is no danger, vulnerability, or risk, when in fact there is, and are required to hide our fear, are the most dangerous of all relationships. If we ignore our fear in a vulnerable interaction, we are much more likely to set ourselves up for being hurt. Feeling the fear doesn't mean you don't take the risk; it just means you take the risk more consciously, deliberately, compassionately, and self-respectfully.

Because our egos have taken on the job of denying not only our need for approval and acceptance, but also denying our *fear* of disapproval and rejection, if and when we do decide to take any risks in our relationships, we take them in *the most unsafe of all circumstances.*

So if you hurt me in a conversation, I cannot simply tell you "that hurt me," and you cannot simply accept that you did, even if you had no intention of doing so. I must behave defensively and so must you. The true source of the hurt cannot be explored with curiosity and compassion. This is so because the hurt is embedded in our need for acceptance and approval, which we have all agreed is a shameful need that we need to hide from each other. So I won't tell you that you hurt me. Instead I may look to hurt you back, or withdraw to lick my shameful wounds and nurse resentment toward you.

If I do tell you, it will be in an accusatory, angry way, making sure I don't show you my hurt and need, only my anger. And then of course you are more likely to respond defensively, maybe tell me I am "too sensitive," or that I took it the wrong way, and dismiss my hurt. There will be no feeling of compassion or empathy, and no curiosity in either of us. There will be no healing in the moment, only more hurt, disconnection, and defensive anger. In this scenario, we are moving inevitably towards becoming enemies. And the shame of acknowledging our vulnerability to each other, and the compulsive need to avoid the experience of that shame, guarantees we will eventually become permanent enemies. We may remain civil toward each other if our relationship is relatively unimportant, but if we matter to each other, and therefore have the power to threaten each other's physical and/or personhood safety and wellbeing, escalation into some form of violence— emotional and/or physical—or the suppression of feelings into some form of deadness and depression are a certainty.

We lie to ourselves and each other about the hurt and damage to our personhood caused by the ways our egos force us to relate to each other. And we navigate every one of our conversations, from trite to crucial, within the narrowed, disabling, and destructive bounds set by our egos' need to avoid any exposure of our vulnerability to each other.

This is our "normal" condition as humans today. There is no point in arguing that it should not be so. Maybe in some ideal/real possible world, this condition would not exist. But we don't live in that world; we live in this one. Arguing with reality only seems to embed more deeply what we may be trying to change. We need to start from where we are, not from some rational/moral/wishful notion of where we "should" be. This is where we find ourselves for now. It is generally not safe to include the recognition of our need for approval and acceptance in our conversations with each other. We need to approach the challenge of changing this condition with great respect and compassion. In a sense it is no one's fault. And it is everyone's problem to solve.

# chapter thirteen

# Can We Be With Each Other Safely and Courageously?

## Dialogues Continued

**Lou:** So let's see where we are. Gabe, I see you're back.

**Gabe:** For the moment, it was good to get outside, out of this room. Being outside made me feel I could leave if I really felt I should. Mack talked to me, and that was helpful. He told me he felt like I was inside his skin, feeling what he was feeling. He knew the rage. It didn't scare *him* like it scared you. I feel comfortable with him. He wanted me to stay. A couple of others said the same thing, said they felt something was here for me and they respected my honesty.

    Mack and Liz got me to look at being embarrassed about leaving and made me see I was afraid of disapproval. They know how much I hate that. They do too. But there it was. Motherfucker. Gina told me I scare her to death but didn't want me to leave either. That really surprised me. That took some guts. Mack also got me to see I feel safe with him. I wouldn't have called it "safe," but I saw what he meant. And I liked what you said in your piece about having to respect our vulnerability and protect it, that it wasn't just about feeling it in front of everybody, and that sometimes you need to be a tough guy, just not all the time. I don't know. We'll see. I'm here for now.

**Lou:** Sounds like a lot happened on the break. I'm glad you felt all right about returning. There were a number of things in what you just said that we could look into that relate both to the Truthplace and safety. But I am wondering what you want to do right now.

**Gabe:** What's to look into?

**Lou:** Well, for example, it seemed to bother you in some way that your rage frightened me.

**Gabe:** I don't know if it bothered me. I just thought you were a wimp for being afraid.

**Lou:** So it was just a judgment thing, no other feeling?

**Gabe:** I don't know what you're fishing for, but I have a feeling I don't want to go there. Let's just leave it all for now. Okay?

**Lou:** For sure. You may not feel this applies to you right now, Gabe, but for me it is essential to have the courage and permission to both step into and step away from our Truthplace, essential for the discovery of what is true for us in an authentic, moment-to-moment way. But let's open it up to some more feedback from the rest of you.

**Willa:** What do you mean "step into" and "step away" from the Truthplace? I thought the whole point was to get there and get good at staying there.

**Lou:** If we impose a new set of "goods" and "bads" on this process of discovery and unfolding we will subvert the process. If being in contact with the Truthplace becomes the new "good," the new acceptable (i.e. compulsory) way to be in our new "Truthplace seekers" tribe, and vice versa not being in contact with the Truthplace becomes the new "bad," the new unacceptable, shameful way to be, then the ego has once again brilliantly co-opted the process. Now it has become compulsory for us to always have access to our Truthplace, and to always *want* to go there! We're no longer allowed to not want to go there, to not want to know the truth of the moment. We're bad if that's what we choose.

**Willa:** But I want to be there!

**Lou:** No problem then. Just go there.

**Willa:** But is that my ego wanting?

**Lou:** Only if it feels compulsory, like you have to, or if you don't you're failing, or not being good, or something really bad is going to happen. Those would be signs of the ego at work. Going there is not necessary.

**Willa:** But if I want to live a certain way it *is* necessary.

**Lou:** Yes, if you *want* to live a certain way, *want* to have certain consequences, it is necessary.

**Willa:** So?

**Lou:** Like I said, if you want to live a certain way then do whatever is necessary to live that way, do whatever helps you accomplish that goal. No problem.

**Willa:** I don't know why I'm feeling frustrated right now.

**Lou:** You could pause and drop in.

**Willa:** Hmm. (Takes a moment) I feel angry. I feel angry that I can't be connected to myself all the time. It feels like I'm being cheated out of being me! Hmm. The anger is getting even stronger. Wow, I am really pissed off that this happened to me! And now I'm a little scared. I'm losing control. I'm not supposed to be angry. I feel guilty. But boy am I pissed! Why can't I be me?! Why can't I be connected to what's true for me?! Why?! It's not right! I feel robbed! Fuck you, whoever did this to me! Fuck you! Fuck you! And why the fuck can't I be angry?! Fuck you, whoever you are! Jesus!

**Lou:** Surprise.

**Willa:** I'll say!

**Lou:** Definitely not the ego at work now. The ego doesn't like surprises, doesn't like its host to be out of control, to be spontaneous.

**Willa:** Yeah I can feel the Critic/Terrorist/Doubter revving up for an attack. I can feel the "fearful maybe" creeping in. "Maybe I'm crazy." "Maybe I'm being an egotist." That's a good one. That really bites. Fuck you. Fuck you!

**Lou:** Right now you are on the frontline of your own personal self-recovery battlefield. The need, that native desire to be yourself, whatever that may be in a given moment, is right there inside you, calling for expression and feeling the pain and outrage of being suppressed. And your particular ego's need to conform and suppress and be safe by never being angry is also right there, doing its best to stop you from risking your acceptability. And you are able to be with both, be present to both, as the battle unfolds right now in this very moment, right in your own felt experience, not just in your head. Powerful, eh?

**Willa:** (Now crying...and not speaking for a while) When you said the word "pain" it hit me like a punch to my heart. I've been so lost for so long... (sobbing) so long. I'm so sad. What a loss. I feel so sad for myself. And so mad. And so sad. Back and forth.

**Lou:** It is both sad and outrageous that we have to chew off pieces ourselves in order to be safe—vital pieces.

**Willa:** Jesus. I certainly didn't expect this. But I'm glad to know this about me, to know I'm alive and kicking inside. I don't want to ever suppress this "me" again.

**Lou:** You don't but your ego has not changed its mind. The Terminator will be back.

**Willa:** Wow! Thanks for the memories! Jesus! Fuck you, too.

**Lou:** Sorry.

**Willa:** Shit. I wish you weren't right.

**Lou:** I know. I wish I wasn't too.

**Willa:** Really?

**Lou:** Sure. Look. At this point in my own evolution I would never give up the work of waking up for the trade off of going back to sleep. But does it suck at times? Sure. Do I choose unawareness over awareness sometimes? Absolutely. I feel it is important to keep it a choice and not a "have to." But does that work against my own evolution at times? Yes. But I'd rather err on the side of permission than on the side of compulsion.

Here are a couple of really important things regarding choosing and not imposing your will upon an unfolding discovery process: First of all it doesn't work. It would be the equivalent of trying to make a plant grow faster by pulling it upwards out of the ground. The truth is you're going to take it right out of the ground it needs in order to evolve according to its true nature.

Also, when you start to turn things around and head in the direction of using your awareness more deliberately and purposefully in order to include more of your own experience within it, you really don't know what you're going to bump into. Stuff may come up that up until that moment you may have been completely unconscious of. All of us have some degree of trauma in our lives. Being human involves experiencing lots of significant hurts and frightening events, and many of these experiences may have been scary enough to have had to be buried in unawareness. So as you open the door to this buried stuff, you need to be very respectful. It got buried because it felt too frightening, painful, or overwhelming at the time of it happening—like Gabe's experience of the suicide of his brother.

If you let the ego now take over your exploration, your process of opening up, and the ego insists that you have to keep feeling into something that's come up that feels really frightening or overwhelming, then you are abusing yourself, not healing yourself. There needs to be courage, but there needs to be compassion and gentleness about this as well. If we turn our awareness inwards like the harsh light in a law enforcement interrogation room we are re-traumatizing ourselves. When you are doing a self-inquiry, a dropping in, it is really important to keep the permission to stop doing it at any time you feel the need to, otherwise we create another cult full of prescriptions and proscriptions, and full of self harm.

**Willa:** Not simple.

**Lou:** The method is simple; we are complex.

**Mack:** This "safety" thing has a few us spinning a bit. On the break, after we read the paper, Frank, Liz, Gabe, and I talked for a bit. Safety is a concept none of us would have ever considered as a need. We all felt we were good at taking care of ourselves, protecting ourselves. It's funny, but none of us felt that had anything to do with needing to be safe. "Needing to be safe" sounds weak and powerless, just like needing approval does. And yet obviously if we are protecting ourselves we are keeping ourselves "safe' from some kind of threat.

For me, I see I focused on the power side of the equation, the aggression it takes to take care of me, not on the need to protect me. Saying it out loud it sounds kinda stupid. Like who's kidding who here? When you said we rely on each other not to harm each other physically, that rang a bell. I'm aware if someone wants to really do me physical harm, even if they're weaker than me, they could figure out a way to do it. In fact at times I'm afraid my wife is gonna take a knife to me when I'm asleep. You saying what you said just kinda busted my denial about safety. Like of course I need to be safe and I need other people to respect that need. It still feels shameful to acknowledge that, but I'm getting that's my Critic. I think we all kinda get this now—not liking it but getting the truth of it. And I think we all liked what you said about the stupidity of pretending we don't need each other's care and protection, pretending we can't be damaged or destroyed physically. It's just this need for approval thing that really bothers me and the others.

**Lou:** So it's not so shameful to need physical safety, but it's really shameful to need safety from the hurt and harm of rejection?

**Mack:** You got it.

**Lou:** And the shamefulness around needing protection from rejection is still really convincing? Feels really true, like you really should be ashamed about that?

**Mack:** Right.

**Lou:** So it sounds like that's kind of what's so for now. There's no room for questioning that belief for any of you in this moment, correct?

**Mack:** Hmmm. I didn't think of questioning the shame, just avoiding it.

**Lou:** Shame really works, doesn't it?

**Mack:** Say more.

**Lou:** What we call "shame" is really an amazingly powerful feeling experience. It's really awful. Like I described in the paper that was about the Critic, shame, at its most intense, is frightening, terrifying, because it feels so convincing and so self-annihilating. It feels like your "self" is being squashed, crushed, emptied of all value and acceptability. The feelings in your chest and belly, and up in your face, make you want to hide, disappear, or run away. If you're not overwhelmed by the fear, then rage will take over, murderous, violent. You want to annihilate the "shamer," kill them, obliterate their power to make you feel the shame. At its worst it can make you feel suicidal or homicidal or both. So no wonder we all want to avoid feeling shame.

**Mack:** What's going on with me and my wife has pushed me too close to that fire too many times.

**Liz:** I think Mack, Frank, and I have felt what he just called that "fire" in our relationships. It sounds like Stew has, too. I don't know about Gabe. So I think we know what you're talking about is real. That rejection is really powerful, hurtful, frightening, and shaming, too. But we seem to be too ashamed of *that* shame, ashamed of *all* those feelings that rejection causes, if that makes sense. And it does feel convincing. It feels really *necessary* to avoid it. So we don't know what to do that would be different in a good way. You talk about safety. Well for me it feels like there is no safe way to challenge that shame, and that shame about shame. It feels utterly humiliating.

**Frank:** Precisely.

**Mack:** I couldn't have said it better.

**Gabe:** If it's true, I don't want to know about it. I don't ever want to feel it. And I'm beginning to really worry it's true.

**Stew:** I'm hearing this music in my head right now. It's a howling sound. Howling! Coming right up out of my chest and my belly. I can hear it. There's a really dark song coming.

**Lou:** I once wrote a little piece I called "A Thank You Letter to the Proprietors of the Black Hole Hotel." It went like this:

Dear Sir and Madam,
   This is a note to thank you for the utterly agonizing experience you provided for me while staying as a guest at your Black Hole hotel. The experience you created for me was exquisitely devastating. Your in-room entertainment system was all I could have asked for. The piped-in sound effects of howling and screaming were incredibly convincing and completely darkened my soul. And the walls coming alive with the faces of people laughing hysterically and pointing their fingers at me was a brilliant and effective touch.
   When I laid down on the bed those dark sheets you provide seemed to embrace and pervade me with feelings of shame and humiliation. I sank into the most tortured sleep I have ever experienced. My nightmares were vivid

and horrifying. I awoke in the morning feeling utterly lost, depressed, and worthless. The call to suicide has never felt sweeter.

Thank you for providing me with an experience I will never forget.

Sincerely,
a thoroughly devastated guest.

**Stew:** Cool. Maybe I'll call the song the "Black Hole Hotel."

**Lou:** So listen, Liz, thank you. You really dug right into the guts of this, the real battleground this can be. The shame of the shame is so accurate. That's the last nail in the coffin. One layer of shame is challenging enough to confront. Put another layer of shame on top of that, and you're really sealed in...or out. It's totally forbidding and forbidden. It is incredibly important that we can actually describe this, name it, and talk about it. We're already busting the shame about the shame just by speaking about it. We're breaking the enforced silence. Willa's outrage is part of breaking that silence also. This is serious. This is very much a life and death battle. When the shame, and the shame of shame, has you pinned down, the analogy I used before really fits. Those guys who landed on Normandy Beach, pinned down by a merciless rain of bullets and firepower from the Nazis perched on the cliffs above the beach is what it's like. The Nazis had all the advantage. What unbelievable courage to keep pushing on. Eventually we got to Berlin, but fighting all the way and at the cost of great pain. It must have felt hopeless on that beach—futile, suicidal, insane, purposeless. But the fight for freedom from sadistic oppression (from the collective righteous, bully ego of Germany gone berserk) was necessary, no matter the cost. If we had allowed that crazed collective ego to rule, can you imagine how we would be living today? The oppression of freedom would have been staggering.

Likewise, until we confront the darkest of the dark forces within us, feel their withering firepower, confront the despair and futility those forces create, and come out the other side, we will not be free—free to safely care about each other, ourselves, and how others treat us...and talk about it with each other.

And thank you Frank and Mack, and Gabe, too, for your willingness to speak your truth. You speak to the seriousness of this work. We are not in some airy-fairy, "all's good" bubble. Human life is at least as full of darkness as it is full of light, if not more so. "The race to the bottom" is a very real dynamic. We're well on our way. There appears to be less and less accountability and less and less learning from our mistakes in our culture, and more and more identification with the need to be right, all ego-driven, all shame-avoidant. And there will be no easy fixes from what I can see. What you are doing here is what those unbelievably courageous soldiers did at Normandy in fighting external oppression. You are taking on the forces of inner oppression.

**Gina:** Can I say something here?

**Lou:** Seems you need to ask permission. Maybe that's exactly what we're talking about.

**Gina:** I know. *I know. I know.* Do you hear me?! *I know. You didn't hear the tone of that question.* The words were asking for permission; I wasn't. Old form, different substance. Let me put the words differently: I *want* to say something here! Do you hear me now?

**Lou:** Got it. Got it.

**Gina:** Good. At least in this moment *I've* got it. I've got that I've been terrorized out of any sense of safety. That's just how it is for me. That's my battlefield, definitely Normandy Beach stuff. I can barely feel the sorrow of that, but it's kind of *just* there for the first time in my life. And I thank you all for this moment. I feel it just may be possible to have some compassion for myself out of what you all have shared here. And I mean compassion, not pity! That's a first. Enough said. Don't want to invite too big of an attack from the Critic and the Terrorist.

**Lou:** I was going to say, "I can't tell you how much it means to me," to hear you say what you just said. But I realized I can tell you. At least I want to try. To hear someone like yourself, who has suffered serious wounds and not realized it come to clarity and see the reality of your history helps me see my own with more clarity and acceptance and let in the reality of what we're doing here more deeply—the importance of it, the difficulty. We're lucky, you know? Incredible lucky. We're privileged, right? We're not dealing with physical survival and safety, for the most part. Someone in this group may be and just hasn't spoken of it yet, but we are not like people who are living under the life-threatening rule of fundamentalist egos. Ironically that gives us the possibility, *and the responsibility*, of confronting the deeper effects of the wounding we visit upon each other, and the horrendous consequences. You can't do that if you're not physically safe. Physical safety trumps all other considerations; all else must wait until that is established.

Most of the others in this workshop have egos that have managed to buy them a feeling of safety that can be sustained to a far greater degree than your ego has managed to buy, Gina. Their defenses against shame, fear, and doubt, against the "bad me," are more effective than yours. Their egos give them at least some periods of safety where the danger of unacceptability and rejection is off the radar. Yours doesn't seem to give you that respite. You seem to never feel safe, never feel acceptable, always feel in danger of a misstep, and then you're shamed into silence about being locked into that permanent internal attack zone.

That you could find a space, namely this one, in which it is finally safe enough to be able to talk about never feeling safe, is really moving to me. It has opened the possibility for you to actually *feel* some compassion and tenderness for your beleaguered self. Being here with all these folks, having the courage to confront there own experience of not feeling safe inside their own skins, and the shame about that, makes it safe enough for you and them to touch a place inside that is *already* safe, a place inside *that is separate* enough from the grip of the ego's twisting and turning, squeezing and squirming efforts at trying to *find* safety. And then from that more separate place *seeing* the self-shaming deal our egos had to buy into *for safety's sake*. *That* feels enormously poignant to me, and rich with the possibility of authentic personal autonomy, power, and freedom.

**Gabe:** We're like opposite poles, Gina. You can't get your heart to stop bleeding, and I won't let mine spill one drop of blood. But you melted me just a bit right now—especially when you told Lou to more or less shut up. That was really brave. But to use that courage to speak about that fucking fear and shame of being wrong and being rejected and hurt, somehow that made it all right for me to let in what I've done to myself, to my heart, to have a little compassion for being jammed into the choices I've made and then getting stuck there. Like Liz, Mack, and Frank, I do feel really stuck there.

**Lou:** Compassion and courage. Wow. For me right now I feel so enriched, so filled up by how and what each of you have done here. I have this feeling in my heart that's hard to describe. "Full" catches some of the feeling. Full of a quiet aliveness, kind of like the feeling I get on a dark night looking up into the sky and seeing the moon and the stars there. All that space. All that quiet light and deep dark. Peaceful. Awesome. Way beyond my grasp. And safe in the moment.

We're going to need to leave this here for now. As you know, we're scheduled to meet again in two weeks for a half-day's work. But before we close for today let me just say a couple of things:

Compassion and courage really kind of sums up what we're called to summon on this wake-up trail. Compassion includes being open to our vulnerability, to our needs, to our hurts, to our fears, to our deep dependency on one another. And courage means staying true to ourselves, staying authentic, risking rejection and disapproval when speaking the truth in the moment requires it. Courage and compassion are both required to stare down the evil eye of shame, to acknowledge its frightening power. It takes courage to say, "No. I am not going to let you bully me, push me off my truth," compassion to know I will need the support of others not to run from myself in fear and shame. It takes courage to seek and ask for that support.

You have all summoned both your courage and your compassion many times during the time we've spent together.

We also need methods that help us counter the pull of our egos back into conditioned, automatic, rigid, compulsive ways of thinking, acting, and feeling, methods that we can use as individuals and as groups. We will always be two-sided persons, with a side seeking, loving, and embracing our truth, and a side programmed to avoid, fear, and reject it. So the methods we use need to embrace both sides. .Our practice, whether as individuals or in groups, needs to include both courage and compassion. So I am going to leave you with another document that kind of formalizes or gives structure to what we've been practicing here. It describes methods you can use for yourself and in groups. You may want to create a support group based on the understanding of the ego and the Truthplace that we have uncovered here. So a group method is included.

Over the course of the next two weeks I encourage you to be in touch with each other, if that feels right to you. Practice using the methods, if that feels right. And we'll see what emerges when we meet again in two weeks. May your own truth set you free. See you then.

# chapter fourteen

# Resource Document

The two-sided method we have been working with includes "spotting/telling on our egos" and "dropping into the Truthplace." The practice of this method has a specific usefulness that I would like to clarify. It is, however, a method that only becomes useful after some personal experience that breaks through and/or breaks down our image of ourselves as totally defined by our egos. This "breaking" experience varies widely from individual to individual, as we have seen within the group portrayed in this book. It can be a "small" moment or a "big" moment, and every degree in between. And it can be a breaking that feels good or feels bad. What breaks is the delusion (believed belief) that "I know everything that is fundamental to who I am." The consciously-held belief that there are no significant, meaningful unknowns about who I am gets broken in a way that can't be fully "fixed."

Another way of saying this is that the Convincer's power to hold the host in its trance of belief has been dealt a fatal blow. The Convincer has been exposed as a hypnotist and a con artist, not a truth teller. The host's unfailing belief in the Convincer's view of the "truth" has been shattered and cannot be fully restored ever again. We have seen that this disillusionment can be a positive one, but it is at the very least disorienting, and can also be very negative, even devastating. It appears to be a necessary inner event if we are ever to discover the presence of our Truthplace and the reality of our personal awareness. It is only then that any guidance from our Truthplace can become consistently available.

We have seen how we can use our "personal awareness." It is that aspect that can "see" both the workings of our ego *and* be present to our Truthplace, that can see the Seeker/Inflator/Convincer and the Critic/Terrorist/Doubter teams at work within us. We can use our personal awareness to see and tell on our ego's machinations. *And we* can use our personal awareness to drop into our Truthplace. We can see when we are largely caught in the grip of our egos and be with that truth. And we can see when we are listening to our Truthplace and be with whatever truths are merging from there. Our Personal Awareness allows us to respond to both these sides of ourselves consciously and usefully.

This two-sided approach of seeing/telling on our egos, and of dropping into our Truthplace, becomes useful because in the wake of disillusionment we discover that we are in fact "two-sided" beings. One side of us is a collection of our conditioned interpersonal survival strategies—our "egos." And the other side of us is a collection of all of our native inner capacities that we are calling the Truthplace. It appears to me that, for the long run, these two sides will be co-existing within us moment to moment. They will be sharing our inner space. And one side or the other will occupy more or less of that space, moment to moment. That balance will be constantly shifting, depending on what a given moment contains.

Practicing this two-sided method keeps increasing the amount of space, or inner ground, occupied by our native selves. Every time we connect with our Truthplace that ground is more and more securely held. With practice, we inhabit an inner place/space from which flows, more and more broadly and deeply, an organic, wise responsiveness to our own experience moment to moment, instead of the rigid, conditioned reactiveness of our egos. We experience more and more autonomy from our own unique ego—not the disappearance of the ego, but autonomy from it. We develop more and more of a sense of our own personal authority—an authority based, not on the rigidified, black or white, good or bad thinking of our egos, but on a fuller awareness of everything that is happening within us (including both our egos' reactions and our Truthplace knowings), as well as a more sensitive awareness to what is happening outside of us, *from one moment to the next.*

This method is very much a "moment to moment" method, not a "breakthrough" method. Breakthroughs, and breakdowns, may occur as a result of using this method, but they are not the goal of the method. The outcome of using this method is living our lives with more and more awareness of what is happening *inside of us* from one moment to the next. There are other "consciousness raising" methods that are specifically designed to produce breakthrough experiences and shifts in our consciousness. These are very helpful along the path. What "breakthroughs" break through is our conditioning, our egos. Our egos are put "on hold" or transcended for a period of time. And then a more direct and a fuller experience of different aspects of our native self is allowed to emerge into our personal awareness.

These experiences are very valuable because they help us know that there is much more to our native selves than the limited experiences our egos will allow us. But the ego has only been temporarily put "on hold" or transcended. It is not gone. We may feel genuinely liberated following a breakthrough, and for the moment we are. But, like the Terminator, the ego knows..."I'll be back."

So we need day-to-day, moment-to-moment methods to secure the inner ground opened up by our breakthrough experiences. The two-sided method described in this book is that kind of method. We need to keep spotting our ego's automatic efforts to co-opt whatever ground our native self has gained, "tell on our ego" (at least to ourselves), and then drop again, freshly, in "this moment," into our Truthplace, if possible. We once again use our personal awareness to connect to the felt, living truth of our inner experience of this moment, *whatever* that experience may include.

## Dropping Into the Truthplace

This practice of "dropping into the Truthplace" is not new. Many others, especially in the last hundred years, have pointed to and used this capacity in describing their work on themselves and their work with others. Freud, and many others in his time in history, had grasped that there is more to us than what we are consciously aware of. Ever since that time, the notion that there are active forces within us that we are not aware of has become more accepted as a psychological truth, although still not widely in the general population. All sorts of methods for accessing this "something more" have been developed over the last hundred years or so. In addition, in the West, especially from the 1950s on, the understanding and practice of meditation methods have become widespread and have introduced us to a "something more" within us that is becoming more accepted as a spiritual truth.

Freud didn't call it the "Truthplace," but he was accessing this source through his method of "free association," which allowed his patients to access their "subconscious minds." By allowing their personal awareness to be more inclusive, they experienced revelatory insights about themselves. Others have called their methods by different names but all are directing awareness to the same space/place within the body/mind. I am going to mention a teacher who has been particularly clear about using our personal awareness to access this deeper source of knowing. His work has been pivotal in raising our collective awareness of this inner resource.

Eugene Gendlin is a psychologist whose research led him to discover that patients who have access to what we are calling the Truthplace get more out of therapy than clients who don't have this access. He realized that everyone has this resource within them but have varying degrees of access to it. So he decided to put together a way of teaching people how to deliberately access this powerful resource. He developed a method that he called "Focusing," and wrote an instruction manual by the same name (see list of reading resources in Appendix A). This manual taught people how to use his method. His method is essentially the same as the one we have been using, i.e. moving your awareness down into the center of your body and waiting there for what he called a "felt sense" to emerge into awareness. The specific content or message within the felt sense is always meaningful, but the real power of the method is the connection it facilitates to what I named earlier as "insight knowing." He describes how by taking time out with yourself, calming the mind, and listening within, a clear knowing can emerge around anything you choose to explore. It can be used to clarify the nature of an "upset" you are experiencing, to explore a personal question or decision, or to regularly check in with yourself to see what is emerging within you on this deeper level. The continuing evolution of our genuine personhood emerges from this inner resource.

Gendlin wrote a highly valuable guide to finding this inner resource, and several other books that explore the uses of his method and the broader implications of his view of how our personal inner evolution unfolds. Many others have also written useful descriptions and guides regarding deepening and broadening our inner awareness. There will be a section at the end of this book called "Resources" (Appendix A) in which I will identify a number of the resources that relate to supporting the expansion of our awareness of the "more" within ourselves.

# Why Spot and Tell On Our Egos?

Moving our personal awareness into the neighborhood of the Truthplace and keeping it there is one side of our two-sided method for becoming incrementally more aware, more authentic, more open, more compassionate, more creative, and wiser. But what makes the other side of the method—that is, spotting and telling on our egos—important to this inner evolution?

It is important because we now know that the ego doesn't ever step aside permanently. It is dedicated to doing its job. It will actively and creatively seek to step back into control. And it will do so through the activity of any one or all of its host management team members.

We all hunger desperately for permanence—permanent acceptance, permanent safety, permanent peace, permanent self-esteem, permanent love, permanent abundance, permanent health. And deep inside we are terrified of impermanence.

The ego preys on this hunger and fear. It turns this very human hunger and fear into a compulsive, rigid quest for control—of control over every experience or action that promises the safety and satisfaction of permanent positive outcomes. Positive outcomes, of course, are ones that create safety, feel good, and bring us "good stuff."

So if you are diligent and successful on this alternative path of incrementally waking up to more of who you are, you can be sure your ego will be right there to seize control of whatever positive outcomes you experience. The Inflator will take credit and make you feel superior and powerful for making it happen. The Seeker will make you compulsively seek more and more of that "positive." The Convincer will make you believe you finally "found the answer" and that you should be able to keep "it" permanently available. The Seeker/Inflator/Convincer will be right there at work alongside your genuine steps into freedom from them.

Likewise, if you have discovered positive outcomes and the good effects of those outcomes diminish or go away completely, the Critic/Terrorist/Doubter will be right there and go to work making you feel ashamed of losing the good effects, terrified you'll never have good experiences ever again, and making you doubt that "getting it and losing it" is *not* your fault. A "fearful maybe" will arise that somehow it is all because you are doing it wrong. The ego will whack you around for not being in better (i.e. complete) control of the process of waking up itself.

Your ego knows that in your spiritual seeker/self-helper tribes that the ego itself is viewed as a "problem," as "bad," so it knows it has to do its job even more stealthily undercover than in "unenlightened" tribes. The host can't appear to be in the grip of the ego, so the ego must hide itself from both internal and external view. In seeker/self-helper tribes the reality of an inner life is acknowledged. So when the ego goes to work on a member of this tribe the rule becomes that the host must believe and appear as if he or she is totally aware of everything going on inside themself. The host must be made to hide any sign of hiding anything, any sign of needing to appear a certain way i.e. any sign of an ego at work. The Convincer will convince the host that he or she is completely aware of his/her ego, has let it go, and is not in its grip. Operating in stealth mode and fooling the host is the ego's most powerful skill.

None of these ego machinations is our fault. It's all automatic. The ego operates independently of our genuine intentions to become more and more open, aware, authentic, and inclusive. But we now know it is actively opposed to those intentions. So we shouldn't be surprised or embarrassed when the ego shows up. I said earlier that we need to decriminalize the possession of an ego. We all have one and they don't give up. We need compassion in the process of seeing and exposing them.

So this is why we need to not only consistently *spot* our egos at work, we need also to consistently "tell on them." The ego wants to hide. So if we are hiding our egos from one another, then we are doing exactly what our egos want us to do. We are preserving their possession of us, rather than deepening our conscious possession of them. And we are maintaining our abandonment of our real selves.

## Two-Sided Persons

There is that set of words again—"real selves." What is that? This question is a broader and deeper one that is at the heart of all spiritual and psychological inquiry and exploration: "What is our true nature?" What is a human being? What does it mean to be "fully realized" as a human being? How is it that what we call "spiritual" can co-exist with the psychological and animal within us? Are we fooling ourselves about having a higher potential or a higher nature? Is all our seeking and inquiring just the result of tricks of the mind or brain, or just the ego at work? How do we account for human brutes and human saints? Are we born a full *human* person, or must we develop into one? Are we capable of evolving in some ways by choice, or does our DNA determine the path of our development entirely? Is there a true experience-able human essence, a "native self," or just a bunch of concepts about ourselves? Where do we go to answer these questions? To brain science and research? To religion? To spiritual teachers? To psychologists, psychotherapists, and psychiatrists? To our own conclusions and opinions? To some other source within us? How do we know? How do we discover what is fundamentally true about us? Can we? And perhaps even more puzzling, how come there is so much confusion, argument, and passion over the many different answers to these questions? We have even killed each other over disagreements on the answers to these questions, haven't we?

Rather than falling into a complex conceptual attempt to answer those questions, I am going to stick to where we are *now*...in our own direct experience. We now find ourselves in a distinct group of human beings. We have all had a direct personal experience, happily or unhappily, that has led us to the discovery that we are *aware* of certain very significant aspects of our own experience of ourselves we didn't know before, and that we are still *unaware* of other very significant aspects of our own experience of ourselves. We have become aware that we are not whole, that we are divided within between what is seen and what is actively and passively hidden from our view.

If you have not had a personal, felt experience of this division you will not believe it exists. It will be outside of your experience and sound and feel "false," "not real," "crazy." No argument will convince you otherwise. If we are truly split within, the only way you come to know that this is so is by some directly-felt experience of that split. And once your own experience has bumped you over the barrier between not knowing and knowing you are split within, then you can't go back. At times, you may wish very dearly that you could, but you can't. *You have been disillusioned.* Living that shift can suck, but is ultimately totally worth it, and ultimately the only reality-based way to go.

*Consciously and openly* becoming a two-sided person is actually a great step forward in our personal and collective evolution as humans. Why? For one thing, it happens to be so. It happens to be an accurate description of our current state of being, for the great majority of human beings. We are humans with both a personal essence *and* an ego, living side by side, consciously or unconsciously. Accepting that you are probably never going to be totally one or the other allows you to move between the two more fluidly and authentically, and to move from moment to moment from within the inner embrace of your personal awareness, which holds *both*. This personal awareness is a natural capacity. It is not a capacity you have to create; it is one each of us has to discover within us, and then dedicate yourself to doing whatever is necessary to develop access to that capacity and to thwart the ego's intention to block your ability to access the rich resource of your Truthplace.

For another thing, by using our personal awareness to create more frequent and lasting access to our inner Truthplace, and then living and relating from that source rather than under the continuous control of our egos, guarantees the discovery and unfolding of our natural selves. It is from within the Truthplace that our natural selves emerge into our awareness, moment to moment. Then we don't have to theorize and debate about what constitutes our natural selves. We will discover whatever that may be through our own direct experience.

And spotting and telling on our egos subverts the endless repetition of experiences and results driven by ways of thinking, feeling, and reacting that are conditioned, automatic, and rigid. It would be a very powerful evolutionary step forward for us to practice talking and listening to each other with this double-sided awareness as part of our moment-to-moment conversations. Can you imagine? It does not seem possible right now, right? But can you imagine? I call these conversations "conscious conversations." And they are entirely possible, given the right conditions. And they are necessary for the full recovery of our natural selves.

## Creating Conscious Conversations: A Suggested Group Practice

Using this two-sided method of both spotting our own egos and dropping into our Truthplace is both a point of departure and one of continuous return. We need to practice this method in order to do our own separate, individual, consciousness-raising work. The method used and described throughout this book, and specifically in Chapter Eight, facilitates this individual work. So also do several of the approaches described in some of the books listed in Appendix A.

But we also need the company of fellow travelers if we are to make real and sustain our individual evolution. If we don't share and use our deepening awareness in our relationships with others, we will not break the oppressive rule of our egos, and in particular the painful and frightening tactics of the Critic/Terrorist/Doubter.

This means that we practice both being personally aware of our two-sidedness moment to moment, *and we are willing* to tell someone else about our experience of this split. Our egos were created *within past relationships* that forced us to split off and hide important aspects of our human nature. Becoming whole again can be fully realized only by continuously coming out of hiding *within new relationships* that are safe enough to do so. Keeping the process of recovering our natural selves from the grip of our egos secret only means the ego continues to rule. Any "recovery" will eventually be co-opted and subverted by the ego.

We also need the support and wisdom of fellow travelers to help us keep our balance between these two aspects of our human experience. We need help catching ourselves when we are in the grip of our egos and don't realize it, when our egos have successfully fooled us. We need to share with each other whatever we have learned by our own direct experience that helps us to keep waking up to *both sides* of our human experience.

The only way to do this is in conversations with those whom we have established a sufficient degree of safety. In conversations in which we can describe to each other our shifting feelings of opening and closing, of safety and danger, of connection and disconnection, of attunement and lack of attunement, of defensiveness and authenticity, and of the comings and goings of all our various emotions and feeling states, conversations in which we can describe the present state of our contact with our Truthplace and the tug of war between self-expression and self-suppression, between our courage to say what's so and our compassion for our fear of rejection and abandonment.

So what agreements would we need to make with each other for such a conscious conversation to feel safe enough, not just in one given moment, but moment to moment as the conversation moves along a lengthier path? Some suggestions are listed below.

## Guidelines for Groups Practicing Conscious Conversations

- Members of the group having the conversation must have some awareness of being two-sided beings and be interested in exploring a conversation that takes this reality as its starting point.
- Members would acknowledge that as we begin it would *not* be immediately safe enough for us to have these kinds of conversations because of the nature of our egos. Genuine safety will be incrementally created by acknowledging the ongoing riskiness of exposing our egos to each other.
- Members understand that the lack of safety in our conversations is because all of them happen, to one degree or other, under the sway of the *ego's rules*. Members maintain an awareness of these ego rules. These rules include:
  A. Talking about the experience of interpersonal safety and danger in our conversations is shameful and forbidden because it exposes our vulnerability to one another.
  B. Any open expression of fear, need for approval, or dependency will be dosed with shame.
  C. Shame is not to be revealed and talked about in conversations. This too will be dosed with shame.
  D. Defensiveness should not be named as such; should not be acknowledged.
- Members agree to watch out for, and speak about, doses of shame, fear, and self-doubt applied by the Critic/Terrorist/Doubter for violating these rules.
- Members initially focus on sharing descriptions and experiences of their unique egos—what their current and historical "goods and

bads" are, upsides and downsides of their ego experiences, what made them aware of their ego, and how their particular ego's defensiveness typically shows up.

- Members share their experience of contact and/or loss of contact with their Truthplace. They describe their practices for strengthening their contact with their Truthplace.

- Members agree that there is no purpose to this conversation other than the exploration of the experience of the group's conversational space regarding the ego, the native self, and the Truthplace.

- Members share only their direct felt experiences of their own ego and their own Truthplace.

- Members refrain from giving advice, analyzing others, "helping" others, or evaluating others.

- Members describe explicitly both recent and past experiences of challenging moments regarding choosing between love and power, autonomy and dependence, truthfulness and lying, showing and hiding.

- Members describe newly discovered awareness of the machinations of their own egos and new manifestations of their Truthplace.

- Members also describe experiences of the above as they occur within the group conversation.

- Members regularly check-in and share their experience of safety within the group, as well as when it feels unsafe for them. They describe what they need to increase their sense of safety within the group.

- Members agree to take breaks every half hour. During these breaks they first do a body scan. They then move their awareness down from their thinking minds to the inside of the trunk of their body and focus there for an extended period of time. After doing so, they share with each other their experiences of their bodily sensations, intrusions of their ego, and manifestations from their Truthplace.

- Members make agreements with each other about being helped when they are being defensive, and what that help would look like.

- Members agree upon a group strategy of how to respond when two or more members get caught in an ego-driven conversation.

- Members agree that if something emerges in conversations outside of the group context, which is relevant to the continued opening and deepening of the group conversation, that they will be committed to finding a safe enough way to describe whatever emerged outside the group within the group itself.
- Members of the group agree to rotate who chairs the meeting. The chairperson holds that role for four sessions. The chairperson is responsible for beginning each conversational session with a guided "dropping in" exercise, as well as for guiding the "dropping in" exercise during breaks.

These agreements, understandings, and principles could function as guidelines for a group to practice conscious conversations. They would help members create enough interpersonal safety so they could slowly feel their way along a path of increasing authenticity, awareness, empathy, and attunement as they talk and listen to each other about their most meaningful subjects. Members could depend on each other for an accepting embrace, and still have their own two feet to stand on when they need to act autonomously. If members followed these agreements faithfully, their "practice" conversations would become springboards for taking their individual and collective "self-recovery" into all the important aspects of their lives.

# chapter fifteen

# Living In a Two-Sided Inner World
## Closing Dialogues

**Lou:** Welcome back. I am eager to hear how the past two weeks went for each of you! I want to make clear from the beginning that this final session is not about getting a grade on your experience. What we are shooting for is to continue our exploration as people who are deeply interested in being more intimately aware of their inner experiences as they unfold moment to moment. There is no endgame here. There is no good or bad, pass or fail, better or worse. There is simply your own experience.

That said, knowing we are two-sided folks, we know the ego will be at work judging, evaluating, second-guessing, distracting, terrorizing, and planting doubts. This I am sure will be part of what you experienced over the last two weeks, and will be happening as we talk today. So we will share about that as well as about whatever happened for you regarding using your personal awareness to drop in to your Truthplace.

Let's take a moment right now to drop in and see more of what's up for us in this moment. Just spend a few moments dropping down into your body and noticing what's there. (Pause)

Okay. Good. See if you can keep some contact with your body while we talk today. Who wants to start?

**Mack:** I've had a helluva two weeks. Some of the folks here are aware of what's happened already. We've been in touch. We even met together a couple of times and that was amazing.

But to catch everybody else up, I've been living separate from my wife for eleven days and counting.

(Several "wows," "holy shits," "you're kidding me," some applause, etc.)

Yeah. I know. I'm as surprised as you are. Speaking of dropping in, I just felt something like a bomb of softness go off in my chest from your reactions. Embarrassing. But I like the feeling. One of the few times in the last eleven days I've felt anything but anxiety.

So anyway, yeah, eleven days ago I decided to stay in the small apartment I keep in the city and leave my wife in our home upstate. She never comes into the city, hates it. So it really keeps us separate...physically at least. And that is a huge deal. I feel like I've been going through some kind of withdrawal...and I haven't felt this close to picking up a drink or doing a line in years! I've doubled down on my AA meetings.

**Stew:** Jesus, Mack! How did you do it!? You were so tied up about it!

**Mack:** Tell me about it. I still am. But you know that moment in that session where what "I really thought" slipped out, and then I looked at that? Well that's been stewing in me since then. I mean I *knew* I had to leave her—at least separate for a while. I knew it. It just scared the shit out of me. And you all saw the trouble I had admitting that fear. Well the day after we broke for the two week hiatus, I was in the apartment, taking a shower after a workout, and this anger jumped up in me and I said out loud, "I'm actually fucking afraid to take care of myself!!" It just hit me. I believed I couldn't be all right about myself without her approval. The truth of that belief just really hit me in the gut. And that meant I had to stay even if it was really hurting me. It meant I couldn't take care of myself if it meant I'd lose her approval.

I mean, none of this is news. But something just turned inside, and my rage was more at that belief than at her or at me for being the dreaded wimp. I hated that belief and what it did to me, but even more I saw it wasn't true. Yeah, I'm afraid...fucking terrified. But I'll never be all right with myself if I, me, can't take care of myself, protect myself. You know what I mean!? I had to get some balls and punch through that fear. So I told her I was taking a break from the relationship, and that I didn't know for how long.

**Gabe:** You know I'm proud of you, man. That took real courage.

**Liz:** You know what, and I've told Mack this already, what he's doing and going through made me respect my boyfriend's decision to leave me. I can see he took care of himself. It wasn't about hurting me. It was about him listening to the pain he was in because of me...and respecting it. That's self-respect, isn't it?

**Lou:** Absolutely. That is living, hard-won, self-respect. It's the opposite of self-betrayal for the sake of preserving acceptability. This is an instance in which the need for autonomy trumps the dependent need for acceptance and approval. That dependent need doesn't go away. Choosing against it is painful and frightening. But the loss of *self* suffered by betraying your own truth would be more destructive and painful. It is a moment when making a "power move" is following the path of personal truth more than making a "love move" would be. And as Gabe pointed out it takes real courage—shaking in your shoes kind of courage—because the need for embrace and acceptance is not being denied. The leg is not being chewed off to get out of the trap.

**Mack:** I'll tell you what's been the hardest: sticking with it; not caving and going and seeing her. Every day my mind is talking to me, telling me I'm wrong, I'm the problem, or maybe she's changed. Maybe if I just talk to her right I can get through. Or I'll never have love in my life again. And she's talking to my friends, too, telling them what a prick I am. I have had some calls from people who don't really know what's going on and I can tell they don't buy my story. That's been really hard. If I hadn't done this workshop and hadn't had some of you to talk to I'd be back with her right now and probably would have bailed on this session with some fucking lame excuse. I'm getting stronger. I can feel it. I'm grateful for that.

**Lou:** Who got together during the two weeks?

**Gabe:** Before the two-week break, Liz, Mack, and Lucas, and I had all discovered we live near each other. So we decided to meet for coffee, which we did, and that was so good we met a couple more times.

**Willa:** I talked by phone a couple of times with Gina and a couple of times with Matt. We found we could really connect right away.

**Matt:** Mary and I had a long talk by phone too.

**Lou:** That's great! Like I said, we really need each other and these kinds of conversations. I'm glad. Let's finish up with Mack's news and then we'll hear from the rest of you.

**Mack:** It feels like really early days with this for me. It reminds me of when I first gave up drinking. A day at a time. There's a lot to tell, but here's the big take away for me: I denied my dependence on alcohol for a long time. I thought I could bend alcohol to my will when it was bending me like a goddam pretzel. Well I thought I could bend my wife to my will too, when she was bending me totally out of shape. Another moment of recognizing real powerlessness. I hate it. But denying it always gets me in trouble. When I said what I really thought was I had to leave her, that was recognizing the truth...I am powerless to change her.

But, like with alcohol, I had to see my dependence on her first, and stop denying that, stop denying that she was controlling me, not the other way around, because of my fear of letting her go, of losing her love. I hate feeling dependent; it really shames me. But I see how if I have to keep lying about it to myself then I can't make a choice about what to do about it. And it rules me from behind my back.

**Lou:** Like your shadow.

**Mack:** Yeah. Exactly. And I'm getting this courage thing—being really afraid and doing it anyway. That's new. I feel pretty brave right now. I hope I stay strong.

**Gabe:** Liz, Mack, and I all have Critic/Terrorist/Doubters that are ferocious when it comes to admitting needing people. Lucas is not as fucked up about it. He had gained a little ground on this before this workshop. But when we all talked together we all knew we shared that shame. And knowing that somehow really de-fanged it. We could even laugh at how crazy we were in our efforts to avoid feeling dependent. We were all members of the "Hate the Needy" club.

**Lucas:** Being a part of Mack's struggle admitting his "weakness" and then finding his strength made me really close to him. He felt like a real brother—and Gabe too, and Liz a real strong sister. It helped in a bunch of ways, but one way is I can keep better connected to my own inner experience even when my wife doesn't get it. I think she will eventually, but in the mean time I don't have to make her get it for me to have it. And I can love her where she is.

**Liz:** I felt proud to be a part of our conversations. Can you imagine?! Me! Proud of talking publicly about shame and needing!

(Lots of laughter)

**Lou:** So it sounds like a big part of what worked for you guys was what we've been calling "telling on our egos?"

**Gabe:** Come to think of it, yeah. I didn't get why you were making such a big deal about it before, but I see why now. There's something about not having to hide the Critic/Terrorist/Doubter that's actually an incredible relief—for that matter the Seeker/Inflator/Convincer too. I mean for sure I'm not letting my guy buddies know about this, at least not yet, but having some folks to talk with about this shit...I would never have believed it could be a relief.

**Mack:** It reminds me of how AA felt after going to a bunch of meetings—safe, hopeful. There was a way out of the black hole. People who had been there and back. It saved my life.

**Liz:** You know what else? These guys are a very different version of "man" for me. There is something very attractive about these guys. And I feel equal. I don't feel like I have to be careful or calculate my moves with them. It feels free. It feels scary, too, like I don't know what's going to happen; I can't predict. And I'm worried about getting hurt if I let them in too deep.

**Lou:** These are guys who are in this moment in touch with both their hearts and their balls.

**Liz:** Good way to put it. And that means I don't have to "mind" them. They can take care of themselves, and not in that bullshit macho way, but for real. And the cat's out of the bag. They've admitted they need my approval and fear my disapproval! We're not bullshitting around anymore!

**Gabe:** Whoa girl! Let's not go too far with this!

**Liz:** Hey, c'mon Gabe. You know I need yours just as much.

**Gabe:** Oh....Yeah....That's right. I forgot. That's what makes it safe, doesn't it? We've admitted we're all at risk of getting hurt. Wow. I forgot for a moment...or my ego got freaked.

**Lou:** And admitting that takes down the shame about being vulnerable, being hurt-able.

**Lucas:** So true. After this workshop, and sharing with these guys, I can feel more clearly that I got hurt by my wife's not getting what I had discovered, how I had changed, after that intensive workshop I took a while back. She sure didn't mean to, but my heart was open, more deeply than ever, and I needed her to see me, to feel that change, to be there with me, and she just couldn't. It was like it all just bounced off her. I didn't know about the C/T/D back then, didn't know my ego would react and jump back in, didn't really know how much I needed not just her approval but for her see me and feel me, if that makes sense. It's like validating. I didn't see how my ego didn't want me to admit that it hurt when she couldn't.

So it surprised me when I shut down. I felt free and figured I had broken through permanently.

Lou: So getting it and losing it makes more sense now.

Lucas: Yes. There is another thing emerging for me, and it is coming out of doing the practice and being down in my body. This is a belly thing, a belly feeling. My heart's in this one too, but it's coming more from a feeling in my belly. The best way I can put it is: "I *want* someone who can meet me from over in her Truthplace." I feel this strong desire. Maybe it will be my wife, maybe not. We'll see. I have this fantasy of looking this woman, whoever she ends up being, in the eye and her looking back, and this "I see you" going back and forth between us. There's curiosity, separateness, groundedness, recognition, attraction, and time, lots of time, no hurry, and no words, at least to begin with. I want that with someone. It could be with a friend, too. With the woman there's a sexual thing to it, but that doesn't have to be there for the rest of it to work.

Lou: Two self-possessed people. In the book my wife and I wrote about the qualities of authentic adulthood (*A Conscious Life*), the first one we identified we described as "I'm over here and you're over there." It captured what you're describing—two separate people deeply grounded in and owning their own experience, and as a result completely open to the experience of the other; people who are connected to both their love and their power, as Martin Luther King might put it.

Lucas: That's it.

Mary: Being grounded in and owning your own experience is dangerous.

Lou: Say more.

Mary: Well...you see people more clearly. You see their lies and defenses. You see what they're hiding. You see the discomfort they don't want you to see. You see their self-doubt. My Sacred Heart vision didn't change much over the past two weeks. It stayed present in me as a kind of assurance as I did the dropping-in practice. Like it kept giving me permission to know what I know, to see what I see. It kept taking away the shame, fear, and doubt about what I saw. And boy I saw a lot. For example, I am surrounded by saint egos!! They're everywhere! The priests, my fellow nuns, all the people trying so hard to be "good." So many of them have totally bought the "unworthy" thing. And so many others think they're holier than thou. I think if I didn't have that Sacred Heart presence saying, "That's true, and don't worry, and that's true, and don't worry, and that's true and don't worry," I would have gone down the shame hole. I kept getting there's nothing wrong with me. I'm not the problem! The fucking ego is the problem. There I go cursing again. That's been happening a lot too.

(Laughter)

It's funny but then not. I really am pissed. I feel like I was sold a bad deal, living a life feeling like I was always about to do something bad, something wrong, when what was "wrong" was simply my seeing and feeling what was true all along. The people who had trouble with what I saw were the problem, not me! I feel so sad and mad. I'm not sure what to do with all this new awareness! It still feels dangerous to be me.

But don't get me wrong, I feel really good inside. It's hard to put words on—so many feelings side by side. I'm scared to death. But I'll tell you all this: I ain't buying in to what feels like bullshit anymore. For the first time in my life I feel fully here, present and accounted for...by me! By my own authority!

(Lots of hoorays and applause)

**Lou:** You know, it's interesting; one source of truth within us is the heart. So the Sacred Heart being there for you in the way you describe makes a lot of sense to me.

**Mary:** But what's amazing is how different this experience of that heart is from what I was taught to believe about it. If this is what Jesus was all about then this is the first time I have experienced Jesus actually loving *me...as I really am*—not forgiving me for who I am, but loving me. Unbelievable.

**Gina:** I wish I felt a connection to a presence inside me like yours. I've had a really hard time staying present inside myself. There's just so much anxiety and fear inside my body, so many fearful, critical, worrying thoughts running around in my head. I tried to do the dropping-in exercise every day these past two weeks. I just couldn't sit with myself for very long trying to look around in my body for the Truthplace. That just didn't work at all. What did work was writing. I've used writing, you know like personal journaling, for a long time. It's the only way, besides talking with someone friendly, that I seem to be able to find a thread of discovery that leads me to some discovery or understanding that feels useful and true. Writing it down helps me hold onto it too.

**Lou:** I've found writing very useful too, and other ways of dropping-in as well.

**Gina:** Really? I thought I was doing something wrong or failing. One thing that has gotten painfully clear to me is that I do have an ego and it is relentless. It's on a 24/7 red alert status. But I am seeing it now. I didn't know it was my ego before. It's still hard to realize it's not me, but I am seeing the Seeker always telling me how I'm supposed to pay attention to everybody else, making sure they feel okay, making sure they don't feel I'm judging them. I see the Convincer making me believe that being a loving person and never criticizing or complaining is the only way I can be and be good. I see the Critic and the Doubter jump on every sign of hurt or anger or care for myself and just smothering them. I really feel under siege. I can only look and write for a while and then I have to put it down and try to do something else. That's hard too!

**Lou:** You are definitely not failing. The whole idea here is to do our best to stay true to our own experience, wherever that takes us. That includes staying true to your experience of what actually helps you do that and what doesn't. Sticking to a method of tuning into your experience that doesn't actually help you do that just because it may have helped someone else or because someone else suggested it is clearly the ego at work.

The *experience* of each of our paths is so unique, so personal, so differently colored by our different interpersonal histories, our personalities, our cultures, and our physical make up. But we are so conditioned to not listen internally, and to not trust that listening will take us anywhere useful, that there is often this terrible, disruptive interference that we bump into when we turn the corner inside...when we start spotting the ego and turning our attention back to something truer to who we really are, to what we really think, to what we really feel, to what we really know. And some of us will experience more of this interference than others. Some of us have been hurt and terrorized more profoundly than others in our history. Our egos are a response to that history.

And the level of interference in each of us will vary greatly over time. There will be times it shuts us down completely. Spotting this interference that the ego creates is a vital part of moving into a more intimate attunement with ourselves and with each other. And being able to share it with each other is vital. So thank you for this, Gina.

**Gina:** That helps.

**Willa:** When I talked with Gina by phone last week and she told me about what she was experiencing I really felt grateful to her. Her description of what the Critic and the Doubter were doing inside her helped me see my own ego at work. It really did. We're actually a lot alike. We have pretty strong saint egos, like Mary, too. I have to say I envy Mary her Sacred Heart presence. It reminds me so much of the feeling I got inside when I experienced that blue light when I was with my teacher. It was totally reassuring and loving. I miss that big time. But I also like the feeling I'm getting of being my human me. That enlightened, blissful me is mind-blowing for sure, but there's something about the way I'm sitting inside my own skin, ego and all, that feels content, at least in this moment. I feel strong. Safe. Regular. That may be a funny word to use but it fits somehow.

**Lou:** Touching into the groundedness of your own presence can feel like a miracle and no big deal at the same time. That's what "regular" captures for me.

**Willa:** That fits.

**Lou:** I love these kinds of conversations. We're using words, just like most conversations, but we're using them to capture and express meaningful, real, in the moment felt experiences and direct knowings. Your saying just now "that fits" is you saying that my words accurately capture some felt truth of your own experience. And you can feel and check inside yourself if my words "fit" or not. If they do then I know, and you feel, that I have "felt" you, not just heard your words. You have that experience of "feeling felt" by someone else. That's rich. I love feeling that connection, that intimacy, that mutual, moment-to-moment discovery and unfolding of each other. Rumi, the sufi poet, had a great friendship with another mystic named Shams. In describing what their friendship meant to him, Shams said to Rumi:

> "What frees you is not words, but rather someone's presence, their actual being. That is the scripture you must attend to."
>
> (Coleman Barks, *Soul Fury.*)

**Gina:** You know Willa I felt like that with you too. When you described your Critic you were talking about mine. I felt felt. That was wonderful. For me, that was like Mary's Sacred Heart or your blue light coming to me, being with me! We can be that sweet presence for each other...if the ego doesn't take over.

**Willa:** I'm with you. What I'm just getting the hang of is this—and this is even more surprising to me—if the ego does take control, and I see it, I can be present to *that* and talk about *that* and if you get what I mean, because you've owned your own ego, if I feel you feeling what that feels like for you, then right then and there the ego has lost its grip again. We're connected and owning what's real. Crappy, but real. "My ego's got me right now!" So the ego doesn't have to be completely gone for us to stay connected, true, and open. It actually helps loosen the grip of my ego! Wow. That feels seismic. Liberating. I don't have to get rid of my ego to be real!

**Lou:** That demand to be rid of our egos turns a process of genuine self-exploration and inquiry into another fundamentalist, dogmatic trip. And it undermines, if not wipes out, the safety necessary for talking to each other openly and authentically about our process. Having an ego and being under its sway becomes a failing, a sin, something to fight and control. Being with the Truthplace is "good" and being in the grip of the ego is "bad." One feels better than the other, that's for sure. One allows us more room to move than the other, that's for sure too. One is less painful than the other, that's for sure too. But neither is good or bad; neither makes me better or worse than you.

**Matt:** That's so clear to me right now, right in this moment, but, man, that's hard to hold onto.

**Lou:** You can now count on the ego giving you some shit for having an ego. *Count* on it. And I say "now" because you have all seen it and have a desire to separate from the trance it induces in your own minds. The best way the ego can keep you in its trance is convince you that you must get rid of it to be free. It's like a brilliant jiu jitsu move that uses your own effort to free yourself from its hold on you to bind you more tightly.

**Matt:** Somebody once said, "What we resist, persists." When I spoke by phone with Mary last week, we both realized how much we'd been caught in efforts to suppress, to not feel certain ways, to correct our thinking—she in her religion and me in my cult—a couple of "saints" fully programmed to think in terms of good and bad, in terms of sinning, of having to correct our basic nature, like if we don't watch out all the time we're going to be bad in some way. It feels like Gina has a version of this going on too. And Willa. So how easy and "natural" would it be to now start correcting ourselves for having an ego! Totally automatic! It makes me want to scream right now. It's like I'm fighting an octopus.

**Lou:** Boy, do I know that feeling. And you know what? I need you, someone, to tell me about that experience because *somehow* hearing it helps me with my octopus. I can feel right now a feeling in my chest loosen and let me breath easier and a warm feeling of gratefulness arising, kind of like "thank God someone else knows this too."

**Matt:** That's what it felt like with Mary.

**Gabe:** What are we talking about here? This is sounding a bit too ooga-boo-ga for me.

**Frank:** Yeah. It's making me feel squirmy, a little on the outside-looking-in, too.

**Stew:** Ya know where I go with this? Right damn into those moments when me and my bandmates have a meeting of the souls in the middle of playing a song together. It's fucking magical. That word you used, "presence," comes close to saying it. It's like an altered state. And something just takes over and we're together—really together, like we've stepped out of our little plastic enclosed cubicles into a bigger room together where we can feel each other in the sounds we're making. It's the best.

**Gabe:** That song you guys wrote, "Four to One," always hit me in a way that mixed me up. It's a real rocker but there was always something else to it—something sad, some kind of longing it would leave me with—besides getting me out on the dance floor. It strikes me now that song may be about what we're talking about.

**Stew:** That song was about losing what we're talking about—having it and then losing it. Four becoming one. And then the one's against four being one. We could only write that song after we found our way back to listening to each other. Lou helped us with that. That connection is really tricky to keep. We've lost it again, maybe for good this time. I came to this workshop to look at my part, but more to look at what happens in my connections to women, what makes that "presence" turn to shit.

**Lou:** So Gabe and Frank raised a question. Instead of answering or describing "what's going on," I'm going to ask you both to drop in and look in your chest and bellies to feel what's going on in there for you. Use the method to see if you can tap more intimately into what's going on for you in this moment.

(Pause)

**Gabe:** Wow. That's my ego at work again. And dropping in that way made me feel at ease. I—the real me—actually like what's happening in this room. I never thought I'd hear those words come out of *my* mouth..."the real me."

**Frank:** Me too. At first I felt a little self-conscious that you asked me and Gabe to look inside, like I might find something wrong in there!!

**Gabe:** That's funny. I did too.

(Both laugh out loud, Stew and others too.)

**Stew:** What the fuck are we laughing at!!?

(More laughter; getting hysterical)

**Gabe:** (Finding it hard to catch his breath) I don't know. But it sure feels good.

**Lou:** (Having trouble composing himself) This kind of laughter is a sign that something has lost its grip.

**Liz:** Yeah! Like all of us!!!

(More laughter)

**Frank:** This is the biggest belly laugh I've ever had! We're all fucking crazy, aren't we?!

**Lucas:** This is what happened in that intensive workshop I took. I'll tell you what's lost its grip—besides us—it's fucking shame, that's what's lost its grip!

You're gonna look inside and find "something wrong" in there, Frank!? How ridiculous is that!? What kind of bullshit is that!? How absurd! But knowing it's absurd only happens when shame has lost its grip. You know what I mean? And I can feel the anger in me now for that fucking shame and what it does to me...to all of us. It twists us up, turns us into minefields for each other, makes us enemies, dangerous to be around, dangerous to be ourselves. How fucked up is that???!!!

(Hoots and hollers; "Yeah, fuck shame!" "Right on, Lucas!" More laughter, cheers)

**Lucas:** Wow. Thanks for that.

**Others:** (No, thank you. Yeah.)

**Lou:** You said it for all of us, Lucas. And we said it back to you. That's what we're talking about. We felt what you felt. We all knew what you knew in the moment. Presence. Being. Truth. Authenticity. Openness. Connection. Vulnerability. All at once. The truth shall set you free...in *this* moment.

**Liz:** But we're gonna lose it, right, Lou???

**Others:** (Lots of "boos" and "nos," "Say it isn't so, Lou"; laughter)

**Lou:** (Laughing) You can count on it!

**Others:** (Laughing; booing; "Meany"; "sadist"; "rip-off")

**Lou:** Like my client who always starts his session by saying, "I'm here for one purpose only....achieving a state of permanent bliss."

**Stew:** Permanent bliss. That's what I want too. I'm lucky. I've had a lot of bliss in my life, as a performer singing my songs, people loving them...me—but never permanent. I've chased that bliss pretty hard. Over the past couple of weeks as I looked inside myself I realized that my rage at others came from blaming them for not letting me keep my bliss. It was *their* fault I lost it. Sometimes it was. But a big part of the rage, and then the depression, was that I felt entitled to keep it, like I should never be without it, never be unhappy. I don't know where the hell that came from. I certainly *know better*. But some part of me just believed that was my due, especially if I kept entertaining people, like my reward for making other people happy was the bliss of their permanent adoration back to me. I know this is what fucked it up with my girlfriend and me.

**Lou:** Can you describe how this came to you?

**Stew:** I was pretty good about doing the practice every day for an hour or so. I like being inside my body...for the most part. One of those days I was sitting....Actually I don't sit. I've got this great lounge chair that massages me while I kind of lay out in it. Anyway, I was in my chair feeling very relaxed for me and this picture memory of me and my girlfriend came up, clear as day. She's sitting on the couch, hunched over, sobbing, and I'm standing over her feeling angry.

So I did what you suggested and started looking to see what more was happening in that moment that I may have missed when it was happening. It was kind of like watching a movie and then being in it. I could feel that I was confused, not just angry. I didn't know what to do. That made me mad. I don't like that feeling. What I didn't know was it scared me that I couldn't make her happy, that somehow I kept disappointing her, that she was so angry with me. Blowing up at her, blaming her, felt better than being confused and scared. All this just rolled out inside me. I wasn't trying to do anything. And it just showed up. I didn't like it. But I felt weirdly all right with it all. No shame. Regret, yeah. I can feel that right now.

**Lou:** Nobody likes unpleasant, uncomfortable feelings or outcomes. It's just that they carry important information for us.

**Stew:** Yeah. I get it.

**Gina:** How in God's name can all this anxiety I have be carrying important information for me!? Sorry. I didn't mean to sound so angry. Or like a baby...

wait a minute. Shit! There's the critic again, the shamer. I don't want to go with that voice. I am angry about all this anxiety. That's not being a baby! Damn it! There. I feel better now.

**Others:** (Cheers, whoops, bravos)

**Lou:** Not so anxious?

**Tina:** No! That's a surprise.

**Lou:** I'd like to come back to your question.

**Gina:** First let me say thank you to this gang of fellow lunatics here. Thank you. Thank you. Thaank you. Now let's hear your answer. It better be a good one! Jesus. (Laughimg) I am really getting out of hand.

**Others:** (Laughing along with Gina)

**Lou:** Being endlessly flooded by any unpleasant feeling is debilitating. Anxiety. Depression. Rage. Terror. Shame. It would be hard to find important, useful information being carried by feelings in that scenario. Yes? But that's not natural, right? Feelings like anger, rage, fear, terror, and hurt are meant to tell us about something we need to respond to, and then go.

But what if we're powerless to respond? Or our responses don't remedy the situation our feelings are reacting to? Or our responses make the situation worse? Or we get attacked for responding? The feelings persist and the situation doesn't change. The feelings are not the problem...the situation is. But the feelings are what we are forced to mess with for the sake of our sanity and tribal safety. Any unpleasant feeling you are stuck in, that persists in a debilitating, disempowering, depressing, de-vitalizing way is the outcome of a painful, frightening, historical situation you couldn't change.

So in this sense even these persistent, debilitating feelings are carrying important information about our history, some specific knowledge about the wounds we carry. Your fearfulness, Gina, is a feeling memory of what it was like for you to be a kid. We can go some distance in healing the wounds that generate persistent feelings, but in my experience, never fully. We can uncover and re-claim capacities of our true being, our true nature, which we had to bury in order to survive. We can find our strength, our courage, our tenderness, our will, our self-assertion, our compassion, our bonds, our comfort, our empathy, our joy, our excitement, our creativity...and, yes, our humor, as we are here. These can co-exist with our wounds, and with our egos, given we are willing to keep dropping into this moment and the next more deeply within ourselves, and even more importantly with each other.

**Frank:**  I just want to thank you and the group for a gift that is priceless to me. The gift of myself. At 77 I'm the oldest in the room. But for the first time in my life I'm feeling like a real person, a whole person, or at least close to it. The last two weeks have been a series of quiet, joyful moments for me. Just by dropping in and following my own true experience. Feels like a miracle to me. Late in life but wow. I am truly thankful I got here before I leave the planet.

**Lou:**  I'm so happy for you, Frank. For all of you. I want to share a quote with all of you. It's from a book called "Spacecruiser Inquiry" by a teacher, A. H. Almaas, who I have found extraordinarily clear about both the difficulties and benefits of looking within in the ways you have all been practicing. He's responding to a student who has shared an experience of the upside of what he calls following the "personal thread" of your own moment to moment experience. Here it is:

> "It's exciting, you know, to be yourself. That's what it means to find where you are: to be yourself continuously instead of just having blips of yourself. You're being there, you're being personally you and going through your life. That sense of being there becomes the center of your life......Then there is an intimate and a personal quality to your life. You are finding your truth – not in contrast to somebody else's truth, but yours in the sense that it is personal to you."

We are going to have to wrap it up for today. Like I said, there isn't an endgame to this; there is the moment to moment to moment. I would like to suggest that you think about and talk with each other about how you might continue to support each other on this path. Some of you might want to form a regular group that uses the group practice I described. I have a handout with the guidelines that each of you will get. And my book has a bunch of supportive resources listed in the back.

In closing, I want to thank you so much for sharing with me your openness, your courage, your compassion, your egos, and your Truthplace. I am strengthened and made more whole by being with you in this way. And if we take the ego to be "the ghost in our machinery", then you guys are one powerful bunch of "ghostbusters"!

**Liz:** How about on the count of three us ghostbusters give a great big "thank you Lou!" One, two, three...

**Group:** Thank you Lou!!!!

# Resources

## On Wounding and Healing

*Complex PTSD: From Surviving to Thriving.* Pete Walker, 2013, An Azure Coyote Book.

*Conquer Your Inner Critical Voice.* Robert W Firestone, Ph.d., Lisa Firestone, Ph.D, and Joyce Catlett, M.A., 2002, New Harbinger Publications, Oakland, CA.

*Healing The Shame That Binds You.* John Bradshaw, 2005, Health Communications, Inc. Deerfield Beach, Fla.

*Radical Acceptance: Embracing Your Life With The Heart of a Buddha.* Tara Brach, Ph.D., 2003, Bantam Books, NYC.

*Recovery: Freedom From Our Addictions.* Russell Brand, 2017, Henry Holt & Co., NYC.

*Shame: The Exposed Self.* Michael Lewis, 1992, The Free Press, A division of MacMillan, Inc., NYC.

*The Drama of the Gifted Child: The Search for the True Self.* Alice Miller, 1997 (Revised Edition), Basic Books, NYC.

*The Empath's Survival Guide: Life Strategies for Sensitive People.* Judith Orloff, MD, 2017, Sounds True Inc., Boulder, CO.

*The Psychology of Shame: Theory and Treatment of Shame-Based Syndromes.* Gershon Kaufman, 1989, Springer Publishing Co., NYC.

*The Tao Of Fully Feeling: Harvesting Forgiveness out of Blame.* Pete Walker, 1995, An Azure Coyote Book.

*Traumatic Narcissism: Relational Systems of Subjugation.* Daniel Shaw, 2014, Routledge, NYC.

*Trauma And Recovery: The Aftermath of Violence—From Domestic Abuse to Political Terror.* Judith Herman, M.D. 1997, Basic Books, NYC.

*Trauma And The Soul: A Psycho-Spiritual Approach to Human Development and its Interruption.* Donald Kalsched, 2015, Routledge, NYC

## On Belonging and Personal Freedom

*Eternal Echoes: Celtic Reflections on Our Yearning to Belong.* John O'Donohue, 1999, Harper Collins Publishers, NYC.

*Soul Fury: Rumi and Shams Tabriz on Friendship.* Coleman Barks, 2014, HarperCollins Publishers, NYC.

## On The Formation of the Ego

*Ego: The Fall of the Twin Towers and the Rise of an Enlightened Humanity.* Peter Baumann and Michael W. Taft, 2011, NE Press, San Francisco, CA.

*One Cosmos Under God: The Unification of Matter, Life, Mind and Spirit.* Robert W. Godwin, 2004, Paragon House, St. Paul, Minn.

## On Dropping In and Waking Up

*A Conscious Life: Cultivating the Seven Qualities of Authentic Adulthood.* Fran Cox and Louis Cox, Ph.D. 1996, Conari Press, Berkeley, CA.

*Big Mind – Big Heart: Finding Your Way.* Dennis Genpo Merzal, 2007, Big Mind Publishing, Salt Lake City, Utah.

*Essence: The Diamond Approach to Inner Realization.* A. H. Almaas, 1986, Samuel Weiser, York Beach, Maine.

*Embracing Ourselves: The Voice Dialogue Manual.* Hal & Sidra Stone, 1998, New World Library, Nataraj.

*Focusing.* Eugene T. Gendlin, Ph.D. 1981, Bantam Dell, NYC.

*Focusing Oriented Psychotherapy: A Manual of the Experiential Method.* Eugene T. Gendlin, 1996, Guilford Press, NYC.

*Gestalt Therapy Verbatim.* Frederick S. Perls, The Gestalt Journal Press, 1969, Gouldsboro, ME.

*Listening To Your Angel: The Science of Focusing on your Intuitive Intelligence.* Kevin Flanagan, 1998, Marion Books.

*Power And Love: A Theory and Practice of Social Change.* Adam Kahane, 2010, Berrett-Koehler Publishers, San Francisco, CA.

*Primary Speech: A Psychology Of Prayer.* Ann and Barry Ulanov, 1982, John Knox Press, Atlanta, Georgia.

*Spacecruiser Inquiry: True Guidance for the Inner Journey.* A. H. Almaas, 2002, Shambala Publications, Boston, Mass.

*Spiritual Bypassing: When Spirituality Disconnects Us from What Really Matters.* Robert Augustus Masters, PHD, 2010, North Atlantic Books, Berkeley, CA.

*The Awakening Body: Somatic Meditation for Discovering Our Deepest Life.* Reginald A. Ray, 2016, Shambhala Publications, Boulder, CO.

*The End Of Your World: Uncensored Straight Talk on the Nature of Enlightenment.* Adyashanti, 2008, Sounds True Inc., Boulder, CO.

*The Instruction Manual For Receiving God.* Jason Shulman, 2006, Sounds True Inc., Boulder, CO.

*The Pearl Beyond Price: Integration of Personality into Being: An Object Relations Approach.* A. H. Almaas, 2001, Shambala Publications, Inc., Boston, MA.

*The Power of Focusing: A Practical Guide to Emotional Self Healing.* Ann Weiser Cornell, 1996, New harbinger Publications, Oakland, CA.

*The Power of Now: A Guide to Spiritual Enlightenment.* Eckhart Tolle, 1999, New World Library, Novato, CA.

*The Unfolding Now: Realizing Your True Nature Through the Practice of Presence.* A. H. Almaas, 2008, Shambhala Publications, Boston MA.

*True Meditation.* Adyashanti, 2006, Sounds True, Boulder, CO.

*Your Body Knows The Answer: Using your Felt Sense to Solve Problems, Effect Change, and Liberate Creativity.* David I. Rome, 2014, Shambhala Publications, Boston, MA.

# The Ego: Classifications and Types

There are two broad classes of egos. Each class includes several different types of egos within them. The two broad classes are:

> Self-enhancing Egos
> Self-diminishing Egos

An ego in the self-enhancing class is one which compulsively and rigidly demands that its host lead with self-assertive and autonomous energies in *all* interpersonal interactions; and vice versa, that its host compulsively and rigidly suppress feeling or expressing *any* need for approval from or dependency on the host's significant others.

An ego in the self-diminishing class is one which compulsively and rigidly demands that its host lead with self-denying and submissive energies in *all* interpersonal interactions; and vice versa, that its host compulsively and rigidly suppress feeling or expressing *any* self-assertion of worth, autonomy, or self interest in interactions with the host's significant others.

Ego types that fall exclusively within the self-enhancing class include:

> The Bully
> The Egotist
> The Star
> The Traumatizing Narcissist

The Power Player
The Righteous True Believer
The Sadist
The Avenger
The Macho Jock
The Leader

Ego types that fall exclusively within the self-diminishing class include:

The People-Pleaser
The Saint
The Caretaker
The Servant/Slave
The Victim
The Scatterbrained
The Fuck-up
The Mr. or Ms. Humble
The Masochist
The Guilt Ridden
The Helpless
The Martyr
The Hermit
The Invisible
The Pacifier

Compulsively self-enhancing egos are the ones spoken of in the line from King's quote: "Power without love is reckless and abusive."

Compulsively self-diminishing egos are the ones spoken of in the line from King's quote:"Love without power is sentimental and anemic."

There are also ego types that can exist in either of the two classes of egos. They are:

The Entertainer

The Rebel
The Conformist
The Rationalist
The Seducer
The Manipulator
The Tough Guy/Gal
The Hero

These ego types can be either self-enhancers or self-diminishers.

There are as many ego types as there are human capacities, skills, attitudes, and values. None of the behaviors embedded in those lists of possible ego types are inherently an ego trait. The telltale signs that the ego has co-opted one or more of them is the compulsive and rigid way the ego utilizes the ones it has deemed acceptable, and suppresses those it has deemed unacceptable.

# Acknowledgments

My professional development and evolution as a psychologist is a process that has spanned fifty-five years. Having been in that process for that long means there are an enormous number of people to whom I owe a debt of gratitude for their support and guidance. There are too many wise teachers, too many healing therapists, too many colleagues who partnered with me, and too many encouraging and affirming friends along the way to mention individually and to properly acknowledge for the unique gifts they gave me. Likewise there have been too many clients – individuals, teams, and organizations – to thank for the privilege of working with and learning from in my roles as psychotherapist and consultant. But for all of you, know that you are in my thoughts and my heart accompanied by a powerful feeling of gratitude. This book is the product of all your contributions to my evolution as a person and a professional.

I will take this opportunity to specifically acknowledge my wife, Fran, and my children, Joshua, Sarah, and Laura.

Fran, you have been with me from the beginning. You always saw what was valuable within me that needed to emerge for my own benefit, as well as for the potential benefit of others. And you helped me to confront and change what needed to be changed within me to bring that forth. Your indomitable spirit, your own powerful creativity and artistry, your big heart, and your courage are mainstays and sources of inspiration for me. You have been my strongest ally and deepest friend along the path of waking up that is captured in this book. The walk on that path would not have taken me to where it has without you by my side.

Josh, Sarah, and Laura, I feel profoundly lucky to be your father, and in these later years, to have you as friends, and to be held as a friend by you. I know I learned a lot of what I needed to learn about myself as a father and a person at your expense. I am thankful that I could learn, though often late, and translate that learning into changes that allowed the love and respect between us to blossom and bloom into the deep friendships we now share. The conscious, loving, responsible, empowered persons and parents you have become are a source of great joy for me. And you have each given me two grandchildren, six in all, who I am watching emerge into their own amazing, unique personhoods with your loving guidance. This book would not be what it is without the roles you have played in my life.

Lastly, my thanks go to Paul Cohen and Colin Rolfe of Epigraph Publishers for their expertise and support in turning my written words into such a beautifully rendered physical reality.

A deeply felt thanks to everyone.

And....

*Mi inchino alla fonte sconosciuta e sapiente di tutto*